Bribery and *Blat* in Russia

Studies in Russian and East European History and Society

General Editors: **R. W. Davies**, Emeritus Professor of Soviet Economic Studies, and **E. A. Rees**, Senior Lecturer in Soviet History, both at the Centre for Russian and East European Studies, University of Birmingham

Recent titles include:

Lynne Attwood
CREATING THE NEW SOVIET WOMAN

John Barber and Mark Harrison (*editors*)
THE SOVIET DEFENCE-INDUSTRY COMPLEX FROM STALIN TO KHRUSHCHEV

Vincent Barnett
KONDRATIEV AND THE DYNAMICS OF ECONOMIC DEVELOPMENT

R. W. Davies
SOVIET HISTORY IN THE YELTSIN ERA

James Hughes
STALINISM IN A RUSSIAN PROVINCE

Melanie Ilič
WOMEN WORKERS IN THE SOVIET INTERWAR ECONOMY

Peter Kirkow
RUSSIA'S PROVINCES

Stephen Lovell, Alena Ledeneva and Andrei Rogachevskii (editors)
BRIBERY AND *BLAT* IN RUSSIA

E. A. Rees (*editor*)
DECISION-MAKING IN THE STALINIST COMMAND ECONOMY

Lennart Samuelson
PLANS FOR STALIN'S WAR MACHINE
Tukhachevskii and Military-Economic Planning, 1925–1941

Vera Tolz
RUSSIAN ACADEMICIANS AND THE REVOLUTION

Studies in Russian and East European History and Society
Series Standing Order ISBN 0–333–71239–0
(*outside North America only*)

You can receive future titles in this series as they are published by placing a standing order. Please contact your bookseller or, in case of difficulty, write to us at the address below with your name and address, the title of the series and the ISBN quoted above.

Customer Services Department, Macmillan Distribution Ltd, Houndmills, Basingstoke, Hampshire RG21 6XS, England

Bribery and *Blat* in Russia

Negotiating Reciprocity from the Middle Ages to the 1990s

Edited by

Stephen Lovell
St John's College
Oxford

Alena Ledeneva
New Hall
Cambridge

and

Andrei Rogachevskii
University of Glasgow

in association with
SCHOOL OF SLAVONIC AND EAST EUROPEAN STUDIES
UNIVERSITY OF LONDON

First published in Great Britain 2000 by
MACMILLAN PRESS LTD
Houndmills, Basingstoke, Hampshire RG21 6XS and London
Companies and representatives throughout the world

A catalogue record for this book is available from the British Library.

ISBN 0–333–73694–X

First published in the United States of America 2000 by
ST. MARTIN'S PRESS, INC.,
Scholarly and Reference Division,
175 Fifth Avenue, New York, N.Y. 10010

ISBN 0–312–23127–X

Library of Congress Cataloging-in-Publication Data
Bribery and blat in Russia : negotiating reciprocity from the Middle Ages to the 1990s / edited by Stephen Lovell, Alena Ledeneva, and Andrei Rogachevskii.
p. cm. — (Studies in Russian and East European history and society)
Includes bibliographical references and index.
ISBN 0–312–23127–X
1. Business ethics—Russia. 2. Exchange—Russia. 3. Business networks—Russia. 4. Bribery—Russia. 5. Business ethics—Soviet Union. 6. Exchange—Soviet Union. 7. Business networks—Soviet Union. 8. Bribery—Soviet Union. 9. Business ethics—Russia (Federation) 10. Exchange—Russia (Federation) 11. Business networks—Russia (Federation) 12. Bribery—Russia (Federation) I. Lovell, Stephen, 1972– II. Ledeneva, Alena V., 1964– III. Rogachevskii, A. B. IV. Series.
HF5387.5.R8 B75 2000
364.1'323'0947—dc21 99–054893

This book is printed on paper suitable for recycling and made from fully managed and sustained forest sources.

10 9 8 7 6 5 4 3 2 1
09 08 07 06 05 04 03 02 01 00

Printed and bound in Great Britain by
Antony Rowe Ltd, Chippenham, Wiltshire

Contents

Preface

The main inspiration for this volume was the conference 'Bribery, *Blat* and Patronage in Russia', held over two days in the School of Slavonic and East European Studies, University of London, in June 1997. We would like to thank all those who helped to make this an intellectually stimulating occasion: the speakers, the discussants and the many people who offered their comments from the floor. Julian Graffy and Geoffrey Hosking deserve our special thanks for their support of the project from its inception. We are grateful to the Humanities Research Board of the British Academy for contributing financially towards the conference.

We would also like to thank our two anonymous readers for their constructive and thought-provoking comments. And thanks, finally, to our ever-alert copy-editor, John Andrew.

Stephen Lovell
Alena Ledeneva
Andrei Rogachevskii

August 1998

Notes on the Contributors

Irina Davydova was a Lecturer in Sociology at the University of Novosibirsk from 1991 to 1994 and is currently completing her PhD on the topic 'Moral Traditions of Russian Communities' at Manchester University. Her main interests lie in the study of Russian culture.

J.A. Dunn has been a member of the Department of Slavonic Languages at the University of Glasgow since 1976. He teaches Russian Language and Slavonic Philology, and his main research interests are the Russian language in the post-Soviet period and the Russian mass media (especially television).

Sheila Fitzpatrick is the Bernadotte E. Schmitt Professor of Modern Russian History at the University of Chicago. Her most recent books are *Everyday Stalinism. Ordinary Life in Extraordinary Times: Stalin's Russia in the 1930s* (1999) and (ed. with Robert Gellately) *Accusatory Practices: Denunciation in Modern European History, 1789–1989* (1997).

Mark Galeotti is Director of the Organised Russian and Eurasian Crime Research Unit (ORECRU) at Keele University and Senior Lecturer in International History. Educated at Cambridge University and the LSE, he is an acknowledged expert on post-Soviet security issues, with a particular interest in organized crime. He has served on secondment to the British Foreign and Commonwealth Office and written widely on Russia and the USSR.

Åse Grødeland is a Research Assistant in Politics at the University of Glasgow and Co-director of the ESRC project on 'Public Perspectives on Postcommunist Governance'. Her doctorate (1996) was on the emergence and development of the Green Movement in Ukraine.

Janet Hartley is Senior Lecturer in International History at the London School of Economics and Political Science. Her PhD thesis (School of Slavonic and East European Studies, 1980) concerned Russian local administration, including the judicial structure, in the reign of Catherine II. She has written extensively on the administrative, diplomatic, institutional and social history of eighteenth- and early-nineteenth-century Russia; her publications include: *Guide to Documents and Manuscripts in the United Kingdom Relating to Russia and the Soviet Union* (1987), *Alexander I* (1994) and *A Social History of the Russian Empire 1650–1825* (1999).

Caroline Humphrey is a Fellow of King's College and Professor of Asian Anthropology at Cambridge University. She has carried out anthropological research in the USSR/Russia, Mongolia, Nepal, India and Inner Mongolia (China). She is author of books on Inner-Asian pastoralism, on collective farms in Russia, theories of ritual, and on Mongolian shamanism. She has also published articles on gender, kinship, economic exchange and barter, Jainism, Buddhism, and post-socialist transformations.

Catriona Kelly is Reader in Russian at Oxford University and Tutorial Fellow of New College. Besides numerous articles on Russian literature and cultural history, her publications include *A History of Russian Women's Writing 1820–1992* (1994) and *An Anthology of Russian Women's Writing 1777–1992* (1994). She is also co-editor of *Constructing Russian Culture in the Age of Revolution, 1881–1940* (1998) and *An Introduction to Russian Cultural Studies* (1998). She is currently at work on *Refining Russia: Gender and the Regulation of Behaviour from Catherine to Yeltsin*.

Tatyana Koshechkina is Managing Director of USM (Ukrainian Surveys and Market Research) and an Honorary Fellow in Politics at the University of Glasgow. Formerly she worked in the Institute of Sociology of the National Academy of Sciences, Kyiv, and later founded and became the first Managing Director of SOCIS-GALLUP.

Alena Ledeneva is currently a Research Fellow of New Hall and Affiliated Lecturer at the Faculty of Social and Political Sciences, Cambridge University. She gained her first degree in Novosibirsk, and her MPhil and PhD in Cambridge. Having previously taught sociology and social theory at the University of Novosibirsk, she now teaches courses on Russian politics and society at Cambridge. She has done research in the sociology and anthropology of everyday life, forms of exchange, and the barter economy. She is the author of *Russia's Economy of Favours* (1998).

Stephen Lovell received his PhD from the School of Slavonic and East European Studies in 1998, and is now a Junior Research Fellow at St John's College, Oxford. He is the author of *The Russian Reading Revolution: Print Culture in the Soviet and Post-Soviet Eras* (forthcoming). His current project is a history of the *dacha*.

William L. Miller is Edward Caird Professor of Politics at the University of Glasgow and a Fellow of the British Academy. His recent publications include *Values and Political Change in Postcommunist Europe* (1998), co-edited with Stephen White and Paul Heywood.

Cathy J. Potter is Lecturer in History at the Chinese University of Hong Kong. She has published an article in *Chteniia po istorii russkoi kul'tury (RAN)*, is a contributor to the Solov'ev translation project and the *Modern Encyclopedia of Religions in Russia and the Soviet Union*, and is working on a manuscript on Patriarch Ioakim and the Russian Church at the end of the seventeenth century.

Andrei Rogachevskii is Teaching Assistant at the Department of Slavonic Languages and Literatures, University of Glasgow. He is the author of *Ritoricheskie traditsii v poetike A.S. Pushkina* (1994) and *Zhurnal 'Tvorchestvo' (Moskva, 1918–1922): Ukazatel' soderzhaniia* (with O.S. Figurnova, 1997), as well as of many articles on Russian literature, history and culture. He received his PhD from the University of Glasgow in 1998.

Vladimir Spiridonov is Head of the Laboratory of Cognitive Psychology at the Russian State University for the Humanities. Educated at Moscow State University, he is an expert on research into social representations and mentalities.

Vadim Volkov received his PhD from Cambridge University in 1995. His research interests lie in historical sociology, social theory, Russian Studies, and sociology of the state and violence. Currently he is the Dean of the Faculty of Political Sciences and Sociology at the European University at St Petersburg. From 1999 he will be SSRC-MacArthur Foundation Post-Doctoral Fellow in Peace and International Security.

1 Introduction

Alena Ledeneva, Stephen Lovell and Andrei Rogachevskii

Whatever arguments may rage about continuity and change in Russian society and political culture, there are some areas of life in Russia that most observers tend to regard as eternal. In 1971 the *Great Soviet Encyclopedia* called bribery a 'shameful remnant of the past'; today Russians still experience dismay and frustration, mixed with a certain resignation, when confronted by the palm-greasing apparently so ubiquitous in post-Soviet society. Early in 1998 it was estimated that mere access to an office-holder in a position of responsibility cost around $1,000; the fee for registering a car without enormous administrative delays was $2,000; overall, in 1996 alone more than five trillion roubles (approximately $1 billion) was reckoned to have been drained from the public purse by corruption (Elizarov 1998: p. 6). In the 1997 Transparency International ratings, based on a comparative study of fifty-two countries, Russia was judged the fourth most corrupt after Nigeria, Bolivia and Colombia.[1]

Yet perhaps 'bribery' and 'corruption' are terms too harsh and unforgiving to do justice to the multifarious forms of unofficial transaction into which Russians enter for material, social or cultural gain. Is bribery a crime or a means of survival? Might it not be true that in Russia the unofficial exchange of favours has contributed fundamentally to the social cohesiveness and viability of political systems where the rule of law has (in)famously failed to operate?

We are grateful to Cambridge University Press for permission to reproduce some ideas originally presented in Ledeneva, *Russia's Economy of Favours* (Cambridge, 1998), and to Catriona Kelly for her insightful commentary on a draft of this chapter.

Or is this interpretation a dangerous step in the direction of moral relativism?

These are important questions, but we can only even begin to answer them by defining and explicating our main terms: bribery (the use of public office for private gain) and *blat* (the informal exchange of favours). Before proceeding to this theoretical exposition, however, we should emphasize that the present volume will focus not on corruption as such, but rather on routine 'give-and-take' practices which may (as in the case of bribery) or may not (as in the case of *blat*) generally be referred to as 'corrupt'. Although Russian society is by no means unique in its reliance on unofficial exchange, such practices have been remarkably tenacious throughout Russian history. By giving them centre stage, our intention is to illuminate aspects of Russia's social and cultural history that are often overlooked or downplayed in studies of corruption.

Why this Book Is Not about Corruption

As generally understood, 'corruption' is a generic term that designates a range of practices such as bribery, patronage, nepotism, embezzlement and so on. Whereas the latter terms are used to denote particular types of transaction which together contribute to the spread of corruption in a social system, 'corruption' connotes an attribute of the system itself. Robert Klitgaard (1988), for example, argues that there are not just two actors (a 'client' and an 'agent') involved in any corrupt transaction, but rather three: a client, an agent and a principal (very often the state) which authorizes the agent to act on its behalf. A transaction becomes corrupt when a gap opens up between an agent's actual conduct and that prescribed by the principal's interests, that is, when the agent (for example, the government official) does not obey the codes laid down by the state and deviates from his or her formal duties as a representative of the state's interests.

Most definitions of corruption cover both transactions between agents ('bribe'-takers) and clients ('bribe'-givers) and the direct abuse by an agent of his or her relationship to the state (for example, internal fraud, theft of property and misuse of power). If, however, a *client* abuses his or her relationship to the state (for example, through tax evasion, illegal economic operations, diversion of state property and so on), this is not considered to be corruption, since it does not involve the collusion of an agent of the state. According to this definition, *blat* and other informal practices of 'co-operation' between clients for the sake of 'beating the system' would not come under the category of corruption unless they involved an agent who was supposed to represent the state rather than to 'beat' it; bribery, patronage and nepotism, on the other hand, most certainly would be categorized as corrupt.

However clear this distinction might seem, there is a good deal of disagreement as to what constitutes corruption legally, historically and culturally (see Heidenheimer, Johnston and LeVine 1989). Nor are definitions of corruption independent of moral judgement. At the most basic level, corruption is taken to be 'the use of public office for private advantage' (Palmier 1983: p. 207), the latter term being understood not only in a pecuniary sense but also in terms of status and influence. As Friedrich (1966: pp. 74–5), following Weber, has pointed out, however, the use of public office for private advantage is not always widely perceived in a given society as corrupt. Particularly if an individual making personal gains is simultaneously making a positive contribution to society, many will see such actions as at least acceptable and sometimes even as 'a just reward'. Thus, although corruption usually implies some kind of betrayal of public confidence, the significance of that betrayal cannot be given a universal assessment. Because of the potential clash between an abstract definition of corruption and its application to a complex real world, some authors have distinguished between what may crudely be called 'good', 'bad' and 'ambiguous' — or white, black and grey — corruption (Heidenheimer 1970: pp. 26–7).

The acceptability of particular 'corrupt' practices may vary considerably according to the societies where they occur. Soviet people clearly felt that bribery and embezzlement, on whatever scale, were worse forms of corruption than the small-scale use of public resources for private ends, such as using workers to do private jobs in enterprise time (Lampert 1984: p. 371). To an extent, this ranking of corrupt practices echoes the legal distinctions drawn between various forms of corruption in the Criminal Code and the penalties applied for engaging in them. Some give-and-take practices, for example *blat,* are not on the criminal scale at all. But even in the case of an activity — such as bribery — which is, strictly speaking, illegal (particularly when a bribe has been extorted), some respectable reasons for accommodating it within the category of 'good' or 'ambiguous' corruption can be found. Some of these reasons are value-orientated and relate to general human ideals (a bribe may be essential to save someone's life, family or business, or to help somebody who 'really deserves it', and so on). Others are goal-orientated and rely on a particular interpretation of state interests (for example, the actions of Soviet fixers [*tolkachi*] who bribed apparatchiks in the ministries responsible for their branch of industry might be justified by the need to fulfil the plan). These two modes of reasoning derive from a common source: the confusing nature of the relationship between the public and the private as reflected in both Russian culture and Soviet ideology.

Western definitions of corruption can be very misleading when applied to Russian conditions. Definitions focusing on distinctions between public and private interests or purposes have to confront differences in the economic system and the system of property rights. As Lampert concluded of the USSR: 'it is appropriate to interpret some typical abuses as "organisational" rather than "individual"; the purpose of illegal practices is to further the overall aims of the organisation, not the personal interests of individuals within it' (Lampert 1984: p. 370). The distinction between the organization and the individual, however, becomes blurred, both because organizational success will often bring status and/or material rewards to the individual, and because individual offences may be rationalized in terms of 'the good of the organization'. It is this confusion of the organizational and the personal (which resulted from the ideological norm of self-identification with the purposes of the organization, the Party and the Soviet state) that helped to create a favourable environment for 'give-and-take' practices in the Soviet period. When this confusion was further exacerbated by the collapse of Soviet values in the 1990s, a post-Soviet corruption boom was the result.

The view on corruption outlined above has limitations, not only because public and private spheres often overlap, but also because it does not do justice to the complexity of private actions and motivations. 'Private' give-and-take practices are closely bound up with a range of reciprocities — to do with kin, friendship and relations of mutual help and understanding — which are not necessarily selfish or self-orientated. These personalized relations can bring non-bureaucratic, human codes of behaviour to any level of the social hierarchy or state apparatus (the same action may be called 'nepotism' or 'patronage' at the top of the social hierarchy, while at the bottom of the social hierarchy it will be deemed an 'everyday form of resistance'). Value-orientated codes of this kind acquire particular legitimacy when they operate within a hierarchical and repressive system, and in this case they are known as compensatory codes or codes of hidden opposition. It is precisely the dimensions of 'altruism' and 'compensation', with all their unwritten laws, that are not represented in mainstream corruption studies. Quite apart from this, a focus on corruption *tout court* — that is, on losses incurred by the state and gains made by agents — leaves out those 'give-and-take' practices which might be responsible for and contribute to corruption without themselves being identified as corrupt (networking and informal information channels, for example); it also ignores the advantages clients may gain over the system.

One of the main tasks of this volume, then, is to present the participant's, or 'insider's', view of give-and-take practices located at different points on the legal spectrum, and to place them in their historical, social and cultural contexts. First, however, we must break down these practices theoretically by explaining the distinctions and the connections between bribery and *blat*.

Bribery and Blat*: Differences and Similarities*

Blat is virtually impossible to translate directly into English. As Joseph Berliner, one of the pioneering researchers of the Soviet informal economy, remarked, 'the term *blat* [...] is one of those many flavored words which are so intimate a part of a particular culture that they can be only awkwardly rendered in the language of another' (Berliner 1957: p. 182). Most dictionaries of the Russian language contain the pre-revolutionary meaning of *blat* as 'criminal activity'[2] — although the word was generally used to mean less serious kinds of crime, such as minor theft. In early Soviet times the word acquired a new, 'vulgar', usage: in the expression *po blatu* (by *blat*) it meant 'in an illegal manner' (Ushakov 1935–40). A slightly later Soviet dictionary defines *po blatu* as 'an illegal means of obtaining something by protection or deception' (*SSRLIa* 1950–65). In common parlance, the phrase 'by *blat*' took root as meaning 'by acquaintance' (*po znakomstvu*) and was used to refer to ways to obtain (*dostat'*) or arrange (*ustroit'*) access to goods and services by the use of connections.[3] Although *blat* needs to be viewed in the context of pre-revolutionary Russian 'traditions' of patronage and self-interested giving, it should also be distinguished from them in terms of its extent: the types of everyday 'fixing' encountered in Russian society before 1917 became more widespread and systemic under the shortage economy brought into being by the Soviet state's monopoly over the official distribution of goods and services. The fact that all social strata — even the intelligentsia and the managerial élite — now had to make frequent use of their connections quickly made *blat* a key form of Soviet sociability.[4]

Berliner was not daunted by the cultural specificity of the concept of *blat*, but rather strove to analyse it — and in the process suggested certain criteria for distinguishing *blat* from bribery. He identified one point of difference as the way in which participants enter into the reciprocal arrangement. 'In *blat* there is some personal basis for expecting a proposal to be listened to sympathetically, either for the sake of friendship or because of trust derived from a long business association [...]. In bribery it is only the offer of the bribe which links the two persons involved'. Hence bribery has a somewhat more cynical quality than *blat* and is considered a more dangerous practice (Berliner 1957: p. 191). Bribe-giving must never be witnessed and does not necessarily imply trust or continuity in the relations between the two parties. Bribery is illegal according to a statute in the Criminal Code, while *blat* does not feature there at all.

In contrast to bribery, *blat* requires membership of a certain social network. *Blat* favours are normally provided to people belonging to the circle, to 'one of us'. In such long-term networks of relations or friends, all kinds of favours are possible, and they are not normally paid for directly. This leads us to draw a further distinction: in bribery a direct and immediate payment is usually implied, whereas in *blat* the return favour may or may not take place some time in the future and may take any form. In contradistinction to bribes, defined by the *Concise Oxford Dictionary* as 'money etc. offered to procure action or decision in favour of the giver', *blat* does not imply a straightforward offer and normally excludes money or any other immediate and equivalent repayment. As Crankshaw observed, it should not be thought that

> *blat* has anything in common with simple bribery. It is essentially the product of an under-the-counter mentality which causes friends and acquaintances to combine together to defeat the shortages, and the unlimited, obstructive, entangling red tape of the bureaucratic machine. The motive is self-defence; and the most incorruptible individuals deal in it freely. There is no other way to come through in a land where there is still far from sufficient to satisfy all needs, even at a price. [...]
>
> Straight bribery is quite another matter. *Blat* stands for the exchange of personal favours and is human and warm. Bribery stands for impersonal corruption. (Crankshaw 1956: pp. 74–5)

Bribery implies a conflict of interests resolved only when one is 'compensated' for doing something one would not do otherwise; *blat*, on the other hand, is a form of co-operation and mutual support with a long-term perspective and implies trust rather than compensation for risk. In daily life, to obtain something *po blatu* implies that ordinary people are using their contacts, which may be justified by a situation of urgent need or even on its own terms, as long as these are not seen to exceed modest norms of personal consumption; 'bribery', on the other hand, implies a bribe-taker using a public office and his power for his own material gain — and this is regarded as reprehensible.

Blat is more pervasive than bribery, for it penetrates spheres where money may not be used, either because of the ethics of personal relationships, or because the favour is so petty or so large that it cannot be repaid. *Blat* is widespread both among the poor, who have no money to pay premiums, and among those who would not dare to receive a bribe but would protect or promote someone or something by *blat*. Many people who resist bribery for ethical reasons are quite prepared to use their connections or to 'help' people close to them.

There is, none the less, a close connection between bribery and *blat*. To give a bribe, one has to know how much is to be given and to whom. Such information can only be obtained informally: to give a bribe one has to be recommended as a reliable person in order to guarantee the safety of the bribe-taker; that is, *blat* relations mediate bribery. One needs a chain of *blat* contacts to work out who has to be approached in each particular case, and how this is to be done. With good contacts it may be possible to resolve everything by *blat*, and bribery may not be necessary at all. If there are people in the chain who are not tied by close personal relations, a bribe may quite often be paid. Thus, some links in the chain are secured by *blat*, while others must be paid for directly. The cases where *blat* approaches or mediates bribery create legal problems as well as everyday confusion. This is but one reason why the struggle against bribery and corruption cannot be fully effective: a prosecution case highlights just one link in the chain (between the bribe-giver and the bribe-taker), and fails to target the wider context of *blat* and personal networks.

Because *blat* is not based on immediate payment and is embedded in personal networks, it can easily be disguised by altruistic motives of friendly help. When bribery occurs, profit (not necessarily but quite often pecuniary) is drawn from an official position. In the case of *blat*, even if use is made of an official position, this is done not for immediate profit or for a return favour, but to help a friend, a relative or a 'good person', which enables the donor to maintain a positive self-image. The fact that no money is involved is enough for the transaction to be deemed non-selfish. *Blat* must by definition have an 'affective' as well as an 'instrumental' component, and the two can never be entirely disentangled. The use of *blat* is thus considered less morally reprehensible than the payment of bribes and it is defended by the mechanisms of so-called 'misrecognition' by which friendship is intertwined with the use of friendship. Personal contacts through which a formal procedure is circumvented or access to public resources is gained cannot be seen by the participants themselves as *blat* relations, because they are already perceived as based on or mediated by kin, intimate or friendly relations. Knowingly or unknowingly, people avoid the term '*blat*' when describing their own contacts and personal relations, but are not reluctant to use this term when referring to the informal contacts of other individuals or groups. Thus, *blat* is frequently 'misrecognized' in one's own case, but can easily be recognized in the case of the other.

The concept of 'misrecognition', as we employ it here, was first formulated by Pierre Bourdieu in his critique of economic or objectivist explanations of gift exchange. According to Bourdieu's account, although objectivist explanations lay bare the reciprocal structure underpinning any 'voluntary' act of gift-giving, they overlook the fact that 'gift exchange is one of the social games that cannot be played unless the players refuse to acknowledge the objective truth of the game, the very truth that objective analysis brings to light, and unless they are predisposed to contribute, with their efforts, their marks of care and attention, and their time, to the production of collective misrecognition' (Bourdieu 1990: pp. 105–6).

In other words, if gift-givers openly acknowledge that they are involved in equivalent exchange, and that they expect something of equivalent value in return, this is not gift-giving any more. In the case of *blat*, misrecognition is not collective in the same sense. Misrecognition remains normal for the participants in *blat* transactions, who can practise *blat* only if they recognize it as 'helping out'. From the perspective of an observer, however, any such deal is recognized as *blat*. By a perpetual switching of perspectives one is able to engage in *blat* practices and at the same time to distance oneself from them.

Thus, in the case of *blat*, the 'misrecognition game' is often incomplete, as not all individuals would accept the internal rhetoric of *blat* relations. It is even less complete in the case of bribery. A bribe is more difficult to misrecognize, especially if paid in money, and is therefore considered sinister and corrupt. As Caroline Humphrey explains in Chapter 12, one of the distinguishing features of the *vziatka* (bribe) is that it 'creates a particular, usually short-lived, "negative" social relation between the giver and the taker', and Russians will often go to great lengths to ensure that a transaction is *not* construed in this way.

In order to grasp the rules of the 'misrecognition game', we must distinguish between the language of observation (the outsider's view) and the language of participation (the insider's view, often expressed in terms of mutual help or 'friendship rhetoric'). To draw this distinction is not simply a question of finding clean ways of reporting dirty deals (nepotism as 'support', patronage as 'care' or 'respect', old-boy ties as 'friendship', *blat* as 'mutual help'), but rather of identifying the ethics and rituals which guide these practices and the ways they are expressed in language.

The Legitimacy of Give-and-Take Practices

We have now seen that the assessment of give-and-take practices may vary according to the point from which they are observed.

Variation is also possible on a broader social and historical scale. In traditional societies, for example, gift-giving to curry favour is widespread. It is an accepted practice necessary for building the personal relationships which bind a traditional society together and assure its smooth functioning. In modern societies, many such practices are understood as bribery and condemned as corruption. For this shift to take place, the reconceptualization and redefinition of a form of transaction are required, and in particular its transfer from the realm of the normative to that of the criminal. Over the course of Russian history, many attempts have been made — by, amongst others, theologians, politicians, revolutionaries and industrialists — to re-mark forms of social interaction so as to make them illegitimate, but no cultural revolutions or work ethics have proved strong enough to overthrow Russian society's traditional and heavy reliance on informal reciprocity.

By considering the historical, cultural and comparative aspects of various forms of reciprocity we aim to uncover both the universal and the specific assumptions upon which their disapproval or acceptance rests. For example, 'mutual help' transactions on a moderate scale (like *blat*) seem to be more often accepted, whereas calculative transactions that are orientated towards the accumulation of considerable private wealth (notably bribery) are more likely to be stigmatized. Donors have traditionally found themselves treated rather more leniently than recipients. Other factors that deserve consideration include the particular forms of favour and payment that are employed (for example, sex, commodities, appointments or cash) and the general level of legal consciousness obtaining in a particular society, along with its implications for mapping out the boundaries between privilege and abuse.

'Give-and-take' practices in Russia are often justified as examples of 'forced corruption', both for those who give bribes and for those who take them. In the Soviet period, for example, the system of free medical care and the relatively low wages for doctors would sometimes force a patient to look for either personal contacts or opportunities for bribery and a doctor to accept 'candy, perfume, caviar, sausages, meat and anything else the patients can think of' (Simis 1982: p. 158). Given the structural (both economic and cultural) forces or constraints within the socialist system, one could say that life was impossible *unless* the rules were broken.

People were forced to engage in *blat* practices, if not bribery, to obtain things to which they were legally entitled: medicine, foodstuffs, places at educational institutions and so on. Similarly, for industrial enterprises the only way to obtain the resources to fulfil the plan, and hence to meet the demands of the command economy, was to go through the informal channels laid down by *tolkachi*. *Blat* and, to some extent, bribery can therefore be seen as mechanisms that compensated for the shortages attendant upon the planned economy and for the public disapproval of private gain. Give-and-take provided a bulwark for private interests and 'human' needs against the rigid constraints of the state order and helped Soviet citizens to maintain their standard of living and enjoy a sense of 'beating the system'. These practices were directed at satisfying everyday needs and meeting basic necessities, and so were restricted to the domain of everyday life and carried out on a modest scale. The acceptance of *blat* (and sometimes bribery) as legitimate was fostered in large measure by harsh living conditions, the inefficiency of formal procedures and the inability of state institutions to cope with people's day-to-day demands.

If we take a longer historical view, we can point to three major factors that have tended over the centuries to make systems of unofficial reciprocities both prevalent and relatively accepted features of Russian society. First, the patrimonial nature of political rule based on tradition, personal loyalty and direct dependence, which to a certain extent endured as a feature of the Soviet bureaucratic state. Secondly, the relative weakness of law in Russia, especially law relating to property. Thirdly, the weakness of the market: this was a society where money was always in short supply or of little value, and where market relations were largely subordinate to other forms of exchange, communication and prestige. But our concern in this volume is not only to account for the prevalence of bribery and *blat* in Russian society, but also to explain when, how and why these practices have come to be treated as dubious, wrong, or simply illegal. With this in mind, we should qualify the three factors listed above: yes, Russia has been deeply marked by its traditions of patrimonial rule, yet it has also borne the brunt of (often virulent) modernizing ideologies; likewise, although in Russia the law has often been weakly administered and inadequately formulated, it has remained a nagging normative presence (and sometimes rather more than that); and, finally, although Russians have often affected to despise money, they are not altogether indifferent to it. For all these reasons, we believe, reciprocity is an important and highly contested informal institution which offers rich insights into Russia's social and cultural history.

The Structure of the Book

The chapters are arranged in broadly chronological order, starting with the early modern period and ending in the 1990s. Although reciprocal practices in Russia show significant continuity over the centuries covered by our contributors, their evaluation has often proved problematic and controversial. Cathy J. Potter, in her chapter 'Payment, Gift or Bribe? Exploring the Boundaries in Pre-Petrine Russia', charts the emergence of a discourse on corruption in Russia in the early modern period, taking as her main source legal documents generated by both central and local authorities. By studying carefully the usage of key terms such as *pochest′*, *posuly*, *mzda* and *likhoimstvo* it is possible to trace the evolution (and the inconsistencies) in official attitudes to various forms of give-and-take. Potter argues that, from the end of the fifteenth century onwards, the central government and the Church increasingly sought to draw clear distinctions between payment for services rendered, acceptable gifts, and bribes. Such efforts, however, were not necessarily successful: the process was slow and uneven. Not only were traditional mentalities tenacious, but the financial and legal arrangements of the state administration frequently made it difficult, if not impossible, to make and enforce such distinctions.

In Chapter 3, Vadim Volkov examines a thorough-going attempt to challenge and transform a social system based on pre-modern mentalities and structures: the reforms of the first quarter of the eighteenth century, when the ways of traditional society collided with Peter I's determination to bring concepts of law and legal system into Russian administration. Volkov explains Russia's persistent corruption problem, and Russia's perception that it has such a problem, in terms of an enduring (since Peter) conflict between patrimonial and rational-bureaucratic principles of government. Corruption should be seen not as some deep-seated reflex of Russian culture or of the Russian mentality, but rather as the product of Russia's 'historically specific patterns of rapid modernization'.

In Chapter 4, Janet Hartley shows some of these historically specific factors at work as she investigates the causes and effects of bribery in the administration of justice under Catherine II. In the late eighteenth century, bribery was pervasive in Russian provincial courts for a number of reasons. The prevailing 'culture of bribery and fees' ensured that legal officials were allowed (and even expected) to exact dues from the local population. At the lower levels of the legal bureaucracy, clerks were more or less driven to take bribes by the inadequacy of their salaries. Throughout the legal administration — often even at the higher levels — posts might be filled by inexperienced (sometimes adolescent) and poorly educated personnel. The cause of greater procedural regulation was further weakened by the vagueness of Russian legal codes and the sluggish operational tempo of the courts. In short, the problem was the weakness of the Russian judicial system rather than bribery *per se*.

In Chapter 5, Catriona Kelly shifts the focus away from administrative structures by placing *vziatochnichestvo* in the context of a variety of forms of 'self-interested giving' in Russian élite and popular culture — from peasant practices such as *pomochi* to upper-class practices such as tipping, nepotism and patronage more generally. These practices, and the values that went with them, made Russian society relatively tolerant of give-and-take activities, as long as they were not felt to be unduly abusive of power relations. Kelly then examines hitherto-neglected sources (notably the translated self-help books of Samuel Smiles) to describe the attempts made to inculcate a new ethic of reciprocity in late imperial Russia. These efforts, however, had only limited success: a relatively relaxed attitude to self-interested giving persisted in Russian culture. Somewhat more revealing of the prevailing 'etiquette' of bribery are native Russian advice-literature, journalism and *belles-lettres*. An analysis of this material brings the chapter to its suggestive conclusion: that bribery appealed not only because it was formally similar to customs sanctioned by tradition, but also because it acted as a levelling device (power was contested between bribe-giver and bribe-taker, so that the asymmetry of authority between officials and members of the public was challenged), and so had particular appeal for a culture where anti-statism had been and remained a persistent force.

'Self-interested giving' may have been an accepted part of Russian culture, but the extortion of gifts by officialdom was, by the nineteenth century, recognized as an acute problem. And in the writings of the time there was rarely any doubt who was to blame for this state of affairs: the bureaucracy. Irina Davydova's chapter, however, suggests that our perception of nineteenth-century Russian public servants risks taking its cue from an exceedingly partisan Russian intellectual tradition. Like Janet Hartley, Davydova argues that the Russian bureaucracy was profoundly undermined by the social conditions in which the class of officials was formed. But its position was further weakened by the implacable opposition of the intelligentsia, which monopolized the public sphere to put forward its own concept of public service — a concept that had very little to do with the performance of legal and administrative duties. What is more, Russian social philosophy took up an antagonistic attitude to the bureaucratic ethic of following the rules, arguing instead that only 'love' could provide a valid ethical basis for human relationships. The Russian intelligentsia may, for once, have underestimated the power of its anti-bureaucratic ideas to shape reality.

Davydova is just one of several contributors in this volume to draw on literary sources for illustration. There is often no better place than *belles-lettres* to look for material on bribery, a practice that is by definition under-represented in the sources that social historians generally like to consult. In Chapter 7, Andrei Rogachevskii surveys the huge body of nineteenth-century imaginative writing on bribery. Literary representations, he shows, can shed much light on questions that are raised throughout this volume: the etiquette of bribery, its evaluation by participants and observers, the social acceptability of various practices, the distinction between donor and recipient, intentionality, and actual common practice. Moreover, just as literature can help with our study of bribery, so bribery did its bit for Russian literature: literary depictions of Russian officialdom on the take helped to bring into being a distinctive and highly influential satirical tradition.

In Chapter 8, Stephen Lovell investigates the response of Soviet literature to the 'cultural revolution' of the 1920s — which, among other things, aimed to combat old forms of self-interested giving (and taking), and replace them with a new ethic of *kul'turnost'*. Far from providing a transmission belt for new ethical norms, however, early Soviet literature offers an illuminating commentary on their interaction with actual practices and values. Public rhetoric, far from acting as an impersonal arbiter of social norms, could be adapted by the individual speaker to suit his or her situational ethics. Moreover, literary works of the 1920s provide much evidence of a tension (perennial in Russia) between law and social custom and between the letter of the law and the spirit imputed to it by different social actors. The chapter ends with a necessarily brief coda on 'mature' Socialist Realism and the post-Stalin period: here too, it is argued, literary representations of reciprocity occupy a complex and revealing middle ground between ideology and real social values.

In Chapter 9, Sheila Fitzpatrick examines some of the forms of reciprocity that emerged under Stalin, taking as her main source material collected as part of the Harvard Interview Project in the early 1950s. The command economy and official distribution system brought into being their 'unofficial *Doppelgänger*': a widespread network of mutual-help relations. Despite the official condemnation of *blat*, Soviet citizens came increasingly to find it an essential lubricant to oil the stiff wheels of the planned economy. In addition, Fitzpatrick argues that *blat* became rather more than an unpleasant necessity: the 'friendship rhetoric' that accompanied the unofficial exchange of favours was not just a camouflage for economic self-interest, but rather fostered a peculiarly Soviet form of social solidarity.

In Chapter 10, Alena Ledeneva takes the discussion of Soviet *blat* into the 1990s. She argues that new rules and opportunities emerged with the market reforms and brought radical changes to a social environment where reliance on people always used to be much more important than reliance on money and formal arrangements. This has put give-and-take practices on a quite different footing: nowadays informal contacts are employed not to obtain consumer goods or to meet daily needs but rather to make money and acquire property. Consequently, just as the Soviet system was dependent on its 'counter-economy', so the post-Soviet order has found itself tied to a corrupt and criminal economy. Long-standing Soviet mechanisms of self-help are now enabling post-Soviet *biznesmeny* to help themselves. The interpenetration of the economy, political structures and organized crime puts serious obstacles in the way of Russia's aspiration to institute the rule of law.

J.A. Dunn's chapter foregrounds a subject that no reader of this book will be able to ignore: the ways in which attitudes to bribery are reflected in language. Dunn examines the vocabulary of modern Russian and the etymology and usage of terms pertaining to bribery. He finds that criminal slang (*blatnoi zhargon*), usually a rich source of new words on all manner of social activies, has contributed relatively little on bribery. The terms most current in modern Russian are drawn mainly from three other sources: exoticisms (generally orientalisms), 'respectable' terms and circumlocutions. Such euphemisms, Dunn argues, are generated by the need to 'defuse the potential embarrassment of a situation in which otherwise respectable people are engaged in an illegal transaction'. Language, in other words, plays a leading part in the 'misrecognition game' described earlier in this Introduction.

In Chapter 12, Caroline Humphrey goes beyond commonplace public representations of bribery and focuses instead on the ways in which reciprocal transactions are mediated by and reflected in the discourse of their participants. Here again language is crucial. The Russian term *vziatka* is too specific to be rendered adequately by 'bribe'; it must and can also be distinguished from mutual help, at one extreme, and tribute (*dan′*), at the other. Humphrey investigates the origins and nature of the stigma commonly attached to bribery, the limits of its social acceptability and the etiquette required of donors and recipients. By drawing on examples from contemporary Russia, she enquires whether the connotative field of the term *vziatka* has changed its contours in the post-Soviet period.

In Chapter 13, Vladimir Spiridonov offers a fresh perspective on the affective charge carried by certain terms relating to bribery: that of a practising psychologist. Analysing data collected as part of an independent experiment, he finds that people's emotional responses to 'the bribe', '*blat*' and a range of related concepts, do not coincide with their extremely negative declarative assessments. Spiridonov's research points strongly to the importance of power relations in the practice of bribery. The subjects of his experiment may not have felt any particular affection for the bribe-taker, but they at least respect him (not usually her) as someone who wields power and influence; the bribe-giver, on the other hand, is looked down on as powerless and ineffectual.

In Chapter 14, William L. Miller, Tatyana Koshechkina and Åse Grødeland take their own look at the dynamics of the relationship between bribe-taker (official) and bribe-giver (citizen), drawing on extensive focus-group research in the Czech Republic, Slovakia, Bulgaria and Ukraine. This chapter provides illuminating detail and an important comparative perspective on citizens' strategies for coping with officials in the post-Communist world. Two broad conclusions are drawn from the data collected. First, that to cite long-term cultural factors (such as religion or allegiance to one or other of the nineteenth-century European empires) as determinants of citizens' behaviour and attitudes may be reductive in the extreme; their lived experience of Soviet-style bureaucracy over the past fifty years is a more significant factor. Secondly, that current variations in the relationship between citizens and officialdom are strongly affected by varying experiences of economic transition across the former Soviet Bloc.

In the final chapter, Mark Galeotti seeks partially to rehabilitate 'corruption' as an analytical term. Although informal social networks have traditionally helped the Russian economy and administrative system to function, they have also left Russia vulnerable to organized crime and high-level political corruption. Not only that, corruption has functioned as a peculiarly effective 'tool of governance' in Soviet and pre-Soviet Russia: it devolves responsibility for revenue collection without threatening the state's power to intervene in all areas of economic activity; in the absence of enforceable legal mechanisms, it has the advantage of 'getting the job done'; it reduces pressure for change by buying off potentially powerful élites; and it even helps to preserve popular acquiescence in the political order by giving ordinary people their own (albeit highly inequitable) stake in the system. All these considerations remain valid in post-Soviet Russia, but there are also good reasons to suppose that 'the corrupt art of governing Russia' has reached a new stage in the 1990s. Every society strikes its own balance between formal and informal structures and practices, but the interplay of formal and informal, Galeotti implies, is in danger of becoming socially malignant when formal structures come to be dominated (if not controlled) by informal ones. For anyone familiar with the cronyism of the Yeltsin regime and concerned about Russia's future, there is considerable food for thought here.

Notes

1 Full details located at http:\\www.GWDG.DE/~uwvw/icr.htm.

2 According to dictionaries of etymology (Fasmer 1964, Shanskii 1965), the term *blat* came into Russian from Polish *blat*, meaning 'someone who provides an umbrella, a cover' (*ukryvatel'*); this in turn is taken from Yiddish *blat* which means 'close, familiar' (*svoi*). In its original sense, in the phrase '*Svoi? Stuchish' po blatu?*' (meaning 'Are you one of us? Do you speak our *blat* lingo?'), it was already being used at the beginning of the century. Like much other slang, the term *blat* was probably coined in Odessa, Russia's southern port, known as the leading conduit for linguistic imports (Polivanov 1931: p. 154).

3 *Blat* does not, however, appear in any of the three editions of the *Great Soviet Encyclopedia* (in volumes published in 1927, 1950 and 1970) since, although the term was in wide informal currency, it was banned from official discourse and the practices associated with it were condemned by the Soviet authorities.

4 For more on the peculiarly Soviet flavour of *blat*, see the later chapters by Sheila Fitzpatrick and Alena Ledeneva.

Bibliography

Berliner, J.S. (1957), *Factory and Manager in the USSR*, Cambridge, MA.

Bourdieu, P. (1990), *The Logic of Practice*, trans. Richard Nice, Cambridge.

Crankshaw, E. (1956), *Russia without Stalin*, London.

Elizarov, A. (1998), 'S kogo vziatki gladki?', *Rossiiskaia gazeta*, 18 February.

Fasmer [Vasmer], M. (1964), *Etimologicheskii slovar' russkogo iazyka*, vol. 1, Moscow.

Friedrich, C.J. (1966), 'Political Pathology', *The Political Quarterly*, 37, 1.

Heidenheimer, A. (1970), *Political Corruption: Readings in Comparative Analysis*, New Brunswick, NJ.

Heidenheimer, A., Johnston, M. and LeVine, V. (eds) (1989), *Political Corruption: A Handbook*, New Brunswick, NJ.

Klitgaard, R. (1988), *Controlling Corruption*, Berkeley, CA.

Lampert, N. (1984), 'Law and Order in the USSR: The Case of Economic and Official Crime', *Soviet Studies*, 36, 3.

Palmier, L. (1983), 'Bureaucratic Corruption and its Remedies' in M. Clarke (ed.), *Corruption: Causes, Consequences and Control*, London.

Polivanov, A. (1931), *O slavianskom slovoobrazovanii*, Moscow.

Shanskii, N. (1965), *Etimologicheskii slovar' russkogo iazyka*, vol. 1, Moscow.

Simis, K.M. (1982), *USSR: Secrets of a Corrupt Society*, London.

SSRLIa (1950–65), *Slovar' sovremennogo russkogo literaturnogo iazyka*, 17 vols, Moscow.
Ushakov, D.N. (ed.) (1935–40), *Tolkovyi slovar' russkogo iazyka*, 4 vols, Moscow.

2 Payment, Gift or Bribe? Exploring the Boundaries in Pre-Petrine Russia

Cathy J. Potter

The reputation of Russian officials for corruption and a remarkable receptivity to bribery is long-standing and has provided material sufficient to make the name of more than one talented author. Given the perception of ubiquitous corruption, it is surprising that few historians have explored the phenomenon in Russian society before the 1917 revolutions. Only recently has the topic been addressed in regard to pre-Petrine Russia. N.F. Demidova (1987) included a brief but provocative discussion of *kormlenie ot del* (literally 'feeding from business') in her larger work on the Russian service bureaucracy in the seventeenth century. More recently, P.V. Sedov (1996) discussed *podnosheniia*, the practice of gift presentation (generally accompanied by the expectation of some kind of return), in the official world of seventeenth-century Moscow, basing his work on a careful analysis of the account books of several important monasteries.

Central to all discussions of corruption is the problem of definition. Heidenheimer (1970) began his classic collection on political corruption by offering seven scholars' different approaches to, and definitions of, corruption. Rocca (1992: pp. 402–16) argues for yet

---

I would like to thank those at the School of Slavonic and East European Studies of the University of London for organizing a productive and stimulating conference on bribery, Chinese University for funding my attendance at the conference, and Professor Daniel Kaiser for bringing the text *On Witnesses* to my attention and for suggesting some improvements to some of my translations.

another, anthropological, approach to the problem of definition in his analysis of corruption in modern China. Pavarala (1996) emphasizes the dynamic political process of definition, and Johnston (1996: pp. 321–35) reminds us that consensus still has not been attained. Understandings of what constitutes corruption differ according to time and place, and these differences are reflected in terminology. The Russian term frequently used in formal speech is *vziatochnichestvo.* Its derivation from *vziat′*, 'to take', focuses attention on bribery and/or extortion (Brokgauz and Efron 1892: *s.v. vziatochnichestvo*). Most would agree that bribery and extortion come under the umbrella of corruption. Few would agree that corruption is limited to these examples.

Even limiting the discussion of corruption to bribery and extortion, however, does not solve the problem of definition in the context of pre-Petrine Russia. The aforementioned works of Demidova and Sedov manifest the difficulties of defining bribery in a society that in Weberian terms would be considered institutionally 'irrational', pre-modern and perhaps closest to a patrimonial-bureaucratic state (see Weber 1964: pp. 329–36, 342–5). Demidova locates her discussion of bribery under the heading '*kormlenie ot del*', vividly emphasizing the problem of differentiating payment for services rendered and bribery, at a time when the payment of officials in government services came, at least in part, directly from the people 'served'. This practice was not disappearing in the course of the seventeenth century. On the contrary, Demidova's work shows it was being extended (Demidova 1987: pp. 122–37).

In her discussion, Demidova distinguishes between a series of terms: *pochest′*, *pominki* and *posul*. She defines *pochest′* as a gift in money or kind, generally presented to officials in advance to assure the successful and speedy conclusion of business. *Pominki* were payments, almost always in money, for the fulfilment of a specific item of business within the jurisdiction of the receiving official. Both *pochest′* and *pominki* were accepted and expected supplemental payments to officials from their 'clients', necessary for their support and maintenance. *Posul*, in Demidova's opinion, was a bribe (*vziatka* is the term she uses to clarify the point), condemned by the state and liable to be prosecuted under the law (Demidova 1987: pp. 143–4). Sedov, however, questions the precision of Demidova's formulations. He notes, I think correctly, that the boundary between 'legal' *pochest′* and 'illegal' *posul* was extremely unstable. *Pominki* too vacillated between the poles of 'legal' gift and 'illegal' bribe (Sedov 1996: p. 146; see also Davies 1997: pp. 42–5).

The problem of defining corruption (or more narrowly bribery and extortion) as these concepts were understood in pre-Petrine Russia thus becomes a problem of searching for boundaries, of seeking to identify characteristics distinguishing an acceptable payment for services rendered from unacceptable extortion, an acceptable gift from an unacceptable bribe. The work of Mauss (1967) and more recently of Klitgaard (1991: pp. 211–39), or a cursory reading of most daily newspapers, reminds us that the problem of drawing the boundaries between payments, gifts and bribes is not a problem limited either to Russia or to the early modern period. In so far as corruption and bribery are normative rather than ideal concepts, a precise and universal definition establishing clear and firm boundaries will always elude us. In so far as such concepts are contingent on time and place, it is useful to examine their usage in specific contexts, seeking to grasp their meaning at different points in their evolution.

The purpose of this chapter is a limited one: to explore the usage of terms related to the notions of bribery and extortion as they evolved in Russia over time (*c.* eleventh to eighteenth centuries) in legal documents. This is neither to assume nor to argue that legislators and their laws exclusively and conclusively define corruption, or even bribery and extortion (for the problems of 'legalistic definitions', see Pavarala 1996: pp. 60–3; Johnston 1996: pp. 322–3; and Mény 1996: pp. 310–11). Law does not necessarily reveal 'the view from below'. Nor does it necessarily include all acts that individuals in a society would perceive as corrupt. At the very least, however, it does reveal some of the definitions and boundaries the ruling élite wished to promulgate and, if possible, enforce at different points in time. Given the weaknesses of early modern governments in general, and of the government of pre-Petrine Russia in particular, it may well be that such definitions and boundaries enjoyed but limited dissemination and acceptance beyond the inner circles of the ruling élite. None the less, as it is precisely Russian officialdom which historically is accused of corruption, the official understanding of the boundaries of corruption as it evolved over time is not without significance.[1]

'Posul', 'Pominki', 'Poklonnye'...

Through the seventeenth century, *posul* was the term most commonly used to refer to an offering (or, as the root [*sulit'*, 'to promise', in modern Russian] suggests, the promise of one) made with the intention of influencing the decision of a government official or perverting the course of justice. In different contexts, however, the term and its variations did not always carry a negative connotation or denote an illegal action. In one statute of the late fourteenth century (1397/8) *posul* was used in two different places with two distinct meanings. In one article *posul* unambiguously signified a proscribed money transaction, a bribe:

> [Fine] a person who takes justice into his/her own hands four roubles; a person who takes justice into his/her own hands being one who, catching a thief red-handed, lets him/her go, and takes for him/herself a *posul.*
> [*A samosuda chetyre rubli, a samosud to — kto, izymav tatia s polichnym, da otpustit, a sobe posul vozmet*...]
> (*PRP*: vol. 3, 'Ustavnaia gramota ... dvinskoi zemle', art. 6, p. 163)

Article eight used the same term, *posul*, to describe both an acceptable 'fee for services' and an unacceptable bribe. Here it is declared that the official may collect a fee (*posul*) of four *belki* to fetter an accused person unable to produce surety (*poruki*), but 'the *dvorianin* is to take no more than this' (*bolee togo dvorianinu ne vziati nichego*). Further, once surety had been produced the official 'is not to request a fee or bribe [*posul*] [from the accused?] in irons' (*PRP*: vol. 3, art. 8, pp. 163, 192–3. Compare ibid., vol. 2, 'Proekt dogovora ... 1470/1', art. 5, p. 248).

In legal documents of the fifteenth and sixteenth centuries, *posul* generally indicated an unacceptable payment or bribe. The use of the term to mean an acceptable fee for services rendered did not disappear, but some efforts were made to distinguish the two opposed meanings. In a document from Pskov, the element of secrecy was introduced as the boundary distinguishing fee from bribe. The prince and the *posadnik*[2] were ordered to judge in accordance with the law, 'as God will judge them at the second coming of Christ'. Further, the document stated: 'Neither the prince nor the *posadnik* are to take secret payments/bribes [*A tainykh posulov ne imati ni kniaziu, ni posadniku*]' (*PRP*: vol. 2, 'Pskovskaia sudnaia gramota [XV v.]', art. 4, p. 286). The same document also introduced the notion of the 'excessive' in order to distinguish between the acceptable and the unacceptable, between a fee and bribery or extortion. Article forty-eight (ibid., art. 48, pp. 292, 311, 358) condemned officials who demanded someone's clothing or their horse in return for assisting in a judicial procedure. Such an action was identified and equated with plunder and robbery (*grabezh*), and it was punished as such.

Against this background, the *Sudebnik* or Law Code of 1497 provides evidence of attempts on the part of the Grand Prince to define 'excess'. In the Law Code of 1497, the term *posul* was used only to designate an unacceptable fee or demand on the part of officials and it was put alongside detailed descriptions of the fees that officials were permitted to receive for their services. The first article of the Law Code decisively forbade offering *posuly*, extra payments or bribes, to any of the court officials to influence the outcome of the judicial process (*PRP*: vol. 3, p. 346). The third article sought to establish the fee that the *boiarin* and clerk officiating at a hearing could receive (ibid., p. 347). Article thirty-three (ibid., p. 351) prohibited the bailiff (*nedel'shchik*) from requesting a fee/bribe (*posul*) on behalf of the officiating *boiarin*, on behalf of the clerk, or on his own behalf (compare also ibid., articles 66 and 67, p. 357).

As many scholars have remarked, the Law Code of 1497 condemned bribery and extortion, but sanctions against such practices were not established until 1550. From the point of view of definition, however, the document is important. It provides evidence that by the end of the fifteenth century the government recognized the problem of distinguishing between bribes, extortion and permissible fees and sought a solution. Expressed simply, a fee was what the sovereign or the government decreed as reasonable; a bribe was anything in excess of that. This rather crude definition of the boundary between the legal and the illegal, the permitted and the punishable, proved extremely tenacious.

The sixteenth-century documents provide evidence of increasing restriction on the use of the term *posul*. Its neutral meaning as an acceptable fee faded. Increasingly it came to be used exclusively in the sense of an illegal bribe or extortion. In addition, as researchers have noted, in the course of the sixteenth century simple prohibition and condemnation of *posul*y was superseded by the imposition of harsh sanctions against the practice. The Law Codes of 1550 and 1589 included numerous articles prohibiting bribery and extortion and accompanied these articles with threats of punishment. The 'class' orientation of these sanctions, that is, the operating principle that the lower the class, the harsher the punishment, cannot be missed (*PRP*: vol. 4, 'Sudebnik 1550', articles 1–5, 32–4, 42, 45, 53, 62, 99, pp. 233, 240, 242–3, 246, 248–9, 260; ibid., 'Sudebnik 1589', articles 1–5, 94, 96, pp. 413–14, 423, 424).

The Law Codes of 1550 and 1589 are also interesting because of the use of two additional terms, *pominki* and *poklonnye*, both associated with *posul* and thus with bribery and extortion (for example, *PRP*: vol. 4, 'Sudebnik 1550', articles 45, 47, pp. 243–4; ibid., 'Sudebnik 1589', art. 94, p. 423). Related to *pomnit′*, to remember, *pominki* was used most commonly to designate prayers for the dead. In the *Pskov I Chronicle* the word is used several times for entries of the fifteenth century to signify a perfectly legitimate present or gift (Sreznevskii 1989: *s.v. pomin″k″*). Sreznevskii suggested that in some instances *pominki* referred to a type of tax or duty, but in all the examples offered the meaning is ambiguous, and seems to refer to a gift or present rather than to a required tax or fee.

Poklonnye was derived from *poklon″*, a bow manifesting deference, honour and respect. A *iarlyk*, or edict from the khans of the Golden Horde, given in 1379 to Metropolitan Mikhail, linked *pominki* and *poklonnye* (*SGGiD*: vol. 2, no. 12). Like *pominki*, the word frequently appeared in a religious context. Sreznevskii suggested the meaning of gift or present (*dar″*) for one occurrence of *poklon″* in the *Chronicle of Bygone Years*, under the year 6479 (971/2) (Sreznevskii 1989: *s.v. poklon″*).

In these legal documents the boundaries distinguishing *posul*, *pominki* and *poklonnye* were not defined. The unique characteristics of the respective concepts do not emerge from the contexts in which they are used. Article 94 of the Law Code of 1589 linked the terms *pominki* and *poklonnye*, as they were linked in the *iarlyk* of 1379 to Metropolitan Mikhail. This article defined the fees to be given to bailiffs [*nedel′shchiki* and *dovodchiki*] for travelling to a city or around districts [*volosti*] on business, and added:

> And neither the Grand Prince's bailiff nor the *namestnik*'s bailiff is to take *poklonnye* or *pominki* from the surety [given].

> [*A ot poruki nedelshchikam i dovodchikam poklonnago i pominkov ne imati.*]
> (*PRP*: vol. 4, p. 423)

The precise meanings of *poklonnye* and *pominki* here are not clear, but the proscription is. Government officials are not to help themselves to money or property held as surety for an accused party.

In two documents from 1552 and 1555, *posuly* and *pominki* were joined in the same fashion as *poklonnye* and *pominki* above (*PRP*: vol. 4, 'Ustavnaia zemskaia gramota volostei maloi penezhki... [1552]', articles 9, 26, 28, pp. 191, 195–6; ibid., 'Medynskii gubnoi nakaz [1555]', art. 14, p. 185). Documents from the same period use one or the other of the terms alone (for example, *PRP*: vol. 4: 'Prigovor o razboinykh del [1555]', art. 13, p. 426). In none of these cases is it possible to discern any distinction, whether it relate to size, substance or circumstance, in the usages of the different terms. It is likely that from the perspective of the government, the important point was that *any* exchange of money, goods or advantage outside the defined fees, by whatever name, was illegal.

Historians have asserted that the *Ulozhenie*, or Law Code, of 1649 moved in the direction of more precise and specific definition (see Man'kov 1987: pp. 184–5). In the area of defining corruption and bribery such efforts were not notably successful. *Posuly* and *pominki* continued to be linked and undifferentiated, although both were condemned equally and the sanctions against them were defined. For example, two articles threatened harsh punishment, to be determined by the sovereign, for *boiare* and *voevody* who gave leave to soldiers without the permission of the sovereign in return for *posuly* and *pominki* (see Man'kov 1987: ch. 7, articles 10 and 11, pp. 25, 166–7). Chapter ten of the code dealt at length with the courts, and bribery occupied an important place in the discussion. One article threatened harsh punishment to any court official who accused anyone falsely 'because of a *posul*, or because of friendship, or because of enmity [*po posulom, ili po druzhbe, ili po nedruzhbe*]' (ibid., ch. 10, art. 5, p. 31). Subsequent articles of this chapter elaborated on the issue (articles 6–12, pp. 31–2). In these articles, the definition of *posul* as a bribe, and the acceptance of a bribe as an illegal and punishable act, emerges clearly and decisively.

In other chapters and articles of the Law Code of 1649, however, fluctuation and uncertainty in the meaning of the term *posul* remained. In the majority of cases in this document, *posul* is used to designate an illegal bribe or extortion. On the other hand, article sixteen of chapter ten presented situations when *posul* was acceptable, legal and, in fact, expected. This article stated that if *posuly* were given to a clerk or under-clerk for the purpose of hastening some specific business and the affair was not brought to a speedy conclusion, the official was to be fined (art. 6, p. 32).

Despite over a century of efforts by the ruling élite to distinguish the legal fee from the illegal bribe or gift, to differentiate the terms *posul, pominki* and *poklon"*, the boundaries separating payment, gift and bribe remained blurred in the most important law code of the pre-Petrine period. One must agree with Sedov that Demidova over-defined the terms in her discussion of corruption. At the same time, it is worth noting that while *pochest'* does not enter into the framework of the law (Sedov 1996: p. 147), *pominki* and *poklon"* do, and distinctions of quantity, substance or circumstance which might separate these terms are not identified in legal documents. Moreover, even in the Law Code of 1649, there are occasions when *posul* is considered to be acceptable and apparently legal.

Man'kov's assertion that in the context of a centralizing state *posul* was an atavistic survival of the common law, rooted in the practice of *kormlenie* as a means of paying officials, is difficult to accept (Man'kov 1987: pp. 184–5). From at least the fourteenth century, before one can speak persuasively of a centralizing state, *posul*, when used in its negative sense of a bribe, was condemned. The ruling élite in its legal pronouncements condemned what we would understand as bribery and, as Sedov shows, so did society. Sedov emphasizes the practical problems faced in eradicating the practice, noting that in the course of the seventeenth century the compensation paid by the government to lower officials declined, making 'gifts' an essential supplement (Sedov 1987: p. 147). Pragmatic considerations surely did play a role in the process of defining corruption, or bribery, in establishing the boundary between the legal and the illegal, but it is unlikely that such considerations alone shaped the process. If we start at the other end, with words used in the nineteenth century and beyond to denote corruption and bribery, and trace their usage backwards in time, it becomes apparent that moral and ethical considerations also came to play a part in the process of legal definition.

'Mzda', 'Vziatka', 'Likhoimanie'...

By the nineteenth century a number of words, including *mzda* (*mzdoimanie*, *mzdoimstvo*), *vziatka* (*vziatochnichestvo*), and some words on the *likh-* root (*likhoimanie*, *likhoimstva*, *likhoimets*) meant, or carried the unmistakable connotation of, bribery or graft. In the secular legal sense, and probably in the colloquial sense, these words appear to be relatively late additions to the vocabulary of corruption. Rarely were they used in this sense before the eighteenth century.

Mzda can be translated neutrally as fee, reward or compensation. In reference to religious matters, *mzda* and associated words were condemned as simony from early times, thus crossing the boundary into the realm of the unacceptable. The earliest example of this usage appeared in 1147. A *gramota* of Hegumen Antony of the Kievan Caves Monastery warned that a bishop, or anyone, who established someone (as hegumen) of the monastery '*po mzdie*', or committed any violence against the monastery, would be damned. Likewise, should any of the brothers of the cloister seek the post of hegumen '*mzdoiu*', or by violence, they too would suffer damnation (Sreznevskii 1989: *s.v.* *m′zda* = *m″zda* = *mezda* = *mzda*).

In relation to secular matters and in civil documents, however, *mzda* rarely carried the connotation of reprehensible (and prosecutable) bribery; rather it signified a value-neutral fee, payment or compensation. Thus the second article in the *Russkaia pravda (kratkoi redaktsii)* ruled that a man beaten by an aggressor so that visible marks were left, if he could not himself take revenge, was to 'take for the offense three grivnas, and also payment for the physician [*vziati emou za obidou 3 grivne, v letsiu m″zda*]' (*PRP*: vol. 1, p. 77; Kaiser 1992: p. 119). In this context *mzda* remained firmly within the realm of acceptable transactions, safe from the danger of formal legal prosecution, much less social opprobrium. Similarly, a trade agreement negotiated between the principality of Smolensk and Riga in the thirteenth century utilized the term *mzda* to refer to a fee paid to a court official (*det′skii*) to pursue a complaint (*PRP*: vol. 2, p. 13). An earlier version of this agreement is extant in two different redactions (*PRP*: vol. 2, pp. 62–3). In one redaction, the term *mzda* was not used at all; in the second redaction, the meaning of *mzda* is clarified by the term *naem*, suggesting hire, a wage ('*Azhe dast′ naem det′skomou*'). A *iarlyk* dating from the middle of the fourteenth century asserted that no payment was necessary for the privileges bestowed therein, and equated *mzda* with *poshlina*, a fee or tax (*PRP*: vol. 3, p. 466: '*Ne nadobe im mzda, nikakaia poshlina ni emliut u nikh nichego*…'). Finally, the term *mzda* appeared only once in the Law Code of 1649, again used in a value-neutral sense. Announcing the collection of a tax for the ransoming of prisoners, the article justified such a collection as charity which would call forth a great reward or compensation ('*velikaia mzda*') from God (Man′kov 1987: ch. 8, art. 1, pp. 27–8).

The only early case I have found of a legal document where the term *mzda* unambiguously and directly refers to bribery appears in a text entitled 'On Witnesses'. Article eighteen of this text asserted that no one may testify 'who was convicted for having taken a bribe to testify [*m′zdu priem poslush′stvovati*]'. 'On Witnesses' represents a rough and selective translation of a text borrowed from eighth- and ninth-century collections of Byzantine law. This text was known to churchmen in Rus′ at least by the fifteenth century, perhaps earlier, and its presence in several miscellanies suggests the norms it expressed were current in church courts. As Kaiser proposes, it is likely that these norms exerted 'silent influence' on secular conceptions as well (Kaiser 1992: pp. li, 119). Influence in the realm of terminology, however — such as to equate *mzda* with bribery — evidently came later.

Until the eighteenth century, the term *mzda* appears to have remained remarkably consistent and neutral when used in a civil or secular context. As late as the mid-seventeenth century, a lexicon defined *mzda* as *za[r]plata* and *nagoroda* [*nagrada*] — wages or compensation (Berynda 1653). When used in a religious context, greater ambivalence and ambiguity are evident. The root meaning of payment, compensation or reward remained, but the attitude was ambiguous and there are some indications of the term acquiring increasingly negative connotations over time.

In the eleventh-century Ostromir Gospel (1056–57), *Matt.* 5:12 is rendered '*Radoutesia i veselitesia, iako m′zda vasha iest′ na nebesekh*', with *m′zda* signifying reward or compensation. In a fourteenth-century copy of *Ex.* 23:8 (*M′zda bo oslepliaet*…), comparison with the Greek and Latin words indicates that *m′zda* accurately translates the notion of bribe. In other contexts it is condemned as simony, the buying and selling of ecclesial posts (Sreznevskii 1989: *s.v. m′zda*; cf. *PRP*: vol. 2, p. 106).

The diverging poles of meaning in the religious use of the term *mzda* offer a marked contrast to the consistent understanding of the term in the secular legal sphere. The reconciliation of these poles perhaps originates in a notation in the Hypation Chronicle under the year 6708 (1200/1). 'God recompenses with grace, in contrast to the wages of work [*Bog″ zhe milosti vozdast′ ti protivu truda m′zdu*]' (*PSRL*: p. 712). Wages or payments in the secular sphere crossed the boundary and become unacceptable bribes when translated into the religious sphere. If this is the case, the composers of the Law Code of 1649 failed to note the distinction when they used the term *mzda* to denote a reward from God.

Half a century later, however, there are signs that the understanding of *mzda* in the secular sphere was beginning to shift. In 1701 an act of Peter I firmly condemned *volokita* (foot-dragging or red-tape) and *izlishnoe mzdoimanie* on the part of government officials, indignantly asserting that some people even gave large gifts to officials in order to get necessary documents properly completed in a reasonable period of time (*PRP*: vol. 8, p. 234). This is not a total re-definition of the term *mzda* in the secular sphere. The act condemned officials demanding 'excessive' compensation for the timely completion of necessary documents (which it was presumably the duty of the official to provide in any case), implying that some, undefined, level of compensation was not excessive. None the less, the tone used in the directive is one of moral outrage, reminiscent of the use of the term in some earlier religious texts and in marked contrast to its value-neutral usage in earlier civil texts. By the early eighteenth century, *mzda*, traditionally used in the secular legal sphere to denote acceptable and legal wages or compensation, was moving across the boundary to the realm of unacceptable and illegal bribery and extortion.

Peter the Great's reign was also a significant moment for the term *vziatka* and associated words. By the nineteenth century, *vziatka* and *vziatochnichestvo* were words commonly, perhaps most commonly, used to identify corruption, bribes and extortion (Dal′ 1981: *s.v. vziatka*, *vzimat′*, *brat′*). In the legal documents surveyed, however, these and related terms are not used with this meaning, and in fact are generally not used at all until the eighteenth century. Sreznevskii identified one occurrence of *vziatka* in the *Dukhovnaia Pankrata Cheneia*, dated to 1482, which he defined as something which must be taken (Sreznevskii 1989: *s.v. v″ziat″ka*). In fact, it is difficult, if not impossible, to associate the usage of the term *vziatka* in this document with the notion of a bribe or extortion. Berynda's lexicon of 1653 does not include the term or any of its variations.

The first instance of the term *vziatka* that I have found in legal documents appeared in an act of Peter I, dated 17 March 1714: 'On the responsibility of finance-inspectors [*O dolzhnosti fiskalov*]'. The head finance-inspector (*ober-fiskal*) was charged with responsibility for investigating murky affairs, such as 'All kinds of *vziatki* and theft of the treasury, and other things, that can be detrimental to the interests of the realm [*Vsiakiia vziatki i krazhu kazny, i prochee, chto ko vredu Gosudarstvennomu interesu byt′ mozhet*]' (*PRP*: vol. 8, p. 51). The concern of this act was primarily losses to the state treasury. The intended meaning of *vziatka* is unclear. Bribes and extortion in the modern sense would not be out of place in the context, but it is not clear that this is what the author intended. It is linked to *krazha*, 'theft', and would probably best be translated as embezzlement.

A juridical dictionary of the late eighteenth century (Langans 1788) offers some clues regarding the *vziatka*. The dictionary included the word *vziatka* but did not define it. Instead readers were referred to the word *likhoimstvo* for further guidance. Langans evidently preferred and privileged the latter term. Like *vziatka* and associated words, by the nineteenth century *likhoimstvo* and related words such as *likhoimanie* and *likhoimets* were burdened in general usage with the strong connotation of bribery or extortion (Dal′ 1981: *s.v. likhoi*). *Likhoimanie*, *likhoimets* and related terms are derived from the roots *likh-* and *ima-*. *Likh-* shares the root with *lishnii* and related terms, meaning superfluous, excessive, unnecessary; *imat′* is an archaic form meaning 'to take'. Thus *likhoimanie* and its derivatives quite literally meant to take more than necessary, an excessive amount. In earlier times they indicated greed, avarice or excessive wealth, implied moral opprobrium and were used most commonly in religious texts (Sreznevskii 1989: *s.v. likhoimaniie*, *likhoiman′ik*, *likhoim″*, *likhoim′nik″*, *likhoim′ts′* and so on).

The seventeenth-century lexicon of Berynda also understood *likhoimstvo* or *likhoimenie* as avarice, the act of taking more than one needed of property or goods. The entry warned that *likhoimtsy* would not inherit the kingdom of heaven, emphasizing the connection of the term with religious texts and contexts. Further, while the lexicon does not include an entry for *vziatka*, *vziasheimenie* is identified as a synonym for *likhoimenie*. Like Peter's 1701 directive above, and in the same vein as legal documents from the end of the fifteenth century, the sin or the crime was not in taking (extortion) or accepting (bribery) a payment but rather in taking excessive amounts, in being greedy.

Intriguing in the light of this evolving understanding of bribery is what appears to be a trend, evident at the end of the seventeenth and beginning of the eighteenth centuries, towards the conflation of secular legal concepts and terminology with religious concepts and terminology. *Mzda* began to move from the religious sphere to the secular sphere, and on the journey its neutral, secular meaning of payment or wage began to fade. In the secular sphere, *mzda* retained the negative connotation it originally had in the religious sphere — a payment to gain an office, an advantage, a bribe — and, in the process, moral condemnation of the practice perhaps intensified legal prohibition. Similarly, the legal documents of the end of the fifteenth century identified 'excess' as the boundary between legal gift or payment and illegal bribe, and asserted the right of the sovereign to define 'excessive'. By the eighteenth century, the term *vziatka* made its appearance and was associated with *likhoimstvo*, *likhoimanie* and so on. The latter circle of terms in the middle of the seventeenth century carried strong religious and moral overtones. They were defined by morally and ethically charged terms such as greed and avarice; and, as Berynda reminded his readers, *likhoimtsy* would not inherit the kingdom of heaven. By the beginning of the eighteenth century, legal and moral-religious conceptions of excess appear to have merged in the term *vziatka*, and the tone of Peter's 1701 edict is one of moral outrage.

The timing of this evolution, wherein secular-legal notions were gradually endowed with moral and ethical value, is perhaps not accidental. In the course of the sixteenth and seventeenth centuries a shift occurred in the religious understanding and ethos of spirituality of the Russian élite. The appeal and force of a religion centered on miracle cults and ritual waned in favor of a religion and spirituality that were ethically informed and emphasized virtuous action (see Bushkovitch 1992). Practical considerations played a role in the evolving definition of bribery in Russia; undoubtedly they played a decisive role in the implementation of, or the failure to implement, legal pronouncements. But changing mentalities and an evolving spirituality were perhaps equally important in the search for boundaries differentiating payments from gifts, and both of these from bribes and extortion.

Notes

1 See also Etzioni-Halevy (1979), who argues in regard to political corruption that in some circumstances élites adopt normative codes and role definitions which ultimately act as a restraint on the élites themselves.

2 In Novgorod (and Pskov), a judge who heard cases together with the prince or his representative, the *namestnik* (Kaiser 1980: p. 271).

Bibliography

Berynda, P. (1653), *Leksikon slaveno-rossiiskii*, 2nd edn, Kuteinskii monastyr′.

Brokgauz, F.A. and Efron, I.A. (1892), *Entsiklopedicheskii slovar′*, vol. 6, St Petersburg.

Bushkovitch, P. (1992), *Religion and Society in Russia: The Sixteenth and Seventeenth Centuries*, Oxford.

Dal′ , V. (1981), *Tolkovyi slovar′ zhivago velikorusskago iazyka*, Moscow and St Petersburg, 1850–82, reprint, Moscow.

Davies, B. (1997), 'The Politics of Give and Take: Kormlenie as Service Remuneration and Generalized Exchange, 1488–1726' in A.M. Kleimola and G.D. Lenhoff (eds), *Culture and Identity in Muscovy, 1359–1584*, Moscow.

Demidova, N.F. (1987), *Sluzhilaia biurokratiia v Rossii XVII v. i ee rol′ v formirovanii absoliutizma*, Moscow.

Etzioni-Halevy, E. (1979), *Political Manipulation and Administrative Power: A Comparative Study*, London.

Heidenheimer, A.J. (1970), *Political Corruption: Readings in Comparative Analysis*, New York.

Johnston, M. (1996), 'The Search for Definitions: The Vitality of Politics and the Issue of Corruption', *International Social Science Journal*, 48.

Kaiser, D. (1980), *The Growth of the Law in Medieval Russia*, Princeton, NJ.

Kaiser, D. (ed. and trans.) (1992), *The Laws of Rus′ — Tenth to Fifteenth Centuries*, Salt Lake City, UT.

Klitgaard, R. (1991), 'Gifts and Bribes' in Richard J. Zeckhauser (ed.), *Strategy and Choice*, Cambridge, MA.
Langans, F. (1788), *Slovar' iuridicheskoi ili svod rossiiskikh uzakonenii...*, Moscow.
Man'kov, A.G. (ed.) (1987), *Sobornoe Ulozhenie 1649 goda*, Leningrad.
Mauss, M. (1967), *The Gift*, trans. I. Cunnison, New York and London.
Mény, Y. (1996), '"Fin de Siècle" Corruption: Change, Crisis and Shifting Values', *International Social Science Journal*, 48.
PRP, *Pamiatniki russkogo prava*, ed. A.A. Zimin, 8 vols, Moscow, 1952–63.
Pavarala, V. (1996), *Interpreting Corruption: Élite Perspectives in India*, New Delhi, Thousand Oaks, CA and London.
PSRL, *Polnoe sobranie russkikh letopisei, izdannoe Arkheo-graficheskoiu kommissieiu*, 2nd edn, vol. 2: *Ipat'evskaia letopis'*, 1908, St Petersburg.
Rocca, J.L. (1992), 'Corruption and its Shadow: An Anthropological View of Corruption in China', *The China Quarterly*, June.
Sedov, P. (1996), 'Podnosheniia v moskovskikh prikazakh XVII veka', *Otechestvennaia istoriia*, 1.
SGGiD, *Sobranie gosudarstvennykh gramot i dogovorov, khran-iashchikhsia v Gosudarstvennoi kollegii inostrannykh del*, 5 vols, 1813–28, 1894, Moscow.
Sreznevskii, I.I. (1989), *Materialy dlia slovaria drevnerusskogo iazyka*, St Petersburg, 1893, 3 vols, reprint, Moscow.
Weber, M. (1964), *The Theory of Social and Economic Organization*, trans. A.M. Henderson and T. Parsons, New York.

3 Patrimonialism versus Rational Bureaucracy: On the Historical Relativity of Corruption

Vadim Volkov

Strictly speaking, the term corruption is applicable only to a specific social group: office-holders, or state officials. The phenomenon of corruption, in turn, is inseparable from a specific type of social organization, the state. A bribe makes sense and can be legally defined and punished only where there is a clear institutional separation of the public from the private, that is, of the interests of the community or the state as a whole from those of particular people. Individuals involved in bribe-giving and bribe-taking are using public office and the powers attached to it for private ends. Bribery, therefore, should be seen as a specific transaction between the private and the public realms that undermines the boundary between them. Sociologically speaking, what is subject to corruption is this very boundary, which in every culture is drawn in a different way and undergoes historical change. The phenomena of bribery and corruption emerge together with the bureaucratic system and have by themselves no national or cultural specificity. Any bureaucratic system, however, takes shape against the background of local traditions and practices which it seeks to exclude but which none the less may affect its formal operational logic. Moreover, since the concrete interpretation of the public–private distinction is determined by particular cultural-historical contexts, no pure (that is, uncorrupted) bureaucratic system is possible in reality.

Max Weber, the founder of the sociology of bureaucracy, gave a systematic analysis of the modern rational-bureaucratic form of domination and government. The concept of patrimonialism, a type of social organization which is qualitatively different from if not opposite to bureaucracy, also belongs to the core of Weber's intellectual legacy, but is less prominent in contemporary social thought. Patrimonialism is justly considered an archaic phenomenon more relevant to the domestic economy and the pre-modern state, and this limits its applicability to contemporary issues. This chapter seeks to recover the concept of patrimonialism and demonstrate its background relevance to the main themes of this volume. I shall argue that bribery and corruption in Russia emerged out of a conflict between patrimonial and modern-bureaucratic principles of government and are therefore of historical rather than ethno-cultural origin.

Patrimonialism

In *Economy and Society*, Weber gives a systematic analysis of the pre-modern, that is pre-bureaucratic, type of domination. He calls it 'patriarchal' or 'patrimonial'. In contrast to the bureaucratic type of action or relationship, patrimonialism is 'based not on the official's commitment to an impersonal purpose, not on obedience to abstract norms, but on a strictly personal loyalty' (Weber 1978: p. 1006). Weber keeps to his description of the two basic ideal types of domination so as to articulate the contrasting principles of action within the two frameworks. In the case of the bureaucratic type these are abstract legality, impersonal orientation, rational procedures acquired through special training and determined boundaries of jurisdiction. Patrimonialism, on the contrary, is a type of relationship and action based on tradition, personal loyalty and direct dependence. Both, however, share the characteristic of being, as Weber puts it (1978: p. 1111), 'structures of everyday life'.

The natural basis of patrimonial power is the master's authority as head of the household, as the paterfamilias. This has a number of far-reaching implications. First, patrimonialism is rooted in the necessity to meet ongoing routine demands of life maintenance, that is, it has its roots in the economy, and therefore its inherent rationalities always revolve around personal maintenance. Secondly, a patrimonial relationship involves a strong ethical element, the core of which is strict loyalty and fidelity. This is also an ethic of mutual obligation or reciprocity which tends to become customary. Ethics, which Weber hardly mentions, preferring to talk about custom or tradition, is of vital significance, because it not only helps us to understand how the subjects should and do treat the master and vice versa, but it also sets limits to the otherwise unlimited power of the paterfamilias. Thirdly, the objective basis of solidarity is the permanent sharing of lodgings, food, drink, everyday utensils and so on. This means that patrimonial domination is embedded in the order of things, that is, patrimonial power is exercised through a certain organization of domestic space and relations of physical proximity. Significantly, the three aspects are inseparable in practice: a domestic economy is a type of ethical relationship that can only exist and reproduce itself through the material structures of the household and a fixed spatio-temporal order.

Patrimonial versus Bureaucratic Officialdom

Weber (1978: p. 1013) further elaborates the concept by suggesting that 'patrimonial conditions have had an extraordinary impact as the basis of political structures'. He implies that there is a strong structural affinity between domestic patrimonialism and the organization of the state. We should understand, however, that in this case the political realm as such does not exist. Of course, we can draw this conclusion only if we have in mind the classical conception of politics deriving from the fundamental distinction between *oikos* and *polis*. Patrimonial state-formation proceeds without this division. Its formula is *oikos* = *polis*. This means that the sphere of government that acquires political functions is none the less organized, understood and, most important, reproduced in practice in the same way as the patriarchal household, *oikos*. It also implies that economics, not in the sense given to it by Adam Smith, that is, as the nationwide production of wealth, but in its original sense, as, first and foremost, the art and the ethics of household management, informs policy-making in a fundamental way.

As is well known, the expanding princely manor or court constitutes the first medieval political realm in both Occident and Orient. The occidental court, however, gradually becomes subject to rationalization; this in turn leads to the establishment of bureaucratic officialdom, which operates according to its own rational procedures and impersonal principles independent of the domestic economy. This is the source of the specifically occidental distinction between the private and the public: the household economy becomes a sphere of private interests strictly separated from the official public realm of the state administration — not only in terms of a formal legal-institutional separation but also because personal influence is to a significant degree neutralized. Within this framework, 'public' is synonymous with 'formal' and 'official'. It implies the precedence of the impersonal positions in the official structure over the individuals who occupy them; it also emphasizes commitment to impersonal tasks and procedures over self-interest and emotional attachments. This separation of public from private, or of the office from the household, also formed the normative basis of modern politics and rational government.

Compared to rational-bureaucratic government, patrimonial officialdom is a qualitatively different configuration. The oriental political realm also coincides with the prince's household: here again the structures of the household economy turn into the functionally divided state offices. But the expansion of princely offices and the progress of procedural rationality do not hollow out the value-content of administrative practice, nor do they result in its cultural separation from household values. On the contrary, household law (*oikeios nomos*) becomes the mode of government for patrimonial officialdom and also constitutes the main source of legitimacy for political domination. The continuity of practices that historically and structurally originate in *oikos* thereby becomes the central feature of that which Weber calls the patrimonial state formation.

Through functional division and procedural rationalization, patrimonial officialdom may develop bureaucratic features. Its operational logic, however, remains different. Instead of a division between public and private we have an undivided realm of the personal. The practice of state administration knows no meaningful separation from the material maintenance of the ruler. This is also true of any individual office-holder, for whom administration is a personal affair and a means of subsistence. Relations of personal dependency, patronage and loyalty, which are characteristic of the traditional household and conceived as human rather than functional relations, come to rule the political-administrative sphere as well. To the extent that political-administrative relations retain the structural pattern of the patrimonial household, they are seen by Weber as traditionally sanctioned. Tradition, however, also acts as a natural limitation of the otherwise unchecked power of the master. It would be more accurate to speak of an ethic that both sanctions and checks personal power.

Patrimonial Rationality

In his writings Weber analytically juxtaposes the two ideal types, but he does not reflect much on what comes out of their actual historical encounters and interactions. For Weber, the Protestant ethic is the system of values that matches the development of rational-bureaucratic institutions and supersedes the traditional ethic. Later, he describes bureaucratic office-holding by using his favourite religious term 'vocation' (*Beruf*) (Weber 1978: p. 958). The actual emergence of the modern rational patterns of economy and government was the outcome a series of complex transformations that involved, alongside legal and organizational changes, changes in the prevailing system of values. In Weber's writings the confrontation of the two major types of domination remained for the most part a matter of theory, that is, an ideal-typical comparison.

But what happens, for example, when bureaucratic rationalism is actually forced upon patrimonial structures in an authoritarian manner, as has been the case in many non-Western countries over the course of the last two centuries? What are the possible outcomes of a process of modernization when it is driven by an explicit conflict with the traditional system? We may assume that one of the likely consequences of such an interaction would be a radical re-definition of the traditional ethic in negative terms such as bribery, corruption and abuse of power, and its qualification as 'illegal'. The imposition of an alternative normative and legal framework is likely to change the meaning of traditional practices without changing the practices themselves. Thus, what from the standpoint of rationalized administration is qualified as bribery, corruption and other forms of abuse of personal power could well be acceptable practice within the ethical framework of patrimonialism. With the introduction of the rational bureaucracy various practices involving personal appropriation of institutional power become subject to moral condemnation and penal sanctions. Weber does not account for 'illegal' practices that can continuously subvert bureaucratic domination — perhaps because they do not fit any of his ideal types and seem to lack any institutional autonomy. Still, the advent of rational administration invents a whole new category of criminal or administrative offences which are nothing other than re-defined patrimonial (and therefore traditionally sanctioned) practices. Such a conflict is likely to produce mixed types that combine the two frameworks. Rules of action within combined frameworks we may call 'patrimonial rationality'.

In general, patrimonial rationality is a way of generating and sustaining personal power in the contexts created by the rapid advent of rationalization. To put it simply, it is a way of extending the power of the head of the household beyond the household, as it were, into the official, 'public' domain. Although this synthesis of ideal models may seem a rather mechanistic way of using Weber's analysis, the existence of such a category is logically implied in his juxtapositions. If bureaucratic rationality consists in the conversion of any concrete individual action or activity into an impersonal rule-governed operation, a place should be reserved for the reverse procedure. Patrimonial rationality, then, is the subjection of formal rules to personal discretion. If bureaucratic power derives from the reduction of individuals to functional positions, patrimonial power is generated through the practical articulation of the personal dimension of any administrative relationship. Thus, patrimonial rationality emerges out of the traditional ethic under the impact of rationalization (which seeks to disqualify this ethic). It can institutionalize 'subversive' procedures and work out its own routines. Patrimonial rationality is a means of everyday escape from the 'iron cage' of rationalization without breaking it — a point that Weber may have overlooked behind the facade of the contemporary bureaucratic state.

It should be noted, however, that Weber accounted for the process whereby the patrimonial power of the ruler can be undermined and corrupted. As Mark Lupher (1996: p. 12–13) pointed out in his comparative study of power struggles in China and Russia, Weber described the modification and attenuation of unconstrained patrimonial power as a process of personal 'appropriation' of public authority. 'Manifest' and 'latent' appropriation, as contemporary researchers have it, regularly result in the gradual transformation of official privileges into the personal property and rights of nominally subordinate political and economic élites, a process which can take place under patrimonial as well as rational bureaucratic conditions but which in practice blends the two types.

Muscovite Politics

Weber uses seventeenth-century Russia to illustrate some aspects of patrimonial state-formation. This phenomenon had also been acknowledged by Russian historians in the second half of the nineteenth century, and I shall now use some of their findings concerning the functioning of the state administration in Muscovite Russia to describe the everyday structures of patrimonialism.

The very term *gosudarstvo*, the state, means the domain of the *gosudar'*, the word which was used to address the Russian tsar. Before the term acquired political connotations, it was normally used to designate the head of the household and to invoke domestic hierarchy. In his study of the domestic life of the Russian tsars, first published in 1851, Ivan Zabelin (1990: pp. 48–9) argued that political domination in Muscovite Russia was intrinsically connected with the private law of the household and popularly perceived as such. The distribution and reproduction of political-administrative power derived from the ideas and rituals of domestic life and were in accordance with the basic principles of the patrimonial ethic. This explains why Zabelin and other historians turned to the study of the domestic life of the tsars and the Muscovite noble élite: because domestic life could provide insights into the organization of the state.

The Muscovite political structure coincided with concrete, not ideal, spatial relations. People closest to the tsar, those responsible for the fabric of his everyday life — eating, sleeping or entertainment — or those just assigned to 'being close' (*okolo*) to him, were also assigned to the highest administrative or military positions in the state. The bedmaker, who prepared the tsar's bed and slept in his bedroom (*postel'nichii*), the table server (*stol'nyi*) or other boyars who were 'near' (*okol'nichii* and *blizhnii*), occupied positions of the highest political significance. The boyars serving in these positions could be sent to govern other towns, command the army or conduct foreign policy. The domestic functions of the tsar's servants and their physical proximity to him correlated with their political-administrative status. They could demonstrate personal loyalty better than anyone else and thus could be entrusted to perform key functions in the state.

The Kremlin was a highly differentiated space where the meaning and value of each room, antechamber or porch varied in accordance with its distance from the location of the tsar. Only a narrow category of officials was allowed as close as the bedroom, that is, the tsar's body itself. Others were admitted to his office; a wider group was allowed into the antechamber, while the majority of the hereditary nobles in the service of the tsar had to wait for his decisions and orders at the porch. The right of admission to a certain room — but no further — defined the person's rank in service and social standing. Accordingly, an appeal for promotion and the promotion itself would normally be expressed in terms of changing one's place: a person would be granted the right of entrance into the next room (for example, from the porch into the antechamber), as if moving one step closer to the tsar. The same pertained to other activities, for example, the distance at which the boyar arriving on horseback had to dismount and walk across the square when approaching the Kremlin palace: the less the distance the higher the boyar's social standing. We should not confuse this system with what is known as the 'representation' of rank or social status through certain norms of behaviour. No abstract codified system of ranks and corresponding duties existed at that time. In the patrimonial system the political and administrative status of the person was sustained through relations of physical distance and opportunities that they provided for personal access to superiors.

Administrative and military positions were distributed in accordance with personal loyalty and 'closeness'. This was a form of reciprocity, especially in so far as the administrative positions were the source of personal subsistence. Rather than having its source in a fixed salary paid by the state, the accumulation of wealth was dependent upon the taxation of subjects by officials who sold administrative powers attached to their position to the local population. The granting of such positions to members of the élite as personal favours strengthened the power of the tsar. The boyars, for instance, would ask the tsar to send them to govern a town in order to 'improve their own welfare'. This system of living off private taxation was known in fifteenth- and sixteenth-century Russia as 'feeding' (*kormlenie*). An administrative position 'fed' the person who occupied it, but not in the form of a fixed administrative salary. Rather, it provided subsistence through various forms of 'private' taxation of those who happened to depend personally upon the official. As there was no formal scale of administrative charges and the only regulation was that of custom (which was often interpreted very broadly), the system of feeding provoked an increasing number of complaints from the local population. Formally, it was renounced in 1555 and replaced by a more centralized tax system, but in the absence of efficient controls, *kormlenie* remained as an illegal but legitimate practice and later reappeared as 'bribery' and 'corruption'.

Muscovite internal politics revolved around personal distance or closeness, most crucially in relation to the tsar. Social space was not metaphorical or ideal but physical and concrete. This was the same relationship as might exist between members of a family and its head. Physical distance was the visible measure of a personal relationship. Within the framework of Muscovite politics, however, there was another key variable that defined one's social standing and political-administrative career: family or kinship. Every noble family behaved as a social unit. It had its own genealogy which legitimated its claims for a certain social standing on the basis of the preceding service positions of the members of the family — ranking by precedence. The rank of the family and its members served as the main principle for seating people at the tsar's dinner table as well as the main criterion for nomination to political-administrative positions in the state. The system of correlation between the social standing of the family (family honour), its position in service and its place at the dinner table was called *mestnichestvo*, literally 'placing'. Most of all, men feared to accept a military assignment or sit at a place (*mesto*) at the dinner table that would set a precedent lowering their families' social standing and prospects in service. *Mestnichestvo* gave rise to continuous competition over one's place: in service, at table, and consequently the place of one's own family in relation to other families.

The idea of patrimonialism as the form of life whereby household practices determine the style of the state administration allows us to understand what it meant to do politics in Muscovy. We can see that doing politics involved establishing personal relations, demonstrating loyalty, using kinship, 'feeding' and 'being fed', securing personal profit from administration, and other such activities. 'Politics' here means practical ways of achieving goals and governing other people's behaviour using the traditionally available means. Originally, this 'Muscovite style' of patrimonial politics, unchallenged and unselfconscious — until the rise of St Petersburg.

Petersburg versus Moscow

Petersburg was founded as the capital of the new, modernizing state. Initially, it had military significance — as a fortress and naval base. Its more fundamental function was to reform the state according to the rational principles of the bureaucratic order. And its architectural design reflected this project: geometry, measurement, proportion, symmetry, planning and other rational principles cut the city space into straight avenues, squares and granite embankments. The impersonality of the city space was the corollary of its consciously designed 'publicness'. Consistent with the regularized city space was the building of new governmental offices which had no connection with domestic life whatsoever. Streets had names, houses had numbers. In 1722 Peter the Great introduced the Table of Ranks which had to become the core structure of the regular state. The Table represented a matrix of impersonal ranks that encompassed all possible positions in the state service. The service was subdivided into three categories: military, civil and courtly. Each category was convertible into the other on the scale of fourteen impersonal graded positions (ranks). To each position were attached functional duties, uniform, salary, form of address, privileges and other formal distinctions. At the same time, institutions for professional training were set up. The central idea behind the introduction of the new system was to professionalize the state service by establishing a direct connection between professional performance in the state service and social standing. At the same time, Peter announced a new doctrine of service, which was extremely radical by the standards of its time: one should serve the state, not the tsar. This was a clear articulation of the principle of bureaucratic domination: one should be committed to one's impersonal functions and one's social position should thus depend upon professional distinction. The whole design overtly and consistently rejected anything reminiscent of Muscovite patrimonialism.

Such quick and radical reforms were unimaginable in Moscow, whose traditional architecture and lifestyle would naturally have put up permanent resistance. Since the end of the eighteenth century, comparisons between Petersburg and Moscow have become a commonplace literary and philosophical exercise. With the transfer of sovereign power to Petersburg, the autocrat, the central figure of patrimonial politics, was missing from Moscow. What remained, however, were the powerful kinship and clan structures. Most comparisons of the two capitals note a specific 'family atmosphere' typical of Moscow, which encompassed the neighbourhood-style arrangement of the city space and the humane, 'warm' spirit of social relations. This, of course, is contrasted with the cold and formal Petersburg. In Moscow, noted Belinskii (1991), people were mostly engaged in visiting their numerous aunts and uncles in order to secure career prospects; all gatherings reminded him of a family feast; all the most important questions were decided at table. Petersburg, then, was the city of officials and clerks: people circulated between numerous offices, colleges and departments. 'The young Petersburger is formal, like a business letter', wrote Herzen (1954: p. 39). While in Moscow people naturally used personal connections, marriage, relatives and so on, as a means to make a career or improve their prosperity and social standing, in Petersburg, so the writings of the time tell us, all this was being achieved through service. The comparison may be pursued further, but perhaps this is enough to see that contemporaries tended to ascribe patrimonial features to Moscow and bureaucratic ones to Petersburg.

From this we might conclude that Moscow and Petersburg are two ideal types that turned into reality. This, however, would be a mistake that one is prone to make by thinking ideally-typically. Although we are justified in conceiving of 'Moscow practices' and 'Petersburg practices', when it comes to practice we should none the less speak of mixed types rather than ideal ones.

To rephrase Marx, Peter the Great was making history but in circumstances not of his own choosing — even though he did his best to choose a virgin site for this project. He was making history in the context or against the background of Muscovite politics. The superimposition of a rational bureaucratic framework onto patrimonial structures and the creation of numerous new social institutions forced people to adapt their habitual ways of action to the new environment. The imposition of bureaucratic rationality produced its double — patrimonial rationality, or the articulation of a traditional patrimonial ethic against the formal standards and rules of administration.

According to Peter's project it should have been the Table of Ranks and performance in office, and not the banquet table and personal loyalty, that defined the social existence of his subjects. The fervour and cruelty with which he implemented his project is well known. Actual results, as critics point out, remained modest for a long time. Some historians (for example, LeDonne 1984) have argued that underneath the new Westernized structures little had changed in the way the state actually functioned. But perhaps the significant change was that traditional politics were now forced to take place 'underneath' the new state structures. What had formerly been open, usual, normal and sanctioned by tradition, tended to become covert, illegal and pathological — denounced by the modernized autocracy but still traditionally sanctioned. The confrontation of two alien types of behaviour, the 'way we ought to' and the 'way we used to', was likely to lead to changes in both. Peter's reforms not only provoked endless historical reflections on the nature of Muscovite traditions but also launched a powerful process of creative appropriation by these traditions of the new rational schemes for doing things. Petersburg was not a triumph of modern rationality but the result of an artful adaptation to it. The historian Marc Raeff (1994: p. 340) has made a perceptive observation concerning the effects of the process of individualization in post-Petrine Russia. Russian individualism did not make an appeal to political and legal principles, as in England; nor did it rest on the authority of corporate bodies, as in France. Western individualism was made by a pluralistic society whose constituent units served to check and balance conflicting interests without recourse to the ruler's arbitration or command. In Russia, and following the Byzantine tradition, argues Raeff, individualism meant only the opportunity to have direct access to the ruler on a personal basis, disregarding the intervening links of social groups and institutions. 'As a consequence, enhancing the individual's active role in no way challenged or reduced the power of the sovereign, quite the contrary, the monarch's power seemed the best guarantee for personal security and increased material benefits' (Raeff 1994: p. 340).

Russian literature has spawned a whole genre describing various aspects of bureaucratic life: Gogol′ revealed this new reality to contemporary readers and Saltykov-Shchedrin subjected it to merciless satire. In the gallery of heroes of Russian literature, next to the Byronic hero stands the office-holder (*chinovnik*) — corrupted, skilled in bribery, liable to abuse power — who looks at things with a view to his own personal advantage. He is skilled in the application of strict rules using the 'method of exceptions', whereby the existence of a rule is acknowledged and reproduced through the understanding of what otherwise would have been normal as 'exceptional'. The value of personal favours should rise together with their formal rejection as principles of government. Without the imposition of the impersonal bureaucratic code, no dealings could have been presented as exceptional. Because the system of government based on tradition is derived from the knowledge of customary practice and much less from explicit codified rules and procedures, and because any tradition subjects the normative ('what ought to be') to the actual ('what usually is'), no firm distinction between the normal and the exceptional exists under such conditions. Bribery, corruption and other 'exceptional' practices that have become normal are the legacy not of Russian traditional culture but rather of its historically specific patterns of rapid modernization. These practices tend to intensify and proliferate each time the Russian state and society enter a new phase of modernization.

Bibliography

Belinskii, V. (1991), 'Peterburg i Moskva' in *Fiziologiia Peterburga*, 1845, St Petersburg, reprint, Moscow.

Herzen, A. (1954), *Sobranie sochinenii*, vol. 2, Moscow.

LeDonne, J. (1984), *Ruling Russia: Politics and Administration in the Age of Absolutism, 1762–1796*, Princeton, NJ

Lotman, Iu. (1994), *Besedy o russkoi kul'ture*, St Petersburg.

Lupher, M. (1996), *Power Restructuring in Russia and China*, Boulder, CO.

Raeff, M. (1994), *Political Ideas and Institutions in Imperial Russia*, San Francisco, CA.

Weber, M. (1978), *Economy and Society*, London.

Zabelin, I. (1990), *Domashnii byt russkikh tsarei v XVI i XVII stoletiiakh*, vol. 1, Moscow.

4 Bribery and Justice in the Provinces in the Reign of Catherine II

Janet Hartley

Introduction

'Bribes are the incurable poison of the courts', wrote I.V. Lopukhin, President of the Moscow Criminal Chamber (a court of third instance) in 1800 (Lopukhin 1860: p. 73). D.B. Mertvago, a court procurator, summed up the situation succinctly: 'The judges present in civil and criminal courts blatantly haggled with the accused and justice was sold like an ordinary commercial object' (Mertvago 1867: p. 186). Bribery occurred at all levels of provincial justice, from minor clerks in the lowest courts to presidents of the highest courts of appeals. 'The bigger the bribe-taker, the harder to unmask him', added Lopukhin. A.I. Viazemskii, Governor-General of Penza and Tambov *gubernii* in the 1770s and 1780s, found it necessary to issue a special order forbidding institutions and individuals from accepting bribes from state peasants (Yaney 1973: p. 27). Contemporary memoirs commented on particularly corrupt individuals but also seemed to accept bribery as a way of life. Indeed, memoirists admitted that they both gave and received bribes. Dobrynin, an official in Mogilev *guberniia*, 'confessed' what admittedly he described as his 'sin' in his memoirs. In 1795 and 1796 he received 360 roubles (the same amount as his salary) from a Count Augsberg in return for certifying the standard of his vodka on the basis of seeing only part of his stock. 'The three of us were not unrewarded', admitted Dobrynin, and 'we acted as semi-worthy servitors' (Dobrynin 1871: p. 326). Denis Fonvizin's satire *The Brigadier* (published in

1769) expressed the general acceptance of bribery in the words of the councillor: 'I myself was a judge. It used to be that the guilty paid for his guilt and the innocent for his innocence. In my time everyone was satisfied that way: the judge, the plaintiff and the defendant' (Segel 1967: p. 335).

In law, it became a crime to *offer* a bribe, as opposed to accepting a bribe, only from the reign of Peter I. Even after this, popular perception and the law made a distinction between bribe-givers and bribe-takers. One of the *nakazy* (instructions) from the noble deputies to the Legislative Commission in 1767 stated that it was unjust to punish those who offered bribes (Yaney 1973: p. 34). Another *nakaz* was harsher in its recommendations: the Vereia nobles thought that those who offered bribes should lose their land and rank but that those who accepted them should be executed irrespective of the size of the bribe (*SIRIO* 1871: vol. 4, p. 379). The law of 1802 made a formal distinction between the offences of giving and receiving a bribe, and between impoverished officials and wealthier and more influential bribe-takers.

We can accept therefore that bribery was pervasive in the provincial courts (and for that matter in the highest courts as well). But the existence of bribery raises two broad questions which will be addressed in the course of this chapter. First, why was bribery so prevalent? Secondly, what significance should be given to bribery as a factor in explaining the inadequacies of the administration of justice in Russia? Or, put another way, did bribery matter? These two questions will be examined with reference to four aspects of provincial life in the second half of the eighteenth century. First, the predominantly fiscal and exploitative nature of the contact between the population and all government officials, not merely court employees, is examined. Secondly, the relationship between bribery and inadequate salaries of court officials is assessed. Thirdly, bribery is put within the context of the low educational level of most provincial officials and of the generally poor standards of provincial administration. Fourthly, the significance of bribery is discussed in relation to other defects within the Russian legal system and judicial practice.

Officials and Provincial Society — The Culture of Bribes and Fees

Almost all contact between government officials and the people took the form of exaction of dues in cash, kind or labour. Peasant communes — of both serfs and state peasants — regularly gave 'presents' to local officials to avoid more burdensome duties or simply to be left in peace. V.G. Orlov sanctioned the use of bribes 'for protection' to local officials on his estates in the late eighteenth century. The commune of Nikol′skoe (serfs) sanctioned bribes to local officials on fifteen occasions in the period between 1805 and 1814. It spent over 100 roubles in 1806 and 236 roubles and thirty kopecks in 1813 on 'presents' for local officials (Aleksandrov 1976: pp. 162–4). Serfs were not subject to the state courts except for serious criminal offences. They nevertheless had contact with organs of police administration, including the lower land court (which was not a judicial court). Peasants in Saratov composed a lament in the period 1776–78 on their relations with officials who worked in this organ:

> Now the whole world knows
> How the land captain [*ispravnik*] and secretaries make life impossible for us.
> By the command of their chief, thieving hundredmen
> Constantly make requisitions.
> They treat us inhumanely,
> Something which has never been heeded.
> Does this anger you, heavenly Tsar,
> That You have
> An incorrigible fool,
> A thief as an assessor,
> A rogue as a secretary,
> Who have ruined us completely.
> They did not stop at a chicken or a sheep.
> In the past tyrannies detested the Christian faith,
> The present one tortures us if we do not give money or measure of oats.
> And all our profits and incomes
> Have been used up on the expenses of the [lower] land court.
> ('Zhaloba' 1908: pp. 215–16).

The other main contact with the state came through the recruit levy, and bribery could ensure that unfit peasants were selected or that fit peasants were found to be unsuitable. In the village of Shapkino (Tambov *guberniia*), the district authorities took bribes of forty kopecks per soul at recruiting time, a practice which yielded a sum of 360 roubles and sixty kopecks (Dubasov 1884: p. 557). In 1795, the serfs on a Perm′ estate of G.A. Stroganov paid

460 roubles when they dispatched eighteen recruits — including bribes of twenty-five roubles to the doctor, fifteen to an official of the fiscal chamber and smaller sums to officers, one of whom marked up the height of recruits who were too short (Keep 1985: p. 149). At the same time, elected peasant officials were most likely to be bribed, or pressurized, by wealthy and influential peasants at this time to ensure that the 'right' peasants were selected as recruits. It was also an accepted practice to pay to avoid the recruit levy. Merchants were allowed to pay a fee of 100 roubles for exemption from the recruit levy in the reign of Peter I; after 1775 they paid a recuit tax instead. But peasants (serfs and state peasants) also paid, either individually or collectively, to purchase substitutes to dispatch to the army in their place. These sums could be very large, and put the lesser amounts paid in bribes to local officials in perspective. Prices for substitutes rose from in the region of 250–300 roubles per substitute in the 1770s to 350–400 roubles in the mid-1780s and over 1,000 roubles in the 1820s. The 345 households on an Orlov estate in Nizhnii Novgorod *guberniia* paid 19,688 roubles in the period 1793–1809 for 'receipts' (*kvitantsii*) for thirty-two recruits (Aleksandrov 1976: p. 266). In the early nineteenth century, serfs on the Lieven estates in the village of Baki were paying sums of up to 2,000 roubles per household for substitutes.[1]

Russians were also accustomed to pay to advance their careers and their interests. Dobrynin, the son of a clerk, paid two sums of fifty roubles to a General Aleevtsev, who worked in the governor's office, to help procure the post of registrar in Mogilev *guberniia*, which he finally achieved after approaching other patrons and giving sums of money to junior officials (Dobrynin 1871: pp. 23–30). At the other end of the scale, in 1778 P.A. Pahlen made a gift of a table set worth 2,000 roubles to one of his superiors in order to be made regimental commander (a post which gave a salary of 12,000 roubles a year) (Hassell 1967: pp. 126–7). Prince M. Shcherbatov claimed that:

> All offices can be bought, official positions have begun to be given not to those most worthy, but to those who pay most for them, and even these men, once they have paid, have started to recoup their loss by exacting bribes from the people. (Shcherbatov 1969: p. 251)

During the activity of Catherine II's Measuring Commission in the 1760s, it was common for nobles to entertain and generally flatter the commissioners in the hope that disputed land boundaries would be settled favourably. And it became accepted practice for the wealthier provincial nobles to 'treat' their poorer brethren in the Noble Assemblies to ensure the election of officials to their liking. 'Treating' of electors also took place for institutions of urban administration and for the peasant communes.

Finally, fees were a legitimate part of the judicial system. Civil and criminal cases were initiated when litigants filed a formal complaint for which they paid a standard fee of three roubles (which was increased to six roubles in 1794). It is easy to envisage that at this stage a rather higher 'fee' might help to ensure more speedy action on the part of the court's clerical staff. Fees were also exacted if one or more of the litigants chose to appeal to a higher court.[2] The fees were returnable if the appellant were successful, but were probably imposed in an attempt, albeit an unsuccessful one, as we shall see below, to discourage appeals. After 1775, cases could only be transferred on appeal from the first to the second court of instance if the case were valued at over twenty-five roubles, and a deposit of twenty-five roubles had to be lodged with the court by the appellant. An appeal from this court to the highest provinicial court required a deposit of 100 roubles; after 1796, appeals from this court to the Senate required a deposit of 500 roubles. A further attempted discouragement to appellants was that unsuccessful appeals resulted in not only the loss of the deposit but also a 'fine' of six roubles (raised to twelve roubles in 1794) (LeDonne 1984: pp. 173–4). Although there was nothing improper about this practice in itself it meant that 'paying' for justice was an established part of the judicial procedure.

Bribery — A Substitute for Inadequate Salaries?

In the seventeenth century and before, it had been accepted that provincial officials would supplement their inadequate salaries by 'feeding' (*kormlenie*), that is, living from 'fees', or bribes, for their services. The Statute of Provincial Administration of 1775, which established a new structure of judicial, fiscal and administrative organs for the provinces, also specified salaries at rates which were supposed to attract able candidates and make bribery unnecessary. These salaries, however, varied enormously according to the post. It has been estimated that a single man needed an income of at least 100 roubles in 1763 to live comfortably in St Petersburg and that this had risen to 300 roubles by 1800. At the bottom of the scale, courts were staffed by secretaries, clerks and junior clerks on pay well below this level. According to the regulations, copyists earned between twenty and 120 roubles, junior clerks between twenty and 150 roubles and registrars between 150 and 250 roubles a year. In Tver′ in 1781, a secretary received 250 roubles, a registrar 130 roubles and a copyist sixty roubles (Hassell 1967: p. 162). But, in practice, salaries for lower officials could be much lower. Timofei Kalashnikov started work as a copyist in 1772, at the age of ten, and earned ninety-three copecks for a 'third' (salaries were paid three times a year; this means that he had an annual salary of under three roubles); by 1776 he had become a junior clerk, earning sixty roubles (Kalashnikov 1904: pp. 147–83). In addition, salaries were often paid late, and sometimes not at all.

To put this in perspective, this meant that junior clerks who were paid at the lower end of the scale were earning a little more than parish priests, who earned on average between twenty-five and forty roubles a year in the second half of the eighteenth century, although sacristans and deacons could earn even less (in the 1770s and 1780s, sacristans earned between ten and twenty roubles a year). Priests, however, were able to supplement their income through fees for services and many also had plots of land. Peasant elders who served in the peasant commune could earn sums not much less than junior officials. Peasant elders on the estate of A.M. Golitsyn earned twenty-five roubles a year in the late eighteenth century (Semevskii 1903: p. 249), and their household, of course, also had an income from agriculture and possibly from trading activities as well. This low pay meant that bribe-taking by junior officials was often condoned by contemporaries. G.R. Derzhavin, the poet and Governor of Tambov, was scathing about the poor standards of local administrators but accepted that there was a difference between 'pernicious extortioners' and impoverished clerks who had to take bribes because their salaries were too small to live on (Korf 1908: pp. 380–1). Because the courts relied so heavily on clerical staff for the preparation of the cases it was all the more important that litigants should be sure of the favours of junior staff.

The case that bribery was an acceptable supplement to salaries cannot be made for higher posts in the courts after 1775. Governors of provinces could earn up to 6,000 roubles a year and presidents of the criminal and civil chambers (courts of the third instance and the highest courts of appeal in the provinces) earned between 840 and 1,350 roubles, and councillors in these chambers earned between 600 and 750 roubles a year (the salary depended on the *guberniia*; a small number of *gubernii* where the cost of living was higher, including St Petersburg, paid higher salaries). Yet bribery also occurred amongst high officials. Andrei Bolotov recorded in his memoirs the case of Kolomnin, a *voevoda* (military governor) in the 1760s, who was such a bribe-taker that even on his deathbed he held out his hand for a bribe before signing a receipt (Bolotov 1973: p. 365)! Count R.L. Vorontsov, the Governor-General of the *gubernii* of Vladimir, Penza and Tambov, was supposedly such a notorious bribe-taker that Catherine II sent him a gift of an empty purse on his birthday (Shcherbatov 1969: pp. 249, 291). Derzhavin exposed an embezzelement scandal in Tambov *guberniia* which involved the Vice-Governor (salary 1,200 roubles a year), described by Derzhavin as 'a man greedy for advantage and, it can be said, for dishonest gain', and the relatively highly paid members of the Fiscal Chamber (the highest organ of financial administration in the provinces) (Derzhavin 1876: p. 564).

Bribery as a Reflection of Poor Standards of Administration?

Poor salaries cannot in themselves excuse or account for bribery, and the causes have been sought in a deeper malaise, namely the generally low standards of public life in the provinces which the Statute of 1775 did not seem to overcome. Baturin, a Councillor in the Kaluga Civil Chamber in the late eighteenth century, gave a vivid description in his memoirs of his colleagues. The President was a German, knew little Russian and was dependent on the secretary, the Procurator spoke without any grammatical rules and another Councillor was described as 'proud, base, self-interested and extravagant, conceited and lacking in understanding' (Baturin 1918: 1–3, p. 68; ibid., 4–6, p. 181). An account relating to Tambov *guberniia* in the late eighteenth century listed the following incidents, which are an indictment of the forces of law and order: an *ispravnik* (land captain, rank nine, who presided over the lower land court; after 1775 elected by the local nobility) descended on a village which had not paid its dues, accompanied by soldiers who tortured and beat the village head and other peasants; a *gorodnichii* (provost, rank eight, an urban official in charge of police functions in the town) beat up a priest, stole and ruined merchants' goods and arbitrarily punished citizens (Dubasov 1878: pp. 30–9). The records of the St Petersburg Criminal Chamber included references to eleven examples of junior officials being brought before the court because of drunkenness or other forms of disorderly behaviour in the first six months of 1788. The Secretary of the St Petersburg *Uezd* Court (first instance court for the nobility) was accused of being drunk while reading the evidence for a murder case;[3] a secretary in Kursk *guberniia* was described as 'almost illiterate and did not know any civil law' (Ostrozhskii-Lokhvitskii 1886: p. 561). Disarray and disorder were common features of Russian courts. When Major-General Potapov arrived in Olonets *guberniia* in 1782 he found 'severe disorder' in the conduct of criminal cases, records poorly and carelessly kept, income and expenditure inaccurately recorded, orders unfulfilled, outstanding cases, and cases not settled according to the law. The secretaries of the lower *raspravy* (courts of first instance for state peasants) left court books in disarray and had failed to perform their duties.[4]

Why were standards so poor? One reason was the lack of training and inadequate educational standards of officials at all levels. Another reason was the sheer number of junior posts which were created in the wake of the 1775 legislation to handle local administration. In 1789, in St Petersburg *guberniia* alone there were 388 junior staff (that is, posts outside the Table of Ranks); of these, 127 were aged between eleven and twenty and 157 had started work before the age of fifteen.[5] The consequence of the shortage of staff was that there was little choice over who to employ and at what age; indeed it proved impossible to fill all the new clerical posts at all. In Vologda *guberniia* in 1786, secretaries were needed in all the courts of second instance; in Iaroslavl' and Vologda *gubernii* in 1784 the lack of clerical staff resulted in the employment of economic (state) and court peasants instead.[6] The consequences were almost inevitable. In 1797, the Governor of Viatka, S. Zinov'ev, reported to the Procurator General, Prince A.B. Kurakin, that he had dismissed several officials for bribery the previous year but that because of a shortage of suitably trained personnel he now requested permission to reinstate these officials (Hassell 1967: pp. 172–3).

The problem of filling posts was not confined to junior positions. It proved difficult to attract educated nobles to the estimated 4,000 newly created elected posts for the nobility in the provinces after 1775. Nobles did have to qualify to stand for election — after 1785, when these qualifications were clarified, they had to be over twenty-five years old, hold at least the lowest officer rank and have an income of at least 100 roubles a year (which in practice eliminated the majority of provincial nobles) — in other words, they had to meet certain service and income criteria but no formal educational qualifications were required of them. The problem, however, was not just the low qualifications required but more the difficulty of finding candidates at all willing to fill the elected posts. Despite the abolition of compulsory state service by Peter III in 1762, military life always appeared more glamorous and attractive to young nobles than civil service. Military posts were also usually better paid than the elected posts created for the nobility in the provinces after 1775. In most provinces, judges of the *uezd* court (a court of first instance for nobles) earned 300 roubles a year and were ranked nine, assessors in the upper land court (a court of second instance for nobles) earned 360 roubles and were ranked seven; noble assessors in other courts earned between 200 and 250 roubles a year and were ranked nine or ten. In comparison, the lowest ranks in the army (*praporshchiki*, or ensigns, rank thirteen, and *podporuchiki*, or second lieutenants, rank twelve) could earn more than this, depending on the regiments in which they served. In 1786, the dragoon regiments paid between 145 and 356 roubles to ensigns and between 165 and 396 roubles to second lieutenants. Even more galling, teachers in the national schools established in 1786 (who were mainly sons of clergy) earned 400 roubles a year for teaching higher classes (that is, more than a judge in the *uezd* court) and 200 roubles for teaching the lower classes (the same as many noble assessors). Even senior posts in the provinces were filled by nobles who had already served for many years in the army. Inevitably this meant that administrative posts, particularly in the provinces, were viewed as the inferior branch of service, most suitable for at best a retirement post and at worst for those lacking in sufficient funds and influence to secure a more prestigious post elsewhere.

Although the second half of the eighteenth century saw the cultural development of provincial towns, wealthy and influential nobles still preferred to live in the capitals, serve in the army or central administration and only visit their estates for recreation.

The result of this was massive absenteeism at the noble assemblies which were supposed to conduct elections for posts in the provincial courts — and consequent shortages of staff. For example, it has been estimated that non-residency of nobles in Penza *guberniia* in 1787 was 54.4 per cent, Tambov in 1779 was 57.9 per cent, Voronezh in 1780 was 70.3 per cent, Vladimir in 1784 was 72 per cent and Olonets in 1784 was 86 per cent. There is also evidence that enthusiasm for the elections waned fairly rapidly. Attendance at the Iaroslavl′ assemblies, for example, decreased with time — 705 nobles attended in 1777, 402 in 1780 and 301 in 1783. More distant *gubernii* faced more severe problems. In Viatka, only six nobles appeared at the elections of November 1780, so that most of the posts had to be filled by appointment (Givens 1975: pp. 465, 389, 379).

Poor behaviour, including bribery, by court and other provincial officials was not necessarily condoned and offenders were punished. In Tambov in the early nineteenth century two officials were dispatched as ordinary soldiers for taking bribes (Dubasov 1884: p. 562). But these were small fry (the bribes were for sums of fifteen roubles and fourteen roubles fifty kopecks). In Olonets *guberniia* in 1782 it was the relatively minor officials — secretaries and members of the Lower *Rasprava*, townspeople who were members of the Town Magistracy (the lowest court of instance for townspeople), the Judge of the Orphans' Court — who were accused of a series of irregularities. The secretaries of the Novoladoga *Uezd* Court and the Vytegra Lower *Rasprava* were ordered to be sacked.[7] Some higher oficials were punished; the Governor of Smolensk, Isai Arshevskii, and the *Guberniia* Procurator lost their posts and their ranks in 1763 because of bribe-taking (*SIRIO* 1871: vol. 7, pp. 224–5). But this was due to Catherine's personal intervention in the case and, in general, it was far harder to stamp out corruption further up the ladder. When Derzhavin, as Governor in Tambov, tried to put a stop to an embezzlement scandal in the Fiscal Chamber, in which the treasury had lost 120,000 roubles in a four-year period, he alienated not only the members of the Chamber but also the Vice-Governor and the Governor-General. As a result of 'slanderous' reports by his colleagues, Derzhavin found he had to defend himself before the Sixth Department of the Senate (Derzhavin 1876: pp. 564–75).

Bribery and Justice — The Failings of the Russian Judicial System

Bribery could result in miscarriages of justice. A.V. Markov, the secretary of I.I. Chicherin, the Chief of Police in St Petersburg, accepted a bribe from someone who fell at his feet with the words 'I know everything depends on you: save us father! And here to show my gratitude in advance, 50,000 roubles in gold!' Feeling 'perplexed', Markov was tempted and fell; the accused was freed and his accusers in turn were found guilty of slander, whipped, had their nostrils slit and were sent to Siberia (Kicheev 1870: pp. 99–103). It is also the case that Russian society was aware that advantages lay with the strong and powerful, in which the ability to pay or otherwise influence the course of justice was crucial. One town delegate to the Legislative Commission in 1767 complained that 'Every merchant will prefer to suffer some damage than get involved in a law suit with a nobleman' (Lauber 1967: p. 213). Baturin recorded a case in Kiev (where he had become Director of Economy) where a peasant petitioned against a treasurer. The Lower Land Court (a police organization, not a court) investigated the case, found the unfortunate peasant to be 'discourteous' and transferred the case to the *Uezd* Court where he found himself accused, and found guilty, of a criminal offence and sentenced to be whipped, a sentence confirmed by the Criminal Chamber. Baturin was aware that an injustice had taken place but was helpless to prevent it (Baturin 1918: 4–6, pp. 193–4).

Nevertheless, the evidence suggests that bribery was not perceived by contemporaries as the only, or even the most important, barrier to justice. The main complaints voiced by the noble deputies to the Legislative Commission in 1767 concerned *delays* within the legal system. The majority of cases involving nobles concerned disputes over landownership. Delays, either in consequence of corrupt officials or simply as a result of the time-consuming and complex series of appeals, could ruin the poorer nobles financially and prove as harmful as unfavourable decisions. 'Poor nobles especially bear great hardship' from legal delays, declared the *nakaz* of the nobles of Vereia (Givens 1975: p. 290). In 1779, Governor-General Krechetnikov commented on 'several restless and ill-advised people who, seeing a stop being put to their slanderous designs, by a timely resolution of the case in the courts, contrive to prolong the case by transferring it from place to place on appeal'.[8] The Statute of 1775 established a new appeals mechanism: there were courts of three instances in the provinces from which appeal could be made to the Senate. But the backlog of unresolved cases remained alarmingly high. Indeed, the new structure probably only served further to slow down the administration of justice. Cases could be transferred from court to court within a year, but it was normal for cases to take four or five years to progress from the lowest to the highest provincial courts; in the St Petersburg Civil Chamber in the 1780s there were cases which had been in the courts for over twenty years. Part of the problem was the sheer number of cases which came before the courts: in 1786, 1,441 cases were outstanding in the St Petersburg courts, but this from a total of 53,868 cases which came before the courts in that year. This suggests that the procedures within the Russian legal system in themselves made justice difficult to obtain, irrespective of the calibre of its officials.

There were also weaknesses in the Russian judicial system which were not addressed in 1775. The Statute of Provincial Administration established a new *structure* and framework of provincial courts but neglected more fundamental concerns, namely the lack of precision of Russian legal codes, the lack of training of judges and the slow development of what may be termed a 'legal consciousness'. The Law Code of 1649, which codified criminal and civil laws and established judicial procedures, remained the fundamental source of Russian law, with only parts of it superseded, on an *ad hoc* basis, by further law codes such as Peter I's Military Code of 1716 and by laws and decrees passed by the tsar or the Senate. Further attempts to codify the laws in this period failed. Catherine convened the Legislative Commission of 1767 for this purpose but it had made no progress when it was prorogued in 1768. Alexander I set up a Commission in 1801 to codify the laws. In 1808 Mikhail Speranskii was appointed to the Commission to speed up its work and this resulted in a hastily composed Law Code of 1812, largely based on Napoleon's Civil Code of 1804. Although this code was accepted in principle by the Permanent Council it was never put into practice. Full codification of the laws did not take place until the reign of Nicholas I, when the laws passed since 1649 were published in a 'Complete Collection of the Laws of the Russian Empire' in 1835. In Catherine's reign the consequence was considerable legal confusion. Cases were resolved in practice with reference to various laws, including the Code of 1649, Peter I's

Military Code (even for civilian cases; penalties for rape, for example, were based on Peter's Military Code as well as the Code of 1649), Catherine's *nakaz* (although this was a statement of principles rather than a set of laws) and to decrees passed by the Senate at various times.

The first professor of law at Moscow University was F.G. Dilthey; the first *Russian* professor of jurisprudence was A. Desnitskii, who became a professor of law at Moscow University in 1773 and had been trained at Glasgow University. Guides to Russian laws began to be published in the late eighteenth century; the first was Chulkov's *Judicial Dictionary* of 1788. But little improvement occurred until legal training, and examinations for appointed posts in the civil service, began to take place in the early nineteenth century. Indeed, by making judges and assessors *elected* posts from the nobility, and stating that the qualifications required were only those of service and income, Catherine II assumed that legal training was not necessary, or even desirable (I think it is fair to say the Russian tsars in the eighteenth century exhibited a certain distrust of the legal profession which was perhaps not entirely unwarranted). The nature of Russian procedure suggested that all that was required was an ability to follow regulations correctly, something which a basic education and a military background could be expected to provide. Clerical staff prepared the evidence, which was signed by both parties and then presented to the court accompanied by the relevant laws which had to be applied. Evidence was provided in a series of proofs, of which the most weight was given to confessions, followed in significance by written statements prepared by the clerks and signed by witnesses. Trials were secret and closed. This procedure meant that judges and assessors relied on the work of junior clerical staff and there was little scope for discretion or interpretation of the law. The only exception was when the case reached the highest place of appeal — the Senate or even Catherine II herself — which is one reason why litigants so readily resorted to appeal. A system of procurators had been established by Peter I, and maintained by Catherine in 1775, which was responsible for overseeing the correct application of the laws. Procurators were *appointed* and not elected officials, but their own legal education could be as inadequate as that of the officials they were supposed to supervise.

Catherine's own poor level of legal understanding can be demonstrated by the history of her so-called conscience court (*sovestnyi sud*), which in 1775 was established in each *guberniia* as part of the judicial structure. Supposedly based on her reading of the *Encyclopédie* and William Blackstones's *Commentaries* in French translation, this attempted to introduce elements of the British legal system — namely the concept of equity and *habeas corpus* — as well as allowing for arbitration in disputes within the Russian legal system. Prisoners who were held for more than three days without being charged could appeal to the judge of the conscience court to hear their case. This proposal demonstrated not just Catherine's muddled legal thinking but a total lack of realism about conditions in Russia, where the chances of a prisoner being able to appeal against imprisonment (even if he were aware that he had this right) were slim indeed. As a result, the courts never functioned fully as Catherine intended, although they were set up and, in practice, served a useful purpose in at least some *gubernii* by handling a number of cases concerning the insane, minors and unintentional criminal offences where application of the prescribed penalties could have been very harsh (they never, as far as can be ascertained, acted as courts of arbitration) (Hartley 1983: pp. 306–18).

Furthermore, many arbitrary actions took place in which the victims could not seek redress through the law. Many land disputes never came to court. The nobles of Peremyshl′-Vorotynsk claimed in 1767 that 'the strongest lord takes the best land, clears the woods for plowfields, and seizes more than his share of the common and arable land' (Augustine 1970: p. 400). Serfs, of course, were subject to the arbitrary actions of their landowners and had almost no effective recourse to the law, which played little part in their lives except when they themselves were involved in the most serious criminal cases. Extreme cases of harsh treatment of serfs would more likely provoke revolt, or mass flight, rather than recourse to the law. Indeed, the conduct of law has to be seen in the context of the general violence and lawlessness of Russian life and the inability of forces of law and order to protect the lives of the population. Robber gangs, largely composed of fugitive peasants and army deserters, could terrorize communities. Violence was endemic in both urban and rural life. The Statute of Provincial Administration was introduced in the wake of the Pugachev Revolt, when the failure of provincial government to deal swiftly with the rebels was so forcibly exposed, but there is little evidence to suggest that matters rapidly improved after 1775.

Conclusion

'As for justice 'tis a joke. No such thing exists & its *shadow* covers vice eneough to make me shudder.' Such was the judgement on Russia by Martha Wilmot at the turn of the nineteenth century (Wilmot and Wilmot 1934: pp. 308–9). Such comments by foreign, particularly British, travellers were common. It is, however, debatable how much worse the standards of public life were in Russia in this period compared with elsewhere in Europe. At least in Russia offices were not sold as they were in France and England. Nevertheless, there were features of the Russian judicial system which made the application of justice more arbitrary and unpredictable than in countries where laws had been codified, where there were traditions of legal education and respect for the legal profession and where an understanding of the 'rule of law' could lead to a legal challenge to government procedures or actions. Within this broader context the existence, and prevalence, of bribery within the judicial system were only symptomatic of general arbitrariness, poor public standards and weak procedures in Russia. Bribery was not in itself the major cause of injustice: the weaknesses of the Russian judicial system were more fundamental. A true 'legal consciousness' only took root in Russia in the nineteenth century, as legal training became accepted, Russia acquired lawyers and a proper codification of the Russian laws took place. Only then could bribery within the legal system be seen as a cause for concern and shame.

Notes

1 London, British Library, Additional Manuscripts, 427427, ff. 132–4, Lieven papers, recruit book of the village of Baki, 1814.

2 After the Statute on Provincial Administration of 1775 there were three separate tiers of courts of first and second instance in the provinces according to social estate — for nobles (the *uezd* court and the upper land court), townspeople (the town and *guberniia* magistracy) and state peasants (the lower and upper *raspravy*), from which appeal could be made to the courts of third instance in the *guberniia* — the civil and criminal chambers — and from there to the Senate.

3 St Petersburg, Rossiiskii gosudarstvennyi istoricheskii arkhiv, Sankt Peterburg, fond 1724, opis′ 1, delo 30, f. 20v., journal of the St Petersburg Criminal Chamber, 1788.
4 *Polnoe sobranie zakonov rossiiskoi imperii* (hereafter *PSZ*), vol. 21, no. 15360, pp. 423–30, 3 March 1782.
5 Moscow, Rossiiskii gosudarstvennyi arkhiv drevnikh aktov (hereafter RGADA), fond 16, delo 533, chast′ 2, ff. 139–241, report by Governor-General Brius from St Petersburg *guberniia*, 1787–91.
6 St Petersburg, Sankt-Peterburgskii Filial Instituta russkoi istorii, fond 36, delo 478, f. 69, report by A.R. Vorontsov from Vologda *guberniia*, 1786; RGADA, fond 16, delo 1012, chast′ 1, f. 228v, report by Governor A.P. Mel′gunov from Iaroslavl′ and Vologda *gubernii*, 1784.
7 *PSZ*, vol. 21, no. 15360, p. 427.
8 RGADA, fond 16, delo 729, chast′ 1, f. 285, report by Governor-General M.T. Krechetnikov from Tula and Kaluga *gubernii*, 1779.

Bibliography

Aleksandrov, V.A. (1976), *Sel′skaia obshchina v Rossii (XVII–nachalo XIX v.)*, Moscow.

Augustine, W.R. (1970), 'Notes Toward a Portrait of the Eighteenth-Century Russian Nobility', *Canadian-American Slavic Studies*, 6, 3.

Baturin, P.S. (1918), 'Zapiski', *Golos minuvshago*, 1–3, 4–6.

Bolotov, A. (1973), *Zhizn′ i prikliucheniia Andreia Bolotova*, vol. 2, Introduction by M. Raeff, Cambridge.

Derzhavin, G.R. (1876), *Sochineniia Derzhavina s ob″iasnitel′nimi primechaniami Ia. Grota. Vol. 6: Zapiski*, St Petersburg.

Dobrynin, G.I. (1871), 'Istinnoe povestvovanie ili zhizn′ Gavriila Ivanovicha Dobrynina, im samim pisannaia', *Russkaia starina*, 4.

Dubasov, I.I. (1878), 'K istorii otzhivshago chinovnichestva', *Russkii arkhiv*, 1.

Dubasov, I.I. (1884), 'Tambovskii krai v kontse XVIII i nachale XIX stoletiia', *Istoricheskii vestnik*, 9.

Givens, R.D. (1975), 'Servitors or Seigneurs: the Nobility and the Eighteenth-Century Russian State', unpublished PhD thesis, University of California.

Hartley, J.M. (1983), 'Catherine's Conscience Court — An English Equity Court?' in A.G. Cross (ed.), *Russia and the West in the Eighteenth Century*, Newtonville, MA.

Hassell, J. (1967), 'The Vicissitudes of Russian Administrative Reform 1762–1801', unpublished PhD thesis, University of Cornell.

Kalashnikov, T.P. (1904), 'Zhizn′ neznamenitago Timofeia Petrovicha Kalashnikova prostym slogom opisannaia s 1762 po 1794 god', *Russkii arkhiv*, 10.

Keep, J.L.H. (1985), *Soldiers of the Tsar: Army and Society in Russia 1462–1874*, Oxford.

Kicheev, P.G. (1870), *Iz nedavnei stariny — Razskazy i vospominaniia*, Moscow.

Korf, S.A. (1908), *Dvorianstvo i ego soslovnoe upravlenie za stoletie 1762–1855 godov*, St Petersburg.

Lauber, J.M. (1967), 'The Merchant–Gentry Conflict in Eighteenth-Century Russia', unpublished PhD thesis, University of Iowa.

LeDonne, J.P. (1984), *Ruling Russia: Politics and Administration in the Age of Absolutism 1762–1796*, Princeton, NJ.

Lopukhin, I.V. (1860), *Zapiski nekotorykh obstoiatel'stv zhizni i sluzhby*, Moscow.

Mertvago, D.B. (1867), 'Zapiski D.B. Mertvago', *Russkii arkhiv*, 8 and 9.

Ostrozhskii-Lokhvitskii, I.O. (1886), 'Zapiski Novo-oskol'skago dvorianina I.O. Ostrozhskii-Lokhvitskago', *Kievskaia starina*, 14, no. 3.

SIRIO (1871), *Sbornik Imperatorskogo Russkogo istoricheskogo obshchestva*, vols 4 and 7, St Petersburg.

Segel, H.B. (1967), *The Literature of Eighteenth Century Russia*, vol. 2, New York.

Semevskii, V.I. (1903), *Krest'iane v tsarstvovanie imperatritsy Ekateriny II*, vol. 1, St Petersburg.

Shcherbatov, M.M. (1969), *On the Corruption of Morals in Russia*, ed. A. Lentin, Cambridge.

Wilmot, M. and Wilmot, C. (1934), *The Russian Journals of Martha and Catherine Wilmot 1803–1808*, ed. Marchioness of Londonderry and H.M. Hyde, London.

Yaney, G.L. (1973), *The Systematization of Russian Government. Social Evolution in the Domestic Administration of Imperial Russia, 1711–1905*, Urbana, Chicago, IL and London.

'Zhaloba' (1908), 'Zhaloba Saratovskikh krest'ian na zemskii sud', *Russkii arkhiv*, 46.

5 Self-Interested Giving: Bribery and Etiquette in Late Imperial Russia

Catriona Kelly

Взяток не берем, а благодарности принимаем
We don't take bribes, but we accept tokens of gratitude
(Russian saying, quoted in Dal′ 1880–82: vol. 2, p. 92)

Discussions of bribery often take as their starting-point the question of why bribery should flourish in a given society. Yet the sheer prevalence of bribe-taking, its ubiquity in human cultures, suggests that perhaps the central question should not be 'Why does bribery happen?' but 'In what circumstances does bribery come to be considered wrong?' That is to say, it is the existence of societies in which bribery and patronage excite disfavour that requires explanation, rather than the existence of those in which they are tolerated. Food for thought here comes from an observation in a recent Russian etiquette manual, *The School of Etiquette: Advice for Every Occasion*, which contains a section on business gifts. Visitors to Britain are warned to be extremely careful to make their offerings modest:

> In English business circles, gifts are regarded very strictly. Only a few items may be regarded as gifts and not as bribes. These include calendars, diaries, cigarette lighters, biros bearing the company logo

---

I gratefully acknowledge the financial contribution made by the British Academy, which funded research visits to Russia and Finland in 1996 and 1997 in order to collect material for the general study of Russian behaviour regulation on which this article has drawn, and offer my thanks to Judy Pallot and to Stephen Lovell for useful bibliographical suggestions.

> and (at Christmas) alcoholic beverages. Other goods are interpreted as a way of bringing pressure to bear on one's business partner. If it becomes known in business circles that representatives of certain firms are involved in such actions [that is, the presentation of inappropriately luxurious gifts], then trust may be ruptured once and for all. (Likhacheva 1996: p. 416)

This is the only such warning given in the book, though readers are informed that the Finns and the Japanese may disapprove of large presents.

It goes without saying that the reflection of 'English business behaviour' in *The School of Etiquette* is partial; the activities of a number of British Members and ex-Members of Parliament are just one recent counter-instance that comes to mind. *The School of Etiquette* is surely correct, however, to suggest that public tolerance of bribery is greater in Russia than in Britain, and that the boundaries between gift-giving and bribery are differently drawn. Finally — the point of greatest relevance to my argument here — the book indicates that from the Russian perspective it is the squeamish refusal of a gift on the grounds that it might be a bribe that is extraordinary, rather than the acceptance of a token of the kind of gratitude that has been aphoristically summed up as 'a lively sense of favours to come'.

While it would be a mischievous over-simplification to argue that bribery is an unchangeable feature of Russian society, it has certainly been an endemic one, and its persistence has been furthered, I shall argue here, by the relation of bribery to 'the culture of self-interested giving' in traditional Russian society. Besides making some observations about this culture, I intend also to trace an important, if finally unsuccessful, challenge that was mounted to 'the culture of self-interested giving' by the rise, in the late nineteenth century, of the 'self-help' ethos, with its championing of dignity through independence, whose emergence in Russia was marked by translations of the immensely and internationally popular works of Samuel Smiles, author of *Self-Help*, *Duty*, *Thrift* and *Heroes of Labour*, as well as many other books. The chapter thus traces the conflict of 'etiquette' in two senses: (a) a Westernized tradition of 'civilized behaviour' codified in written texts, such as conduct manuals; and (b) traditional behaviour norms transmitted by face-to-face contact, rather than (or as well as) through printed texts. That is, the persistence of 'corruption' (practices specifically forbidden by law) is related to the prevalence of 'proto-corruption' (reciprocal practices such as patronage) in Russian society.[1]

One possible objection to tracing attitudes to bribery as an issue of mentality is that the picture that emerges is distorted, since structural factors (for example, the immense political and economic power of the state and, by extension, of the state's official representatives; the function of serfdom in reinforcing relations of patronage) are represented marginally, if at all (compare the strictures of Scott 1972: pp. 7–8). I would argue, however, that the approach taken here at least allows one to grasp the part played by attitudes to bribery in the subjective reality of Russian popular culture (a term used here in the broadest sense, to mean the culture of politically and legally non-expert opinion, or 'common sense'). In this culture, bribery has seldom been discussed in terms of structural relations; it was, rather, perceived as an issue of personal and national identity (corruption has been seen as a characteristic of 'bad officials' or of 'backward Russian culture'). And in any case, structural relations are, at least at some level, the product of a society's mentality, reflecting as well as constraining beliefs and values.

My argument that 'self-interested giving' has been widespread in Russian culture runs contrary to the arguments set out in a well-known article by Iurii Lotman, the historian, semiotician and literary critic, which distinguishes between the gift as contract and the gift as self-sacrifice (Lotman 1993: pp. 345–56). Lotman sets out a schema according to which self-interested giving is seen as a Western phenomenon, related to the close ties between church and state fundamental to Roman Catholicism. In Russia and other Orthodox countries, by contrast, Lotman argues, only detached, self-immolatory, disinterested giving has been valued. Though Lotman's binary opposition depends on a neo-Slavophile myth eventually derived from Dostoevskii's 'Legend of the Grand Inquisitor' in *The Brothers Karamazov* (and, as in Dostoevskii, Western tradition is seen as unitary, with Catholicism, Protestantism and socialism representing only insignificantly differentiated masks of one alien Other), it does usefully capture the high status that has been accorded to self-sacrifice and renunciation of the world (*smirenie*) in Orthodox culture. The long history of Orthodox philanthropy comes to mind here (Lindenmeyr

1996). The reluctance of Orthodox culture to legislate for the secular world,[2] however, meant that theology and religious observance had only a weak hold on gift-giving practices in secular Russian society of the late nineteenth and early twentieth centuries; here various forms of self-interested giving were deeply entrenched.

In Russian villages, perhaps the most important social institutions where exchange of gifts or favours played a role were the *pomochi* or *toloka*, respectively the northern and southern Russian dialect words for what Western scholars usually term 'mutual aid'. According to Vladimir Dal′'s authoritative dictionary of the Russian language, *toloka* signifies: '*pomoch′*, the gathering of the village population at the property of one householder, when summoned, to work in a spirit of camaraderie [*dlia druzhnoi raboty*] for a single day; the host treats those who come to help, and thus is able to carry out reaping, mowing, threshing and so on in one go. There are also *toloka* for taking out manure and even for cutting cabbages (known as *kapustki*)' (Dal′ 1880–82: vol. 3, p. 412). The sense that participation in *toloka* and *pomochi* involved an exchange of labour and hospitality is suggested by a proverb quoted by Dal′, '*Darom kormiat, tak na pomoch′ zovut*', roughly the Russian peasant equivalent of 'there's no such thing as a free lunch' (Dal′ 1880–82: vol. 2, p. 274).

A very full description of mutual aid, the customs behind which were uniform throughout Russian peasant culture, has been given by one of the leading contemporary peasant historians, Marina Gromyko (Gromyko 1986: pp. 31–62). Gromyko has distinguished three kinds of *pomochi*: aid rendered routinely for big jobs (carrying out manure, harvesting, sewing and so on); aid given in a crisis (for example, when a cottage burnt down or a family was stricken by sickness); and aid directly requested by the head of a household himself (in the case of an unexpected crop glut, say). Gromyko asserts that the second type of aid was obligatory for everyone, while in the first and third cases a return was expected (Gromyko 1986: pp. 61–2). Even in the second case, however, one may doubt whether total disinterest was always preserved. As another historian of Russian peasant culture, Christine Worobec, has put it, 'households whose destitution was the result of an irresponsible or alcoholic patriarch received neither sympathy nor help' (Worobec 1991: p. 7). Judgements of this kind were based at least partly on an appreciation that improvident individuals are not only 'beyond help' but incapable of contributing to the community in return for aid received.[3]

Another, slightly different, type of self-interested giving was that signified by the word *magarych* (alternatively spelled *mogarych*). This term, of Arabic origin (from *māharǐg*) can be used to signify a round of drinks bought to seal a bargain (especially a horse-sale), the drinks bought by a new worker for his workmates (cf. *prival'noe*, or 'embarkation drink'), or the treat organized by the owner of a new house for the builders who have constructed it. The following elaborate description of the last kind of ritual comes from the memoirs of the painter Il'ia Repin, who grew up in the mixed Russian–Ukrainian settlement of Osinovka, not far from Khar'kov, during the 1850s:

> We knew very well that all these 'Russian' carpenters were as crafty as wizards. They meant trouble; how many *magarychi* we'd had to put on already! Lay the foundations — a *magarych*; set up the 'mother beam' [king-post] — a *magarych*; put shingles on the roof — another *magarych*. And every time you had to treat the whole *artel'* [work collective] [...].
>
> And God help you if you didn't play along; they'd 'build the house on the soul' of the person in the family they didn't like, and he or she would die. When they were always asked to build it on some old grandad whose time had come in any case — well, that was the will of God. Or the same thing might happen to you as had happened to other folks: they'd hide a pack of cards under the icon corner. And the devilment you'd get then — you'd just have to leave: at night the house spirit and the Evil One would raise such a din and such a scare it wouldn't bear thinking about! [...]
>
> Our Mam had worked out a remedy against the wizardry of the carpenters. It stands to reason that she treated them really well, and the *magarychi* that she stood them were good ones; the carpenters were pleased, and when Mam asked absolutely seriously whose soul they'd built the house on, they answered with conviction:
>
> 'Stop fretting, Stepanida, have we no crosses round our necks [that is, are we pagans] or something, or do you think you offended us in some way? We're human beings too and we understand what kind of people we're dealing with and the rest [...]. (Repin 1982: p. 38)

In such situations, self-interested giving functions as a way of averting *porcha* (the action of the 'evil eye'); the drinks and food offered act as a kind of libation, staving off the dangers of contact with something new — a new horse, a new workmate, and especially a new house (compare other *novosel'e*, or 'new house', customs that Repin refers to, such as making the cat go in first so that any occultic upheavals hit it rather than the human members of the household). Self-interested giving is indulged in as much to avert catastrophe (the negative interpretation) as for its value in achieving positive goals of self-advancement. Besides this primal meaning, though, *magarych* can be used more loosely to mean 'hospitality organized as a reward for something [*ugoshchenie, ustraivaemoe v kachestve voznagrazhdeniia za chto-libo*]' (Evgen'eva 1983: vol. 2. p. 213).[4] From here, it is an easy transition to employing the word as a synonym for a bribe in the strict sense, a usage already recorded by Dal''s dictionary of the Russian language in the 1860s, where *vyprashivat' mogarychi*, 'to request *magarychi*', is given as a synonym for *klianchit'*, 'to cadge' (Dal' 1880–82: vol. 2, p. 288). Conversely, the link between *pomochi* and bribery is suggested by an invitation formula quoted by Gromyko, in which the householder requesting help appeals not to his fellow-villagers' sense of collective spirit but to their venality, by emphasizing the hospitality on offer first, and only then the work that will be requested:

> Come over to us and eat our bread and salt; there'll be plenty of nice vodka and beer for our guests; but please heed our plea; help us and other Orthodox folk to cope with the work we have to do. (Gromyko 1986: p. 26)

It is not too long a step from here to the patriarch in Chekhov's story *V ovrage* (In the Ravine, 1900) who, when his coin-forger son is being held in prison, sends to the warder the coercive gift of a silver tea-glass decorated with an enamel inscription reading 'Moderation in all things' (*Dusha meru znaet*).

Russian élite culture also had its traditional forms of gift-giving which easily crossed the border into bribery. The most important of these was perhaps the custom of tipping servants (*davat' na chai*): tips (*chaevye*) were often the price of a servant's silence over matters that required concealment. Vladimir Nabokov gives a nice instance in his memoir, *Speak, Memory*:

> We skipped school; I forget what Tamara's procedure was; mine consisted of talking either of the two chauffeurs into dropping me at

> this or that corner on the way to school (both were good sports and actually refused to accept my gold) [...]. Nor had I any trouble with our wonderful, eminently bribable Ustin, who took the calls on our ground-floor telephone [...] he briskly replied I had a sore throat. (Nabokov 1987: p. 181)[5]

And one Russian etiquette book of the 1890s directly recommends bribery of servants (and household pets) in a strange household in order to get them on one's side: 'When staying in a family, avoid making enemies of the servants and dogs; you should buy them over to your side [*i tekh i drugikh sleduet podkupat'*], the former by means of a handsome gift of money, the latter by means of tit-bits and caresses' (Svetozarskaia 1890: p. 109). In some cultures (for example, modern Britain or the USA), tipping is generally seen as a reward for good service and an incentive to diligence ('a bonus'); in Russian culture it is generally seen as a contribution to the cementing of personal relations ('a sweetener').

The Russian word *vziatochnichestvo* can be used not only for bribery, but for the attempts to further the interests of one's family or social group (see especially Maiakovskii's poem, 'Vziatochniki' (Corrupt Officials, literally 'bribe-takers'):

> Он понял буквально
> «братство народов»
> как счастье братьев,
> теть
> и сестер.[6]
> (The 'brotherhood of nations'
> meant for him literally,
> Do the best by your brothers,
> sisters,
> and aunts.)
> (Maiakovskii 1955–61: vol. 7, p. 135)

Russian peasant culture was characterized by a great spread of kin or pseudo-kin networks, stretching from blood relationships to those cemented by religious ritual (*kumovstvo*, the relationship between godparents) and affection (*kumovstvo* in its alternative sense of an affective tie, with *kum* translatable as 'gossip'; *pobratimstvo*, the relationship between brothers; and *posestrinstvo*, that between sisters). Kin networks were less elaborate in Russian élite culture: by the late nineteenth century at the latest, many educated Russians had given up grappling with the immensely complex traditional terminology of family relationships, and the French terms *beau-frère* and *belle-soeur* were used instead of *shurin* (wife's brother), *ziat'* (sister's husband or son-in-law or husband's sister's husband), *nevestka* (brother's wife or daughter-in-law) and *zolovka* (husband's sister). All the same, the closest ties (those within the nuclear family and between first cousins, for instance) did impose obligations of mutual aid. As a historian of the Russian family has put it, 'failing to use one's influence to advance one's own (however defined) at the expense of others would itself be the cause of social censure' (Tovrov 1987: p. 109). Such support to affective and kin connections can be named in English as 'cronyism' and 'nepotism', but the terms have a condemnatory flavour that is absent from the Russian words *kumovstvo* and *pobratimstvo*. As late as 1902, it was perfectly natural for Mariamna Davydova, a woman from the old, though impoverished, gentry family of Lopukhin, simply to contact an acquaintance when her husband needed a new job: 'I wrote to the vice-governor of Warsaw, Krevsky, who was married to the sister of a good friend of ours. He promised to give Lev a post as a regional director' (Davydoff 1986: p. 59).

One would not wish to be particularist about the Russian situation with regard to these forms of 'self-interested giving'. In Britain, certainly, it is generally argued that traditional aristocratic patronage had gone into terminal decline by the late seventeenth century, challenged by the meritocratic value-system of the new mercantile bourgeoisie (Stone 1974, ch. 4). Though customs such as nepotism and exchange of personal favours did not disappear, they were increasingly perceived as aberrant. When Anthony Trollope, novelist and ex-official of the Post Office, argued in his autobiography that the introduction of Civil Service examinations was regrettable, since the practice of giving job appointments only to those personally known by members of the appointing board to be 'gentlemen' was much safer, he was making himself the spokesman of beleaguered views: 'As what I write now will certainly never be read till I am dead, I may dare to say what no one now does dare to say in print' (Trollope 1955: p. 39). But the customs found in Russia can all be matched in other traditional societies, and 'self-interested giving' functioned in much the same way in these. In Ireland, for example, where mutual aid was known as 'cooring' (from the Celtic *cómhar*), reciprocality was strictly enforced, and participation rewarded by food, drink and entertainments on the same pattern as the *magarych* (Brody 1983: pp. 134–5; Evans 1957: p. 57). Kin networks played (and play) a large role in obtaining employment and favours, and — just as in Russia — the boundaries between gifts, rewards and bribes were (and are) more porous than in Britain.[7]

If the centrality of self-interested giving is far from unique to Russia, it is, conversely, important to appreciate that bribery in Russia was always a contested institution, and one where practices could be contradictory. The terminology is distinctly ambiguous, with, especially, a derogatory flavour in the words for the agents of bribes (*vziatochnik*, *magarychnik*), most particularly if they resort to extortion (*sryv*). Verbs for those who live by bribery are especially hostile in flavour, branding those who accept bribes as parasites and those who live by them as tyrants: *magarychit′* carries the connotations of idleness and profiteering as well as cadging, and *vziatochnichat′* is used both in the sense of 'forcing gifts' out of people (*vymogat′ dary*) or, conversely, prostituting them to one's purpose (as in the picturesque phrase 'to put golden spectacles' on a person, *nadet′ zolotye ochki*) (Dal′ 1880–82: vol. 2, p. 288; ibid., vol. 1, p. 197; ibid., vol. 3, p. 180). While all these phrases relate to an excessive dependence on bribery, rather than an indulgence in the act *per se*, it is likely that by no means all historical subjects would have accepted the fact that exchanges of favours between friends prepared the ground for bribery; a splitting of consciousness along the lines 'I like to help my friends; you take bribes; he's a *magarychnik*' was perfectly possible.

Bribery was regarded by the Russian state, too, with considerable disfavour: voluntaristic relations between officials and members of the public threatened revenue (the notorious venality of customs officials, for example, hampered the proper functioning of the duty system); they also brought the civil service into disrepute, and challenged the top-down governance required for successful autocratic rule by setting up local hegemonies. Accordingly, legal regulation sought to crack down on bribery and underline the incompatibility of bribe-taking with public service. A law of 28 February 1720 (still on the statute books in the late imperial era) set out the requisite qualities of Russian officials thus:

> The general qualities of every person who occupies a position in the civil service, and the general duties, which must always be a

> looking-glass of his behaviour, are: (1) common sense; (2) goodwill with regard to his subordinates; (3) love of humanity; (4) fidelity to the service of His Imperial Majesty; (5) zealous pursuit of the common weal; (6) energy in the performance of his duties; (7) honesty, selflessness and *abstinence from bribe-taking*; (8) just and disinterested judgement of all, independent of their social standing; (9) patronage to the innocent and injured. (Mordukhai-Boltovskii 1912: vol. 3, 'Ustav o sluzhbe po opredeleniiu ot pravitel'stva', art. 705, my emphasis)

Further legislation of 1764, 1775, 1782, 1825, 1845, 1863, 1864, 1865, 1870, 1900 and 1906 was to elaborate the definition of bribery (subdivided into *mzdoimstvo*, or plain bribe-taking, and *likhoimstvo*, or extortion), and impose punishments ranging from a fine (if the bribe was declared, or if it had been tendered retrospectively, that is, only after the desired action had been performed) up to a prison sentence (Mordukhai-Boltovskii 1912: vol. 15, 'Ulozhenie o nakazaniiakh', articles 372–82, 436, 492–3, 499, 805, 807–8, 810, 905, 946, 1069, 1154, 1291).

Although the legal codes expressed strong disapproval of bribery, they also constructed official duties in a manner that made bribe-taking not only possible but likely. The 1720 formulation, for example, invokes incorruptibility as part of a complex of virtues including disinterested philanthropy and diligence, yet simultaneously represents the official as a father-figure who judged petitioners according to his perception of their needs. Exhorted to exercise 'just and disinterested judgement', the official had also to practise 'patronage to the innocent and injured' — a difficult proposition in a society where 'disinterested patronage' was a contradiction in terms. This situation may explain the strange 'attraction of opposites' evident in the second part of Gogol''s *Mertvye dushi* (Dead Souls, 1842), where Chichikov, a corrupt scoundrel and outrageous trickster whose behaviour is described as 'the most dishonourable that can be' (*bestsenneishee*), is treated with surprising clemency, once his dishonesty is exposed, by representatives of the strand of society to which Gogol''s didactic narrative attributes ideal authority, the paternalist gentry.

By the late nineteenth century, then, the concept that bribery was incompatible with state service and the rational behaviour desirable therein was well established, but the Russian legal code had failed to strike at (indeed, it had from some points of view entrenched) those customs which, if not the only cause of bribery, were certainly a vital part of the context in which it functioned: the upper-class tradition of patronage, on the one hand, and the various forms of self-interested giving that were traditional among the Russian peasantry, on the other. Hence the novelty of the notions of probity expressed in Samuel Smiles's books on self-help.

Smiles, a Scot whose mother was a member of a small, exclusive Presbyterian sect, came from a background characterized by highly specific 'mutual aid' practices. As observed by Max Weber in his famous essay, 'The Protestant Sects and the Spirit of Capitalism', these stemmed from an idiosyncratic association of moral self-righteousness and materialism:

> When a sect member moved to a different place, or if he was a travelling salesman, he carried the certificate of his congregation with him; and thereby he found not only easy contact with sect members there, but, above all, he found credit everywhere. If he got into economic straits through no fault of his own, the sect arranged his affairs, gave guarantees to the creditors, and helped him in every way, often according to the Biblical principle, *mutuum date nihil inde sperantes* (*Luke* 6:35) [that is, 'lend, hoping for nothing in return']. (Weber 1993: p. 305)

This kind of mutual aid was associated with 'an immensely exclusive "pride in caste"' (Weber 1993: p. 319), which guaranteed the probity of sect members and their subscription to the code of 'honesty is the best policy'. Dissenters from this code were excluded from the communion, but, conversely, 'the capitalist success of a sect brother, if legally attained, was proof of his worth and of his state of grace' (ibid.: p. 322). In other words, while reciprocity still underpinned mutual aid practices, its functioning had now been systematized, and exchanges were stripped of any sense that a personal favour was being done. The distinction between Protestantism and traditional Catholic or Orthodox practice is sometimes understood, rather simplistically, to be rooted in a division between 'fidelity to the community' and 'personal responsibility' (see, for example, Heretz 1997: p. 70). As Weber's description makes clear, the discrepancy is rather between two different kinds of understanding of the community, with the 'Protestant' understanding holding each member of the community responsible not only for his or her own virtuous behaviour but also for regulating and supporting the moral commitment of others. Furthermore, there was no area of secular life which was excluded from the Protestant code: financial transactions were as subject to scrutiny as, for example, sexual transactions. In strict Protestantism, there were no unlegislated spaces in which alternative modes of behaviour might flourish (the fasting versus feasting cycle was replaced by an emphasis on consistent moderation, just as the cycle of transgression followed by confession became an insistent regulation of each moment of earthly existence).

For Smiles, the two goals of material success and spiritual probity were as inseparable as they were for the members of Weber's paradigmatic Protestant sect. His famous manual *Self-Help* stated the creed thus: 'The road of human welfare lies along the old highway of steadfast well-doing; and they who are the most persistent, and work in the truest spirit, will usually be the most successful' (Smiles 1866: p. 94). Smiles was also an influential pioneer in disseminating the ideology of 'nature's gentleman': '[the gentleman's] qualities depend not upon fashion or manners, but upon moral worth — not on personal possessions, but on personal qualities' (Smiles 1866: p. 398). Among these personal qualities is the refusal of bribes (ibid.: p. 399). In one of his sequels to *Self-Help*, *Duty* (1880), Smiles expands on this assertion, devoting an entire chapter to 'Men who Cannot be Bought'. Before proceeding to eulogize role models such as Sir Humphrey Davy, William Pitt, Sir Thomas Outram, Meyer Anselm (founder of the Rothschild dynasty) and Lord Macaulay, Smiles offers a ringing denunciation of those who fall below the standards of 'nature's gentlemen':

> First, there are men who *can* be bought. There are rogues innumerable, who are ready to sell their bodies and souls for money or for drink. Who has not heard of the elections which have been made void through bribery and corruption? [...] The men who sell themselves are slaves; their buyers are dishonest and unprincipled. [...] [*The Times* says:] 'It is all important that the public service should be pure, and that no suspicion should rest on the name of any official in a post of confidence. It would be an evil day if it were generally suspected that civil servants took backsheesh or *pots de vin*.' [...] In Russia, the corruption of civil servants, even of the highest grade, is most gross. You must buy your way by gold. Bribery in every conceivable form is practised. (Smiles 1880: pp. 70–2)[8]

As well as publication data, memoir sources also indicate that the circulation for Smiles was large. Already by the 1870s he had considerable currency among Russian radicals, as Il'ia Repin recalls in a memoir of a visit to one of the musical soirées held at the Serov household in St Petersburg (Repin 1982: 353). His hostess, Valentina Serova, the mother of the famous painter Valentin Serov and wife of a well-known musician, was herself a composer, but also a *nigilistka* (woman nihilist), who cut her hair short, spurned society ways and earnestly acquired familiarity with a series of sacred texts of the radical movement, 'mighty works of Russian publicistics and literature forbidden at the time', including Chernyshevskii, Pisarev, Dobroliubov, Shelgunov, Antonovich, Georg Büchner, Jakob Moleschott, Feuerbach, Mill, Lassales and Samuel Smiles.[9]

Smiles's works never constituted 'forbidden literature' as represented by Chernyshevskii or Feuerbach, but it is highly indicative that Repin supposed that they did. Indeed, the extraordinary thing about Smiles is that the reception of his work (unlike that of Feuerbach or Chernyshevskii) bridged the gap between official and oppositional values. The fact that Smiles's remarks on Russia's notoriety as a country where bribery ruled were not censored out of Russian editions of his work indicates official approval for the dissemination of such ideas, no doubt as part of the Russian establishment's increasing commitment to modernizing ideologies in the late nineteenth century.[10] But Smiles was just as popular among opponents of autocracy and, unlike Moleschott or Mill, was read in worker circles as well as in intelligentsia circles.[11]

The heritage of 'self-help' is one reason why the early Soviet years witnessed a new sharpness in assaults on bribery, which was interpreted not only as subversive of the Bolsheviks' need to establish central control but also as an infringement of propriety. Decrees on bribery (imposing punishments right up to execution, to be meted out by revolutionary tribunals) were enacted in May 1918 and August 1921. That these measures were intended not only to curb malpractices but to underwrite an entirely new concept of state service is evident in contemporary statements by Lenin. In 1921, for example, Lenin named bribery and *komchvanstvo*, arrogance on the part of officials, along with illiteracy as 'the three main enemies' of the Soviet regime, and histrionically asserted 'If such a phenomenon as the bribe is allowed to exist, if such a thing is possible, then there can be no talk of real politics. There cannot even be an approach to politics, because all measures will be left hanging in the air and will have no results whatever' (Lenin 1941–50: vol. 33, p. 55). The symbolic representations of the new state drew an equally direct link between bribery, official arrogance and backwardness, with Maiakovskii's 'bribe-taker' portrayed as Soviet *samodur*, or petty tyrant, using his office (in both senses) in order to facilitate his sexual peccadilloes and lust for self-enrichment:

Он думает:
как сократить ему штаты?
У Кэт
не глаза, а угли...
А может быть,
место
оставить для Наты?
У Наты формы округлей.
А там
в приемной —
сдержанный гул,
и воздух от дыма спирается...
Ответственный жмет плечьми:
«Не могу!
Нормально...
Дела разбираются!»
(He thinks:
how should he
cut down on the staff?
Kate's eyes...
they're like coals!
good gracious!
But maybe
Nata should hang on to her job,
since Nata is
so curvaceous.
Out there in the waiting room
voices are raised
and the air's thick with smoke,
it's turned blue...
The official sits at his desk
and shrugs:
'Too bad!
Not a thing I can do.')
(Maiakovskii 1955–61: p. 136).

Assaults on bribery in the 1920s sometimes have nuances of phrasing that suggest Smiles's influence: the unsubstantiated assertion, in the first edition of the *Great Soviet Encyclopedia*, that America was internationally infamous for the prevalence of bribery (*Bol'shaia sovetskaia entsiklopediia* 1929–47: vol. 10, p. 639) is possibly traceable to Smiles's claim that, 'in America, the cream of republics, bribery is conducted in a wholesale way' (Smiles 1880: p. 73). Similarly, the term of abuse that Lenin uses for bribe-takers and bribe-givers in a 1919 response to a petition from a peasant is *negodiai* ('scoundrels': Lenin 1958–65: vol. 37, p. 480), the same word that is used in Nadezhdin's translation of Smiles's *Duty* (1903).[12]

Yet whatever the currency of Smilesian and other views that bribery was dishonest and demeaning, many Russians, both before and after the Revolution, accepted that bribery was a fact of life, and that there was nothing so particularly immoral in it, and especially not in *giving* bribes. The state might institute draconian penalties for bribe-takers, but it was difficult getting judges to mete them out, as is indicated by a furious directive penned by Lenin on 4 May 1918, decreeing that those who gave such 'derisory' penalties for bribery as six months imprisonment, rather than execution, should themselves suffer expulsion from the Party (Lenin 1941–50: vol. 27, p. 290). Even four years after the Revolution, and with the execution of numerous prominent bribe-takers, the struggle with bribery had had so little success that, as Lenin wearily put it, 'we know by experience that, in a politically enlightened nation, there would be no bribes, but with us you get them every step of the way' (Lenin 1941–50: vol. 33, p. 53).[13]

If this was the case under Bolshevik dictatorship, it is easy to imagine the prevalence of bribery before the Revolution. And this is made piquantly clear by a special number of the St Petersburg journal *Novyi Satirikon* in 1915, dedicated to lampooning bribery. In 'The History of the Bribe', Arkadii Bukhov showed Noah arguing with the dove over the olive branch ('What use d'you think this is?') but finally agreeing to take it in exchange for admitting the dove and his mate to the ark. Bukhov bewailed the prevalence of the bribe through the centuries:

> From the moment it came into being, the bribe has taken three forms: the bribe accompanied by threats, the bribe accompanied by hints, and the plain bribe unaccompanied by anything. The third

> type, the most serious, has become an epidemic. It's swallowed entire government organisms like oysters, but without bothering to season them with lemon juice. (Bukhov 1915: p. 6)

And in 'The Technique of the Bribe', Evgenii Venskii revealed the astonishing number of activities where corruption of one kind or another played a part, including not only the procurement of a good review for one's latest book, but the placement of an article with a journal editor, and the attempt to secure a place at all kinds of educational institutions (not excluding religious ones, such as the *eparkhial'noe uchilishche*, or church secondary school), or indeed obtain a divorce (the consistory court is described as 'a positive academy, a Sorbonne of bribery skills') (Venskii 1915: p. 3).

Novyi Satirikon also contains suggestive material about attitudes to bribery. Among the copy is an editorial note quoting the conservative journalist M.O. Men'shikov, who had written along the following lines in his *Pis'ma k blizhnim* (Letters to My Nearest and Dearest) in the conservative newspaper *Novoe vremia*:

> If the ordinary person has to pour a little oil into the vast machine of government institutions every now and then, so what? [...]
>
> In the majority of cases it seems to me that the old custom of giving bribes to officials always was and still is merely a reward for getting a job done quickly or out of turn. After all, do not petty officials in government offices still often receive such 'tokens of gratitude'? Indeed they do, and not only in the provinces, but in central offices in the capital too. And anyone will tell you that giving bribes of that kind is really not all that criminal.

The editors of *Novyi Satirikon* self-righteously protested against this sweeping assumption of a consensus in Russian society:

> No, sir! There are eleven of us on the permanent editorial staff of *Novyi Satirikon*, and all eleven of us say to you quite sincerely: every kind of bribe-giving is criminal, and the tortures that Russia is enduring at present are simply because (to adapt your own expression) 'so much oil has been poured into the machinery of government the wheels have been gummed right up'. (Anon. 1915: p. 8)

But despite this ringing statement on the part of the *Novyi Satirikon* team, the majority of humorous items in the special issue depict a situation in which bribe-giving is seen as essential to social survival, and carries no social or moral stigma. For example, 'How I Paid' is the fictional diary of a Jewish artist who outwits the regulations confining Jews to the Pale of Settlement by re-classifying himself as a house-painter (craftsmen were exempted from the usual controls). The re-classification costs him ten roubles to the registration officer at the police station, twenty-five to the head of the house-painters' guild plus ten to his deputy, and then a further five roubles a month to the concierge in his apartment block (D'Or 1915: p. 12). Both in this piece, and generally in the magazine, the assumption is that bribery is an institution driven by the greed of officials, whose demands ordinary citizens are powerless to curb. A refusal to give on the part of the individual would be an act of socio-economic suicide.

The fact that this view of bribery was widely shared is suggested by the circus artiste Charlie Keith's account of a visit to Russia in the early 1870s. As a naive outsider, Keith had to be tutored in the bribery system by Russians. It did not occur to him that he could bribe the police to get his passport back early, and only through the advice of bystanders was he able to defuse a potentially disastrous confrontation on the street. When a *muzhik* kicked Keith's dog, Keith responded by assaulting him; a policeman was summoned, and only with difficulty was Keith persuaded by bystanders that the sensible solution was to buy his way out of the incident, which he duly did, at the cost of two roubles to the *muzhik*, a rouble to the policeman, and a glass of schnapps to the pair of them (Keith 1879: pp. 99–100). For Smiles's countryman, becoming involved in bribery meant a loss of face; for ordinary Russians, failing to pay off minor officials, and risking arrest, was a course that could only have been contemplated by an idiot.

Up to a point, the assumption that bribe-giving was essential was simply a reflection of the extent of bureaucratic power in late imperial Russia, of the near impossibility, for a private citizen, of obtaining redress against officials who refused to carry out their duties. At the same time, the representation of bribery as a problem emanating solely from above would be misleading: it survived at least partly on the basis of the culture of 'self-interested giving', according to which exchange of favours was a perfectly normal procedure, so that the behaviour of an official who insinuated that he required payment seemed not an aberration but a distortion of normal behaviour patterns.

Illuminating evidence about the persistence of the culture of 'self-interested giving' in the late imperial era can be drawn from the work of Samuel Smiles's Russian imitators, the producers of original self-help manuals (in so far as one can use the term 'original' about a genre where authors plagiarized and adapted without any shame whatever). These imitators, while emphasizing the virtues of self-education and other elements of Smiles's creed, tended to take a less stern attitude to bribery than he did. One manual, enticingly entitled *Self-Education as the Path to Wealth*, is less a blueprint for self-reliance than a charter of self-advancement. Since the late eighteenth century, in books such as *The Science of Being Polite*, translated from the French (Anon. 1774), Russian men had been advised to defer to their superiors. But *Self-Education as the Path to Wealth* exhorted them to combine flattery with devious manipulation: 'Playing skilfully on the strings of his vanity, and tuning them to the key that we want, we may extract any sounds from him that we wish' (Anon. 1908: p. 32). The writer defensively admitted that this might not sound too moral, but justified his recommendations by saying that those who responded to flattery deserved all they got. Advice on giving presents conformed to the general principle of expediency rather than strict adherence to moral absolutes:

> There is a saying: 'little gifts cement a friendship'. Like all proverbs, this is only correct up to a point. In reality, friendship has nothing at all to do with presents. [...] It is better neither to give, nor to receive presents. But if you cannot get by without gifts, then adopt the rule: give, rather than receive. (Anon. 1908: p. 42)

The softening of tone apparent here — it is better to give than to receive — becomes still more evident when the writer goes on to suggest that there are circumstances in which it is all right to accept favours (so long as the person extending them is your superior):

> Having done a favour for someone, we will continue to take an interest in him out of the self-indulgent feeling that he ought to be grateful to us. And therefore the same holds in reverse: if a person who might be useful to you later on does you some kindness, do not refuse the kindness. (Anon. 1908: p. 43)

In other words, while it is less stigmatizing to be a giver of gifts (or bribes) than a taker, even acceptance loses its shameful flavour if the 'gift' comes in the form of a downward trickle of patronage, a *noblesse oblige* gesture of condescension. Similarly, an etiquette book of the 1890s suggests that 'subordinates should only give their superiors presents in exceptional circumstances' (Svetozarskaia 1890: p. 44), but in so doing implies not only that such gifts are sometimes permissible, but also that gifts from superiors to subordinates always are.

There are also other cases that illustrate the relatively high degree of tolerance for 'self-interested giving' in Russian culture, as opposed to the Protestant mercantile cultures of north-western Europe. Chekhov's plays, for example, despite their open dependence on the 'poetic realism' of Ibsen's work, are intriguingly different in terms of theme: the corruption scandals that underlie social and personal conflict in *The Wild Duck* and *The Pillars of the Community* fail to figure. Chekhov's flawed patriarchs (Ivanov, or Serebriakov in *Uncle Vanya*) offend against morality not by financial impropriety but on the grounds of their intellectual nullity and emotional sterility. So far as Russian literature was concerned, bribery was mostly the stuff of knockabout farce (the classic case being Gogol''s *Revizor* [The Government Inspector, 1836]) and not of tragedy. In terms of élite attitudes to 'self-interested giving', it is also worth noting that Russian employers of servants never instituted a campaign against tipping on the lines of the struggle waged by British employers of the late eighteenth century against 'vails and perquisites'.[14]

Anti-bribery ideology was equally underdeveloped in the Russian working classes and peasantry. 'Conscious', that is, politically aware, Russian workers, such as Semen Kanatchikov, could read Smiles avidly yet continue to see nothing wrong in patronage networks such as the *zemliachestvo* system (whereby workers arriving in the city from a particular region would form an unofficial mutual-support agency). Traditional 'protection rackets' of this kind were so fundamental to survival in the hostile environment of the big city that there was no temptation to associate them with the contemptible values of 'men who might be bought'. Certainly, there is some evidence that mutual aid was coming under strain in the post-Emancipation period. In the 1890s, for example, an informant from Vologda province complained that the rise in property ownership (*novoe imushchestvennoe polozhenie*) among peasants there had had pernicious effects on co-operation. 'Those admirable survivals of the past, the *pomochi*, are beginning gradually to take on a totally different appearance', he wrote, explaining this by the fact that the householder receiving help now had to provide such expensive treats that it was sometimes cheaper simply to get in hired labour (Gromyko 1986: p. 59). Even thirty years earlier, one observer had noted stresses in the mutual-aid systems of Russian cities, stating that worker *artel'* arrangements sometimes foundered on the reluctance of members to do their bit (Anon. 1863: pp. 17–18). But for all that, the inadequacy of the urban infrastructure, the dearth of institutions such as employment agencies and accommodation offices, meant that *zemliachestvo* and *arteli* were the preferred means of finding a job and somewhere to live; illiterate new arrivals had to rely on the charity of their fellows simply to find their way round the city. What is more, there is some evidence that new money-driven mutual-aid customs were evolving to replace the old, with emigrant labourers making financial contributions to the household budget.

The result of the interdependence of bribery and mutual aid seems to have been a division of perceptions among most Russians, according to which bribery attracted disapproval where it was seen as a manifestation of excessive greed on the part of officials but was tolerated in other cases. This division of perceptions is evident, for example, in proverbs contrasting the *magarych* ritual and the pursuit of naked profit: *Khot' s ubytok prodat', a mogarychi pit'* (Best sell at a loss, but drink a *magarych*); *Barysh baryshom, a mogarychi darom* (Profit is profit, but a *magarych* is given for nothing) (Dal' 1880–82: vol. 2, p. 288). The scene in Gogol''s *The Government Inspector* where the city merchants complain to Khlestakov, taking him for a government official, that the Mayor has violated their social code, not by taking bribes but by failing to deliver in return, remained an accurate depiction of social attitudes long after the play was first performed in 1836.

Crucial in fostering the wide tolerance of bribery may well have been the well-known lack of overlap between the 'bourgeoisie' in an economic sense (that is, merchants and industrialists) and the 'bourgeoisie' in an ideological sense (Rieber 1982; Owen 1981). Though some commentators, such as Mark Steinberg, have argued for the existence of an 'entrepreneurial intelligentsia' (Steinberg

1992: pp. 38–48), this class was significantly smaller than the class of merchant-philanthropists in Britain; conversely, ambitious peasant entrepreneurs made up a substantial proportion of the Russian merchant class by the late nineteenth century. Hence, the ideology of 'nature's gentlemen' proved more appealing to self-educating workers than to self-created businessmen, while critics of corruption and proto-corruption tended to come from sectors of society which were hostile to trade and commercialism and, indeed, in some cases, to *Realpolitik* in a general sense. A typical instance is Tolstoi's attack on peasant networking in his sententious proverb-a-day calendar for peasants, published in 1887:

> [Taking part in the *skhodka*] is not hard for people who do not think about how to judge according to God's law, but only about how to do well by a connection, a brother, a mate. [...] But it is hard to forget your connections, your relations, your mates at the *skhodka*, and to remember only truth and justice, and to judge by God's way, and to consider how as little harm as possible may be done. (Tolstoi 1928–64: vol. 40, p. 22)

The trouble with this guidance, though, is that it flew in the face of contemporary practical reality: a village commune without interest groups was as much an impossibility as a code of 'Tolstoyan business ethics' would have been (commercial activity being perceived by Tolstoi and his followers as immoral *per se*). Equally, while sharing some of the characteristics of the Protestant sects nominated by Weber as the seedbeds of capitalism (self-righteousness, exclusivity), Russian radical groups, such as the Social Democrats, could not conceive of capitalist business activity as compatible with probity in any sense; hence, they were no more successful than the Tolstoyans in evolving a model for ethical commercial practices. Furthermore, their *dirigiste* failure to construct models according to which the ordinary citizen might negotiate with institutions of state meant that they could only ineffectively contest the view that bribery was the best way of dealing with haughty and unhelpful officials. Given that the impact of concepts such as 'business honour' was low, and that the worker intelligentsia primarily understood 'self-help' in the sense of educational, rather than financial, self-betterment, popular pressure against 'self-interested giving' could mount only in circumstances where recipricocity was not forthcoming, and where collective disapproval could not right the situation by shaming the bribe-taker into co-operation.

All in all, the central question for many Russians in the late imperial era was not whether to give bribes, but how to give them. The twilight zone in which bribery languished — tolerated but not usually approved — meant that advice on how to give bribes politely was not (to put it mildly) a standard topic in guides to etiquette. One can, however, get a sense of the etiquette of bribe-giving from literary and memoir sources, which indicate that a more or less delicate refusal on the part of the person receiving a bribe was a standard part of proceedings. In Bulgakov's story 'The Hand-Towel Embroidered with a Cockerel', one of the *Doctor's Casebook* cycle (written just after the Revolution, but depicting a provincial life unaltered since late imperial times), the narrator, approached by a patient with the gift of the hand-towel in question, at first delicately turns down the offering. In the end, however, he accepts it (no doubt judging that there are occasions when personal feelings are more important than professional scruples):

> She looked at me, and her cheeks were swept by a pink flush.
>
> 'In Moscow... Moscow,' — And I started to write the address down. 'They'll fit a prosthesis for you, an artificial leg.'
>
> 'Kiss his hand,' her father suddenly said.
>
> I was so taken aback that I kissed her on the nose rather than the lips.
>
> Then, hanging on her crutches, she unwrapped a bundle, and out fell a long snow-white hand-towel with a crude red embroidered cockerel on it. So that was what she had been hiding under her pillow when I visited. Yes; now I remembered seeing the thread on her bedside-table.
>
> 'I'm not taking it,' I said sternly, and even managed to shake my head. But the expression on her face and in her eyes made me take it after all... (Bulgakov 1982: p. 68)

For the bribe-giver, the situation was that much more dangerous, given the possibility of humiliation if the tactful and temporary refusal of Bulgakov's narrator were voiced more rudely and decisively. This is what is threatened in Dostoevskii's novel *The Brothers Karamazov* (1879–80), when Alesha Karamazov attempts to buy off a low-ranking army officer insulted by Alesha's brother Dmitrii (who has pulled his beard and referred to it as a 'wash rag'). In this particular instance, however, the humiliation is smoothed over, and Alesha is in any case protected to some extent by the fact that the Karamazovs come from a much more privileged social group than the captain. Where bribery of the powerful was attempted by the weak, the dangers were significantly greater. As a parodistic piece of advice literature in the *Novyi Satirikon* bribery number reveals, most of the authority lay in the hands of the bribe-taker, which he might reinforce or not as he chose. The article begins by contrasting 'the good bribe-taker' and 'the bad bribe-taker':

> A good bribe-taker isn't demanding. He's got no side; he's nice to you. He even shakes the hand of his least important 'client'. He asks you to sit down. Enquires how your lady wife and the kiddies are. Wishes you all the best when you leave. But, most important of all, he doesn't talk any rot about 'order' and 'legality', he doesn't put you through it [...]. A good bribe-taker is always at home when he says he will be. You don't have to visit him again and again. His servants are polite. His telephone gets answered. His dogs don't go for you like wild animals.
>
> He takes the bribe without any fuss. You can hand it over. You can put it on the edge of his desk. You can put it in an envelope. In a word, you can do what you like!
>
> Happy the man who has to do with a good bribe-taker.
>
> But the bad bribe-taker, on the other hand — what a nightmare he is! [...]
>
> He fixes appointments at exotic sorts of times. From 7.45 to 8 in the morning. From 9.09 to 9.10 in the evening. [...] But you still can't find him in. [...] He's terribly rude to anyone giving him a bribe. [...] God help you if you give him anything too blatantly. He'll take it, of course, but he'll drop it immediately as though it had burned his fingers, then shrug his shoulders, wave his hands around, walk round the study, swear, shout about ungrateful pigs and so on.
>
> So people handle him in an 'above-board' way, only mentioning what they have in mind at the end of a strictly business-like discussion:
>
> 'Look, Ivan Ivanych, here's the hundred roubles I owe you for the stamps.'
>
> And if the bribe-giver really knows how to read the mind of the bribe-taker, he won't give him exactly a hundred, he'll make it more 'realistic' by handing over, say, 107 roubles 13 kopecks. At that moment even the worst bribe-taker turns into a good one [...]. (Zozulia 1915: pp. 12–13)

Other kinds of bribe-takers mentioned are the 'kind that doesn't take bribes' (that is, only accepts money through a third party); the 'tactful' kind (who prefers 'presents' to bribes, or who will only take bribes from women); the 'cynical' bribe-taker (who fails to do what he promises, a kind fortunately in short supply since other bribe-takers crack down on behaviour that is bad for business); and the 'ordinary' bribe-taker, who simply takes bribes without fuss and does what you have asked him to. Zozulia's vignette also indicates how the proliferation of strategies on the part of bribe-takers led bribe-givers to find ways of fending off humiliation, and keeping the power initiative in the hands of the donor by heading off capricious refusals. This dictated the indirect approach: getting someone else to hand over the goods, 'forgetting' things on the table, and even placing 'bets' that the bribe-taker was certain to win ('I bet it'll start to rain in five minutes from now') so that the bribe could be handed over as a 'debt of honour' (Zozulia 1915: p. 13).

Conclusion

In this account of bribery and etiquette in late imperial Russia, I have shown how the giving and taking of bribes was related to a complex network of different forms of 'self-interested giving' prevalent in Russian popular and élite culture. The two main sources of opposition to bribery were the perception that bribe-taking was incompatible with the efficient running of the state, and the belief that the giving and taking of bribes was an affront to personal autonomy, a belief disseminated, above all, through the 'self-help' ideology of Samuel Smiles. Opposition to bribery, however, was limited to a small section of the educated élite (and not consistently developed even there); elsewhere, disapproval of bribery seems to have come about only where the practice disrupted the concept of reciprocity essential to self-interested giving (where the bribe-taker did not carry out his or her promises, or was unusually grasping, so that he or she could be said to 'live off others').

At the same time, there was a sense that the practice of bribery was potentially shameful, which was expressed, for instance, in the contortions that people went through in order to give bribes. The dubious status of bribery, however, was traceable less to moralistic feelings (a conviction that the practice was 'wrong') than to the identification of bribery with the exercise of power, a power disputed between those who gave and those who received. One of the secondary meanings of the verb *vziat'/vzimat'*, 'to take', from which *vziatka*, the commonest word for 'bribe', is derived, is 'to get the upper hand over someone' (Dal' 1880–82: vol. 1, p. 196): that is, the practice of bribe-giving may be seen as a contestation of social ascendancy. Bribe-taking officials did not want to be wholly in the power of donors (which would have exposed them not only to vilification as *magarychniki*, but also stripped them of the potential to market themselves with other bribe-givers). Donors, on the other hand, wanted their investments of money, goods and favours to produce maximum results. Hence, the practice of bribery resembled an elaborate game in which 'men who might be bought' struggled to assert dominance by capriciously refusing bribes (or neglecting to perform promised favours, as in the case of Gogol''s Mayor Skvoznik-Dmukhanovskii in *The Government Inspector*), while those who gave bribes endeavoured to beguile them with ever more tempting largesse. As in the comparable social institutions of *pomochi*, *magarychi* and *kumovstvo*, there was a complex jockeying for position, in which the self-interested giver and the taker of the gift contested authority. By extension, in some circumstances bribery could be perceived as a levelling device, righting the imbalance of power between officials and those they governed; like the practice of denunciation (Burds 1996: pp. 786–818; Fitzpatrick 1996: pp. 831–66), it could seem attractive to disempowered individuals who had few ways of obtaining their ends by other means. Bribery, then, was well suited to survive in a society such as late imperial Russia, where patronage and collectivism were strongly rooted and anti-statism was well developed.

I am aware that the discussion here might seem to be standing Lotman's contrast of Western 'contract-bound' giving with Slavic 'entrustment of self' on its head. It would, of course, be absurd to argue that there is no such thing as a disinterested gift in Russian culture: on the contrary, generosity is highly valued, not only in religious but also in secular culture. It is, however, perhaps because of the widespread understanding in ordinary life (*byt*) of the gift as an expression of hard-nosed self-interest that the notion of self-sacrifice has played such a large role in shaping ideals of behaviour. That is to say, it is possible that the importance attached to self-denial and open-handed generosity derives less from the ubiquity of these patterns of behaviour than from the fact that, on the contrary, they fly in the face of customary behaviour models, representing, therefore, a heroism that is the more impressive because it is so seldom expected to be enacted in everyday life.

Notes

1 For the opposition between 'corruption' and 'proto-corruption', see Scott 1972: pp. 7–10.
2 As Leonid Heretz has pointed out (1997: p. 73), 'in the traditional Russian view, heaven is the realm of God, while Satan holds sway over the earth and humanity'. The result of this cleavage was an extreme religious eschatology that to some extent took secular wickedness for granted.
3 Compare Scott (1976: p. 5): 'It is all too easy, and a serious mistake, to romanticize these social arrangements that distinguish much of peasant society. They are not radically egalitarian. Rather, they imply only that all are entitled to a *living* out of the resources within the village, and that living is attained only at the cost of a loss of status and autonomy. They work, moreover, in large measure through the abrasive force of gossip and envy and the knowledge that the abandoned poor are likely to be a real and present danger to better-off villagers.'
4 On the *magarych* and *prival'noe* in the context of the reception of new workmates, see Kelly and Smith (1998). Bulgakov's novel *The Master and Margarita* numbers a sleekit individual named Mogarych (he denounces the Master to obtain more living space) among its characters.
5 While studying at University College, Oxford, Prince Feliks Iusupov became known as such a fabulous tipper in the pursuit of discretion that, according to an oral tradition still current among college staff, servants would deliberately hang round his room waiting to be paid to go away. (My thanks to Dr Michael Nicholson for this information.)
6 Maiakovskii's usage here is unusual, but not so extraordinary as to merit comment or explanation by the editors of his *Complete Works*.
7 Recent Irish political scandals which revolve around favours for services rendered (or *post-factum* bribes, depending on one's point of view) include the 'North Dublin Land Re-Zoning' affair of late 1997, in which a government minister was accused of accepting a substantial payment after allowing farming land to be re-classified for building development.
8 The passage is faithfully translated in Smiles 1882 and in Smiles 1903. It is interesting to speculate whence Smiles had derived his information about Russia. Could he possibly have read the English translation of

Bulgarin's *Ivan Vyzhigin* (on which see Andrei Rogachevskii's chapter in this volume)?

9 More than seventy editions of Smiles's works were published in Russia between 1870 and 1917 (for further details, see my *Refining Russia: Gender and the Regulation of Behaviour from Catherine to Yeltsin* [forthcoming], ch. 3).

10 It is worth noting, though, that the attitude to bribery among modernizing officials was itself more than a little inconsistent: finance minister Sergei Witte, for instance, maintained 'a slush fund for corrupt French editors when he was trying to attract investment capital' (McReynolds 1991: p. 129).

11 For example, Semen Kanatchikov remembered borrowing a copy of 'Smail's' from a friend (Zelnik 1986: p. 166).

12 One has to assume that the chime is unintentional, given that Smiles's works were among those that Lenin's wife, Nadezhda Krupskaia, wanted to place on the Soviet index of banned books (see Pethybridge 1990: p. 217).

13 It is perhaps popular indifference to all but the most lurid abuses of 'self-interested giving', rather than the success of the early 1920s campaign against bribery, that explains why the 1926 Criminal Code prescribes comparatively light sentences for bribery: up to five years for cases of bribe-giving and a maximum of two years for straightforward cases of bribe-taking. More severe penalties were dictated only if 'aggravating circumstances', such as extortion, obtained (see *Penal Code* 1934; *Code penal* 1946, articles 117–19). On the failure of measures to stamp out bribery, see Solomon (1996), which indicates that bribery was widespread in law courts in Moscow and elsewhere during the late 1920s; see also Fitzpatrick (1994: pp. 167–8, 97–8) on the prevalence of bribery in attempts by collective-farm workers to get round the restrictions on freedom of movement, and indeed among recruiting officials trying to sign up labourers to work on construction projects. The 1926 law remained on the statute books right through the Stalinist period, and the penalties were not increased until 1962, when the maximum sentences for acceptance of bribes became ten and fifteen years (for the non-aggravated and aggravated forms) and, for receipt of bribes, eight and fifteen years respectively — a change in the law that coincided with a propaganda drive emphasizing individual responsibility: see *Ugolovnyi kodeks* 1964: articles 173, 174, 174^1). Representations of bribery during the Stalin period also indicate a surprising softness of attitude. For example, Zoshchenko's cycle of moral tales for children about the life of Lenin, 'Rasskazy o Lenine' (1939–40), includes a story about how a fisherman tries to bribe the leader with the gift of a smoked fish in order to swing a change in the fishing regulations: what is surprising

is not that Lenin refuses the gift but that he does so in a remarkably tactful manner, so that the worker leaves saying 'My godmothers, I slipped up there', but is not officially reprimanded (Zoshchenko 1981: p. 294). Again, the culture of self-interested giving seems to have played a role: compare Solzhenitsyn's *Cancer Ward*, in which Dr and Mrs Kadmin are severely punished for harbouring a deserter who is not a member of their family: had he been, this would have been a case of mere *shkurnichestvo* (self-serving) and hence 'understandable and even forgivable' (Solzhenitsyn 1970: p. 232).

14 On the campaign against vails and perquisites, see Hill 1996: pp. 64–92. Despite a good deal of unrest about servants as a threat to morality in the late nineteenth and early twentieth centuries (on which see Kelly 1997: pp. 9–34), tipping was treated with surprising tolerance: see, for example, A. Amfiteatrov's story 'Mamka', which mentions quite neutrally that the story's heroine, an upper-class girl turned nurse, 'earned 25 roubles or so including presents, "tips" and so on' (Amfiteatrov 1911: p. 55). The condemnation of tipping as a 'degrading' practice in the early post-revolutionary years (see Figes 1996: plate 55, showing a protest by waiters against *chaevye podachki* in 1917) was to prove as short-lived as the vilification of bribery.

Bibliography

Amfiteatrov, A. (1911), *Baby i damy*, St Petersburg.

Anon. (1774), *Nauka byt' uchtivym: Perevedena s frantsuzskogo*, trans. Ivan Kriukov, St Petersburg.

Anon. (1863), *O byte rabochikh liudei v Sankt-Peterburge i o sredstvakh k uluchsheniiu ikh polozheniia*, Berlin.

Anon. (1908), *Samoobrazovanie — kak put' k bogatstvu. I: Obshchestvo i znanie liudei*, St Petersburg.

Anon. (1915), 'Chto komu nravitsia', *Novyi Satirikon*, 35.

Bol'shaia sovetskaia entsiklopediia (1929–47), 66 vols, Moscow.

Brody, H. (1983), *Inishkillane: Change and Decline in the West of Ireland*, London.

Bukhov, A. (1915), 'Istoriia vziatki', *Novyi Satirikon*, 35.

Bulgakov, M.A. (1982), *Sobranie sochinenii*, vol. 1, Ann Arbor, MI.

Burds, J. (1996), 'A Culture of Denunciation: Peasant Labor Migration and Religious Anathematization in Rural Russia, 1860–1905', *Journal of Modern History*, 68, 4.

Code penal (1946), *Code penal de la République Soviétique Fédérative Socialiste de Russie* [1946], trans. J. Fonteyne, Brussels, 1951.

Dal', V. (1880–82), *Tolkovyi slovar' zhivogo velikorusskogo iazyka*, 4 vols, Moscow.

Davydoff, M. (1986), *On the Estate: Memoirs of Russia before the Revolution*, London.
D'Or, O.L. (1915), 'Kak ia platil', *Novyi Satirikon*, 35.
Evans, E.E. (1957), *Irish Folk Ways*, London.
Evgen'eva, I.P. (ed.) (1983), *Slovar' russkogo iazyka*, 4 vols, Moscow.
Figes, O. (1996), *A People's Tragedy: The Russian Revolution 1891–1924*, London.
Fitzpatrick, S. (1994), *Stalin's Peasants: Resistance and Survival in the Russian Village after Collectivization*, New York.
Fitzpatrick, S. (1996), 'Signals from Below: Soviet Letters of Denunciation of the 1930s', *Journal of Modern History*, 68, 4.
Gromyko, M.M. (1986), *Traditsionnye normy povedeniia i formy obshcheniia russkikh krest'ian XIX veka*, Moscow.
Heretz, L. (1997), 'The Practice and Significance of Fasting in Russian Peasant Culture at the Turn of the Century' in M. Glants and J. Toomre (eds), *Food in Russian History and Culture*, Bloomington, IN.
Hill, B. (1996), *Servants: English Domestics in the Eighteenth* Century, Oxford.
Keith, C. (1879), *Circus Life and Amusements (Equestrian, Dramatic and Musical) in All Nations*, Derby.
Kelly, C. (1997), '"Who'll Clean the Boots Now?" Servants and Social Anxieties in Late Imperial St Petersburg', *Europa Orientalis*, 2.
Kelly, C. and Smith, S. (1998), 'Irrational Recreations' in C. Kelly and D. Shepherd (eds). *Constructing Russian Culture in the Age of Revolution, 1881–1940*, Oxford.
Lenin, V.I. (1958–65), *Polnoe sobranie sochinenii*, 55 vols, 5th edn. Moscow.
Lenin, V.I. (1941–50), *Sochineniia*, 35 vols, 4th edn, Moscow.
Likhacheva, L.S. (1996), *Shkola etiketa: Poucheniia na vsiakii sluchai*, Ekaterinburg.
Lindenmeyr, A. (1996), *Poverty Is Not a Vice: Charity, Society and the State in Imperial Russia*, Princeton, NJ.
Lotman, Iu. (1993), '"Dogovor" i "vruchenie sebia" kak arkhetipicheskie modeli kul'tury' in Lotman, *Izbrannye stat'i*, vol. 3, Tallinn.
McReynolds, L. (1991), *The News under Russia's Old Regime: The Development of a Mass-Circulation Press*, Princeton, NJ.
Maiakovskii, V. (1955–61), *Polnoe sobranie sochinenii v 13 tomakh*, Moscow.
Mordukhai-Boltovskii, D. (1912), *Svod zakonov Rossiiskoi Imperii*, St Petersburg.
Nabokov, V. (1987), *Speak, Memory: An Autobiography Revisited*, Harmondsworth.
Owen, T. (1981), *Capitalism and Politics in Russia: A Social History of the Moscow Merchants, 1855–1905*, New York.

Penal Code (1934), *The Penal Code of the Russian Socialist Federal Soviet Republic*, London.
Pethybridge, R. (1990), *One Step Backwards, Two Steps Forward: Soviet Society and Politics in the New Economic Policy*, Oxford.
Repin, I.E. (1982), *Dalekoe blizkoe*, Leningrad.
Rieber, A.D. (1982), *Merchants and Entrepreneurs in Imperial Russia*, Chapel Hill, NC.
Scott, J.C. (1972), *Comparative Political Corruption*, Englewood Cliffs, NJ.
Scott, J.C. (1976), *The Moral Economy of the Peasant: Rebellion and Subsistence in South-East Asia*, New Haven, CT and London.
Smiles, S. (1866), *Self-Help, with Illustrations of Character, Conduct and Perseverance*, London.
Smiles, S. (1880), *Duty*, London.
Smiles, S. (1882), *Dolg*, trans. S. Maikova, St Petersburg.
Smiles, S. (1903), *Sobranie sochinenii v 6 tomakh pod redaktsiei M.N. Nikol'skogo*, trans. N. Nadezhdin, St Petersburg and Moscow.
Solomon, P.H. (1996), *Soviet Criminal Justice under Stalin*, Cambridge, England.
Solzhenitsyn, A. (1970), *Rakovyi korpus*, Paris.
Steinberg, M.D. (1992), *Moral Communities: The Culture of Class Relations in the Russian Printing Industry, 1867–1907*, Berkeley, CA.
Stone, L. (1979), *The Family, Sex and Marriage in England 1500–1800*, Harmondsworth.
Svetozarskaia, K. (1890), *Zhizn' v svete, doma i pri dvore*, St Petersburg.
Tolstoi, L.N. (1928–64), *Polnoe sobranie sochinenii*, 90 vols, Moscow.
Tovrov, J. (1987), *The Russian Noble Family: Structure and Change*, New York and London.
Trollope, A. (1955), *An Autobiography*, Oxford.
Ugolovnyi kodeks (1964), *Ugolovnyi kodeks RSFSR*, Moscow.
Venskii, E. (1915), 'Tekhnika vziatki', *Novyi Satirikon*, 35.
Weber, M. (1993), *Essays in Sociology*, trans. H.H. Gerth and C.W. Mills, London.
Worobec, C. (1991), *Peasant Russia: Family and Community in the Post-Emancipation Period*, Princeton, NJ.
Zelnik, R. (ed. and trans.) (1986), *A Radical Worker in Tsarist Russia: The Autobiography of Semen Ivanovich Kanatchikov*, Stanford, CA.
Zoshchenko, M. (1981), *Izbrannoe*, Leningrad.
Zozulia, E. (1915), 'Vziatochniki: Bezkhitrostnye nabliudeniia', *Novyi Satirikon*, 35.

6 Bureaucracy on Trial: A Malaise in Official Life as Represented in Nineteenth-Century Russian Thought

Irina Davydova

А судьи кто? — Who's to judge?
(A. Griboedov, *Gore ot uma* [Woe from Wit])

Iurii Lotman once remarked that 'the Russian bureaucracy, while an important factor in state life, hardly left any trace in the spiritual life of Russia: it created neither its own culture, nor ethic, nor even its own ideology' (Lotman 1994: p. 27). For anyone closely acquainted with Russian literature of the nineteenth century — which I here take to include *belles-lettres*, drama, journalistic criticism and socio-philosophical writings — Lotman's observation impresses by its acuteness. Reflected in the mirror of Russian culture, bureaucracy could see only its satirized image. We do not find the representative of the state civil service featuring as a truly positive hero. The civil servant is either 'a little man' (as introduced by Gogol′) — a poor, miserable being, appealing to the sympathy of the reader (who hears how a suffering human soul peeps out through the bureaucrat's uniform) — or a corrupt cynic living off bribery ('for what are hands given if not for taking?': Kapnist 1960: p. 358). At best, as with Lev Tolstoi's Karenin, he is a dull and unsympathetic character in a novel.

A historical anecdote nicely exemplifies the public attitude to the bureaucratic state: allegedly Karamzin was once asked to characterize in one word the state of affairs in Russia; he replied

'Everyone steals' ('*Voruiut*'). It seems that everything written about the bureaucracy at that time intended its public exposure. Bribery and corruption appeared to be a prime feature of Russian official life. The assault on the bureaucracy has often culminated in speculations about the 'Russian soul', which allegedly denies 'the state's or even any functional constraints', thus resulting in 'the negation of moral obligation and duty in general, so esteemed in the West'. In so doing, it is argued, it really tries to derive all morality from the idea of love and prefers this morality to the law (Veidle 1955: pp. 122–3; see also Il'in 1956: pp. 313–4; Losskii 1957: pp. 49–56, 72).

From such accounts it appears that the perceived corruptibility of the bureaucracy can be explained in terms of the backwardness of Russia and the peculiarity of its culture, that is, the customary practices of its population — and this is broadly convincing. But Lotman's observation opens another perspective on the issue. Why did the bureaucracy not create an image for itself in Russian culture, why did it have no publicly valued voice? Why was society's attitude to this group so negative? Seen from this angle, the presentation of the class of civil officials in literature ceases to be merely a source of information about the bureaucracy's real-life vices and becomes a matter for reflection in its own right. But before pursuing these questions further, let us first examine some of the 'objective' factors that may have pushed the Russian bureaucracy in the direction of venality.

Social Conditions of the Formation of the Bureaucracy in Russia

The class of state officials in Russia emerged under conditions rather unlike those experienced by their Western counterparts. First of all, for a long period the civil service was deprived of public respect. Historically this derived from the low social position of administrators (*d'iaki* and *pod'iachie*) in the Muscovite state: they were the Grand Prince's men, often his serfs. The development of the institutions of Moscow administration between the thirteenth and seventeenth centuries was marked by permanent conflict between the increasing importance and influence of the officers of the chanceries (*prikazy*) and their low prestige in the eyes of nobles, who continued to see this post (*d'iak*) as one of low rank and to associate it with lack of family honour (*rodoslovnoi chesti*).

Peter the Great's reforms challenged but did not change this disposition. Many of the nobility prefered military service to civil service and avoided studying law and other necessary subjects even in schools for the privileged classes, not to mention schools with a mixed intake.[1] As a result of the old prejudice against service in the chanceries, many of the bureaucracy were non-noble by birth. They were recruited, however, not from the urban bourgeoisie and professional classes as in the West — where the lawyers, university teachers, ministers (in Protestant lands) and so on were ready to serve their polities — but rather from among the children of clergy, low-ranking clerks and soldiers — that is, from groups which lacked a sense of estate-membership or professional honour (Raeff 1983: p. 211; 1966a: p. 108; 1957: p. 7). The system of regular salaries, introduced in the late seventeenth century, offered rather small compensation for state service. Salaries were barely adequate to maintain a single nobleman in service, certainly not his family, nor were they paid regularly or in full. It was not unusual for the government to pay a part of the salary in 'Siberian goods' (that is, furs) or grain — leaving to the official the task of marketing it (Raeff 1966a: p. 61). All this, together with the enduring Muscovite tradition of a 'gift of gratitude' from the interested person to the official (*posuly* and *pochesti*),[2] complicated the establishment of a proper bureaucratic ethic. The boundary between bribe and gift was too thin to restrain corruption, and it was of a purely moral, not a procedural nature; moreover, gift-giving was always an accepted form of reciprocity in the villages, whence many of the clerks originated.

Thus a disrespect for bureaucracy can be seen as partly rooted in the status-consciousness of the nobility. In the nineteenth century, as before, the demonstration of contempt for bureaucratic ranks continued to be accepted as good manners by the gentry (Lotman 1994: p. 38). It was especially characteristic of the beginning of the nineteenth century, when, as the author of a book dedicated to the centenary of the State Secretariat wrote in 1902, 'it was even inappropriate [*neumestnym*] for a nobleman to enter the civil service' (Zaionchkovskii 1978: p. 27). This attitude played a negative role in the formation of the new class of career officials, as many of the most bright and ambitious noblemen tended to avoid civil service. It also lowered considerably the prestige of the official service ethos, which was seen as no more than conformism and submissive obedience to superiors, as prescribed by the Table of Ranks. One of the best formulations of disrespect for this ethos is found in Chatskii's retort: 'I would serve, but servility is so disgusting! [*Sluzhit' by rad, prisluzhivat'sia toshno*]' (Griboedov 1951: p. 38).[3]

Analysing the Russian experience, Marc Raeff emphasizes the lack of mediating social structures in Russian society as the main obstacle to attempts to introduce the Western European modernizing pattern: 'in Muscovy we do not meet with the solid, permanent, often very strong and powerful corporations and constituted bodies that provide the framework of premodern European society and that were used by the well-ordered police states in disciplining and modernizing society' (Raeff 1983: p. 186). The result was an over-centralized bureaucracy socially and culturally isolated from the rest of society, whose extensive activity was yet expected, in the absence of other social forces, to implement modernizing policy. Indeed, the low-born officials did not share even the limited attachment to their localities or the paternalistic concern for peasants that noblemen at times displayed (Raeff 1966a: p. 108). More than a century after the Petrine reforms, a critic defined the administration as:

> an office proletariat, semi-ignorant, semi-occupied, used to living at someone's expense and to considering Russia as a conquered land. The bureaucrat sees himself as a citizen of another land located somewhere not even in the state, but above it, and as is usual with humans, gradually comes to the conviction that the nation exists for his benefit rather than vice versa.[4]

Weak professionalization was another characteristic feature of the Russian bureaucracy. In Germany, training in the law became a prime requirement for administrators and in the long run pushed out the non-professionals (the noblemen). In general, due to their shared educational background, practical training and experience, administrators there developed a degree of coherence, consistency and stability in their outlook and behaviour — a certain ethos, in other words (Raeff 1983: pp. 21–2). In Muscovy, on the other hand, chancery clerks started their professional life as teenagers and learned everything by experience as they passed through the various stages of their career (Serov 1996: ch. 1). As the administrative system was rather simple, apprenticeship was sufficient to ensure the necessary level of competence and promotion on the basis of seniority seemed justified. Peter the Great's reforms rapidly expanded the bureaucracy without underpinning it by the development of an effective education system. Despite all efforts made by government in this direction, in the second half of the eighteenth century the ordinary Russian bureaucrat, as before, was required to be only barely literate when entering the civil service and acquired all necessary practical knowledge in office. Although promotion was meant in theory to be based on performance and length of service, in practice it was the latter that had real significance.[5] This lack of educational training and of objectivity in the assessment of abilities and competence, not to mention the absence of competitive examination of state officials, placed much power in the hands of senior administrators and thereby opened the door to nepotism and favouritism — two other vices of Russian bureaucracy.

By the second half of the nineteenth century, the Russian bureaucracy was surely no longer as deficient in its ethic and professional competence as the above account would suggest. Several decades of educational and occupational change, along with the reforms of Alexander II, had a significant effect on the *modus operandi* of Russian officialdom.[6] But in an important sense the damage had been done: the bureaucracy had acquired its unenviable reputation and found itself permanently estranged from a large and vocal section of the educated public.

Intellectuals versus Bureaucrats

Paradoxically, the product of the hard-won state educational system was not an educated civil service but a community of oppositional intellectuals. Whilst the government intended education to deliver necessary skills and knowledge, as well as inculcating the civil virtues requisite in a well-regulated state, what it in fact led to was a culture which flourished independent of official life and a politically radical intelligentsia, rather than a knowledgeable, service-orientated élite. This became evident in the 1840s, when the shortage of students, which had hampered the development of universities and grammar schools, changed to an overflow (many of the new students coming from the lower classes). The Minister of Education, Uvarov, stressed in a secret circular: 'As the aspiration for education is growing everywhere, it is time now to think how to prevent this excessive aspiration for the highest matters shaking the existing order of civil estates by arousing in young minds the impulse to acquire luxurious knowledge [*roskoshnye znaniia*]' (Miliukov 1931: p. 793). Another instruction issued ten years later, in 1850, expressed misgivings about the fact that many of the graduates from St Petersburg University did not join the service but stayed in the capital participating in the publishing of newspapers and magazines.[7] The history of uneasy relations between the intelligentsia and the state is not of prime concern here, but a few comments are in order.

The encouraging and often liberal policy[8] toward the educational system under Alexander I changed to a repressive and prohibitive one during the reign of Nicholas I. One can understand the regime's suspicion of education, given the revolt of 14 December 1825 and its aftermath: many Decembrists acknowledged under interrogation that it was enthusiasm for Enlightenment ideas that had led them to Senate Square.[9] The urge to control the education process, as well as all other spheres of cultural production, pushed the government and intelligentsia on to different sides of the barricades. As education itself became an arena for ideological struggle it was likely to produce radicalism rather than loyalty. Indeed, student unrest became a routine feature of university life. Bureaucracy, being the most loyal and dependable instrument of autocracy, was highly oppressive and suspicious of any expression of free thought. The intelligentsia repaid it with hatred. In this struggle, the bureaucracy had at its disposal the suppressive force of the state apparatus, or rather it was itself this apparatus, while the intelligentsia possessed a symbolic power to form public opinion, which it used effectively.

For the prime domain of the intelligentsia was literature, which from Alexander I's reign onwards played an increasingly significant role in shaping the world-view of young people. The sentimentalist novel of the early nineteenth century had, as P.N. Miliukov put it, 'from being a pleasant pastime for adults, turned into a primary school of worldly idealism [*zhiteiskogo idealizma*] which teenagers went through' (Miliukov 1931: p. 315). Soon *belles-lettres* and literary criticism were established as a kind of forum for the expression of political ideas. Stages in the history of literature in the second half of nineteenth century roughly correspond to those in social and political thought, and also match up with the successive generations of the intelligentsia. The literary disposition of the intelligentsia helps us to understand why the definition of this group is so amorphous when stated in terms of social class and so rigorous when it concerns ideas and world-views (see, for example, Fedotov 1967). In fact, the intelligentsia could be defined as the public of certain progressive magazines, together with their producers.[10]

This is by no means to say that *all* those we can regard as belonging to the intelligentsia were alien to the state service. There were always exceptions such as G.P. Danilevskii (1829–90), a writer of popular novels who also made a brilliant career as a state official (although because of his official status he had to adopt a pseudonym in order to be published in *Sovremennik*). A gap still existed, however, between government and intelligentsia. And so the trial of Vera Zasulich (who shot at the St Petersburg Governor and was acquitted by a jury in 1878) was a real triumph for the latter. Despite censorship, the government's attempts to control cultural production were unsuccessful. It was the intelligentsia which ruled the field of social and political ideals from the late 1840s. This circumstance explains much of the low public prestige of the bureaucracy, and the apparent absence of a culturally articulated ethos of obedience to the law and of honest, just, useful state service.

The intelligentsia's radical views meant that criticism of the bureaucracy was subsumed to criticism of the autocratic system in general. In radical discourse, bureaucracy — the official world — was identified to a large extent with autocracy and was lambasted for its loyal service to the latter. *Golosa iz Rossii* (Voices from Russia) by Herzen and Ogarev[11] accused bureaucrats both of violating the rules (through bribery and corruption) and of following the rules too closely (through their reliance on paperwork: Russia is described as 'a Kingdom of papers' and 'a country of useless formalities').[12] Bakunin took the negation of the sick state to its extreme. He did not even agree to a constitution: as he wrote in *Statism and Anarchy* (1873), 'one would have to be an ass, an ignoramus, or a madman to imagine that any kind of constitution, even the most liberal and democratic, could change this relationship of the state to the people for the better' — namely, the relationship of suppression and parasitism (Bakunin 1990: p. 62). Bakunin's analysis is interesting not so much as a statement of fact, but as a statement of values, and one based on an articulation of national difference via an opposition of typical Russian and German officials. Bakunin believed that German administration and bureaucracy approached the implementation of the ideal which the 'administrations and bureaucracy of every other state strive in vain to achieve', for 'the mass of the German population consists of literate, industrious, relatively well-educated not to say learned persons, who are also submissive and obedient to the authorities and the law' (Bakunin 1990: p. 103). In Russia, on the other hand,

> the great mass of our officer corps has remained just as it was before — crude, ignorant, and in almost in every respect completely mindless. Military exercises, carousing, card-playing, drunkenness [...] systematic almost legalized thievery in the upper ranks [...] however a human heart can still be found, an instinctive capacity to love and understand mankind, and in the right conditions, under a good influence, the ability to became a fully conscious friend of the people. [...]
>
> It was left to Germans, and in particular German officials and officers, to solve a seemingly insoluble problem: how to combine education and barbarism, learning and servility. It makes them repulsive and at the same time highly comical in a social sense, systematic and merciless villains in relation to the masses, but valued individuals in respect to state service. (Bakunin 1990: pp. 77–8, 79–80)

Bakunin explicitly prefers the Russian officer, as described above, to the German one. Why is the crude and often corrupt Russian better than the honest and educated German? Because of his ability to step beyond official duty for the sake of other more important things such as humanity and solidarity with the people. The German officer is 'ever capable of slashing or hacking apart dozens, hundreds, thousands of people at the least sign from his commanders', not because of hatred, but precisely because he is a good officer (Bakunin 1990: p. 80). Bakunin strongly dislikes the bureaucratic ethos (allegedly inculcated in Germans) and here he was merely an extreme representative of views widely held in the Russian intelligentsia. Although Bakunin acknowledges that 'the Germans seek their life and liberty in the state', for him this is the wrong historical course. The following dialogue, which opens the second part of *Voices from Russia*, published in 1856, depicts the gap between 'life' and 'career service' clearly:

> *A friendly chat*
> Official: My goodness! We haven't seen each other since we left the university.
> Non-official: Yes, it's been so long — in the meantime you have managed to become somebody [*ty mezhdu tem uspel vyiti v liudi*].
> Official: And you of course have got married and acquired estates?
> Non-official: Neither. But while you were becoming somebody I was trying to remain a human being. [*No v to vremia kak ty vykhodil v liudi ia staralsia ostat'sia chelovekom*.][13]

Of most interest to us here is the shift in the concept of service. If the Decembrists tried to win influence amongst top civil servants, to give a positive example by their own blameless service, to reveal cases of the poor exercise of official duty in order to create an atmosphere of intolerance of corruption in which fear of public exposure would work as a restraint — if, that is, they saw themselves as a part of the state and responsible for it[14] — the radical intelligentsia understood its civic duty very differently. What they valued was not service to the monarch or the Fatherland (the ideological equivalent of the state) or even to society. They gave top priority to service to 'the people', which required a moral code very different from the bureaucratic one, or so they believed. Fedotov, a bitter critic of the 'high-principled and rootless' (*ideinaia i bespochvennaia*) Russian intelligentsia, characterized this code as 'a petty system of prohibitive norms, necessary for keeping at a distance from an enemy with whom one could not fight. Candidly, the enemy was the Russian state and its power' (Fedotov 1967: pp. 110–11). Lavrov's *Historical Letters* (1869) served to ratify this tendency to equate society with people, civic duty with revolutionary activity. Lenin's famous statement that in Russia every honest man becomes a revolutionary, though certainly an exaggeration, had some basis in reality. Impractical political idealism could easy lead to disillusionment and amorphousness of moral principles. As a young man wrote in his diary in January 1841:

> Why should one care to acquire knowledge when our life and society are in contradiction with all great ideas and truths, when any attempt to put into practice thoughts about justice, about the good

and common welfare, is stigmatized and persecuted as a crime? Why cultivate high-minded aspirations in ourselves? (Miliukov 1931: pp. 325–6)

As already mentioned, the notion of duty acquired a specific meaning in radical discourse. It was seen as a 'debt' on the part of an educated person towards the people whose labour created the civilization and culture which the educated person enjoyed while the people were deprived of its fruits. This duty was tinged by a feeling of guilt and dominated the whole world-view of the Russian intelligentsia. As Frank emphasized in his 'Ethics of Nihilism' (first published in 1909):

> Morality, moral evaluations and moral motives have an exclusive place in the soul of a member of the Russian intelligentsia. If it were possible to characterize in one word the frame of mind of the intelligentsia, this would be moralism. The Russian intelligentsia accepts no absolute values, no criteria, no orientation in life apart from the distinction of persons, actions, situations as morally right and wrong, good versus evil. (Frank 1967: pp. 178–9)

What is more, this moral universe was centered on the people, the happiness of the working masses, of the majority. One might wonder why this populist ethos did not result in the emergence of a layer of honest, responsible, industrious officials. The answer is that it did on those occasions when the intelligentsia did not withdraw from public service. For instance, the populist ethos contributed a lot to the improvement of local administration via the *zemstva* in the 1880s and 1890s. But generally the intelligentsia, *qua* intelligentsia, was most involved in particular areas of *zemstvo* activity — notably education and health. Moreover, the radical wing preferred struggle for great political goals to the routine of 'small deeds' (*malye dela*) and derided the *zemstva* (as Saltykov-Shchedrin did in *Pis'ma k teten'ke* [Letters to Auntie], published in *Otechestvennye zapiski* in 1881–82).

The 'Ethic of Love' versus the Bureaucratic Ethic of Following the Rules

According to the dominating discourse of the intelligentsia, everyday life in Russia consisted of many semi-traditional ways of interaction, including those in formal institutions. Formal rules tended to be negotiated in terms of an understanding of moral obligations. Many observers depicted the general cultural atmosphere in Russia as lacking the 'middle area of culture' — a definition introduced by Berdiaev (1946) — that is, well-institutionalized forms of social interaction and an orientation towards 'bourgeois' values. Personalization of any kind of social relations and disregard for formal rules was one of many manifestations of this general spirit. 'I can't live other than according to my heart, but you live according to rules', says Kitty in *Anna Karenina* — a sentiment that recurs in literature as an expression of the quintessence of the Russian soul:

> So love is the main spiritually creative force of the Russian soul. Without love the Russian is an unhappy being. Basically, the civilizing substitutes for love (duty, discipline, formal loyalty, the hypnosis of appearing obedient to the law) in themselves are not his way. (Il'in 1956: p. 314)

N. Losskii cited Kitty's words to illustrate his argument that this 'living by the heart, not according to the rules' was prevalent and indicated a very individual approach to the personality of the 'other'. He even related the personalistic and particularistic ethics (*konkretnaia etika*) developed in Russian philosophy, as opposed to the legislative ethics (*zakonnicheskaia etika*) of the West, to this characteristic feature of the Russians (Losskii 1957: p. 72). It might be argued that the philosophers were simply objectively observing a genuine 'Russian character' with its anarchistic tendencies and disregard for law and rules, of which corruption was but one manifestation. Corruption, however, cannot be explained simply in terms of the ethnic/cultural peculiarities of the Russian population (such as communal forms of life among the peasantry). To be sure, disregard for law and formal rules was rooted in traditional forms of life in Russia, but to a large extent it was also a result of the alienation of the educated public from the state. Philosophers articulated in their ethical systems above all the attitudes of the educated public, not those of officials in a rule-bound administrative system.

The basis of the ethic articulated by Losskii and others is not duty, but love. 'Love' should be understood here very widely, to include not only love between man and woman, and for their children, but for any other person; according to the Gospel, love is a prime relation to any human being — and even to all the universe. Obviously, many of the Russian philosophers built their ethics of love directly on an interpretation of Orthodox Christianity (V. Solov'ev, B. Vysheslavtsev, Losskii, Frank). But the atheist Petr Kropotkin also centered his ethic on spontaneous sentiments of solidarity. He believed morality to be a natural product of the evolution of the practice of mutual aid, which is characteristic both of nature and of humans. In line with his anarchism, Kropotkin also preferred 'to keep ethical problems distinct from the problems of law' (Kropotkin 1924: p. 25). He thought that the empirical (that is, scientific) ethic should infuse in men ideals 'that would provoke their enthusiasm and give them the necessary forces for building a form of life which would combine individual energy with work for the good of all', rather than justify legislative norms (Kropotkin 1924: p. 23; see also Kropotkin 1901).

In this context even Kant — in contradistinction to modern Western interpretations of his ethical formalism[15] — was cited as an authority. His categorical imperative was seen to establish the sovereignty of morality — as an expression of the 'all-triumphant force of absolute moral law' rather than as a duty to follow any particular rule (Frank 1949: pp. 85, 245).[16] As Frank argued:

> a truly correct moral decision is determined not by observing the letter of the moral law, not by soulless obedience to an abstract rule without attention to the particular needs of real life; it is determined only by *love*, whose requirements are always concrete; in other words, it consists in the relatively best implementation of a moral truth — of what Aristotle called in an untranslatable word the *epieikes* — what is 'suitable', 'appropriate', 'concretely correct'. (Frank 1949: p. 229)

To be able so to act, one should possess a certain moral tact, that is, be a person of certain moral qualities. But that is to say that morality is not so much about norms which must guide actions as about the inner state of the person. This too was explicitly articulated by Frank: 'For all the holiness of some norms of the moral law or "natural law", the notions of good and evil in their prime meaning can be applied only to the spiritual order of the internal being, to the *moral state of the person*' (Frank 1949: p. 245).

There is good reason to believe that the view of morality here typified by Frank retained its force for many generations of the Russian intelligentsia. Take, for example, the following description of life in Russia, written in the mid-twentieth century:

> In Russia, at least in old Russia, there was something which perhaps does not exist any more anywhere else: the feeling of very extensive freedom, not political of course, not that which is protected by the law and state, but the absolutely different kind which sprang from the tacit assurance that your fellows would judge any of your actions 'according to humanity', starting from a general feeling about you as a person, rather than according to the conformity or non-conformity of your action to the law, decency, categorical imperative, or this or that formally established rule. (Veidle 1956: p. 127)

The type of morality outlined here does not necessarily deny rules and contradict the establishment of an ethos of lawful state service, but it stresses that rules are not the most important thing in life. It sets high standards for the person, leaving at the same time considerable moral freedom concerning behaviour in a particular situation. The positive face of this freedom is accentuated in the words of Veidle cited above. The negative face of the lack of legislative discipline, when combined with amorality, could be, and was, ubiquitous corruption among officials.

This 'Russian' ethic, based on the Christian ideal of love, can be regarded as being pre-modern and traditionalist. If it is compared with Zygmunt Bauman's *Postmodern Ethics*, however, we will find many parallels. There is the same stress on the non-sufficiency of moral rules and codes; on responsibility — being for the other — as the essence of morality; on the acute difference between morality and conformism; on the social context of coexistence, of 'being with others', as a ground for moral behaviour (as opposed to the societal, super-individual agencies of training and enforcement); on the unresolvable character of moral antinomies; and on the freedom of moral choice, given that the moral call is intrinsically personal (Bauman 1994). Maybe this affinity is not accidental. After all, postmodernism is a product of disillusion in the 'legislative authorities'; the Russians never had such illusions.[17]

Conclusion

The negative image of the bureacracy in nineteenth-century Russian literature had great circumstantial plausibility. The class of bureaucrats was formed in unfavourable conditions. Groups and structures ready to be co-opted or prepared to take an initiative in the modernization of society were not strong enough in Russian society; the system of secular education was poorly developed; there were virtually no groups of professionals from which the bureaucracy could be recruited. Above all, the bureaucracy never enjoyed public prestige. The nineteenth-century administrative system was gradually reformed after Emancipation in 1861, but it still concentrated too much power in the higher official positions (for example, a superior had the right to dismiss a clerk without clarifying the reason; indictment for official abuses also depended on the superior, not on juridical bodies); it did not have a mechanism of competitive examination for officials; and salaries for the majority of bureaucrats were very low indeed.[18] All these were structural factors supporting corruption.

Futhermore, the Russian bureaucracy was in unfavourable conditions to develop its own ethic. First, it had to oppose the prevailing moral code, with its tendency to negotiate formal rules through the personalized understanding of moral obligations. Secondly, the most obvious justification of bureaucratic activity and rigid adherence to bureaucratic rules — social usefulness and the performance of civic duty — was challenged by the intelligentsia. The idea of 'serving' society/the people had already been appropriated by the radicals.

Over the last twenty years, however, several historians have argued convincingly that the bureaucracy did not deserve its appalling reputation (see, for example, Lincoln 1982; Pintner 1980). Regarding the latter half of the nineteenth century, Dominic Lieven writes: 'If the bureaucracy's lower ranks in the provinces were not over-impressive, taken as a whole the civil service had left the era of Gogol far behind, particularly, of course, as regards the central ministries and the administrative élite' (Lieven 1989: p. 25).

My concern in this chapter has been to explain *why* the Russian bureaucracy received such a raw deal. Criticism of the bureaucracy in the nineteenth and early twentieth centuries was marked by a hostility and disrespect which, above all, originated from the intense political struggle between government and intelligentsia. Our contemporary picture of the tsarist administration as extremely corrupt and open to bribery is in part a stereotype derived from the radical discourse which was itself a product of, and a weapon in, this struggle. Thus, a contemporary author supports his argument that Russia never had a proper bureaucracy (that there were no bureaucrats, only *chinovniki*) by referring to the writings of Gogol′, Chernyshevskii, V. Rozanov, L. Tikhomirov and others (Kantor 1997: p. 194).[19] Although he acknowledges that there was a group of 'liberal bureaucrats' in the era of 'Great Reforms', who exemplified the ideal of 'honest bureaucratic service', he stresses that such figures were not typical. In fact, the very term 'bureaucracy' has predominantly negative connotations in modern Russian.

So although the administrative system after Emancipation improved significantly, no equivalent change in the public attitude to bureaucracy accompanied this positive development. There is, however, some evidence that the assessment of the bureaucracy by the intelligentsia changed with the modification of its attitude to the state, which in turn was a result of a re-evaluation of its own position and ethos after the revolutions of 1905 and 1917. Thus Sergii Bulgakov, in his article for the renowned collection *Iz glubiny* (Out of the Depths), first published in 1918, put into the mouth of one of the participants in the dialogue 'At the Gods' Feast' the following words:

> In general this so-called intelligentsia is no more than Russia's misfortune and absolutely unnecessary to it. We need competent professionals, educated specialists, but not these unacknowledged rescuers of the world who everywhere give alarm but often are of no use in work. Well, for them there is no more contemptuous word than 'bureaucracy', but do we have anywhere a more disciplined, responsible, industrious group of educated men other than the bureaucracy? (Bulgakov 1967: p. 148)

In similar vein, Fedotov noted that 'being a member of the intelligentsia and being businesslike are not compatible' (Fedotov 1967: p. 117). Losskii argued that after the reforms the situation in the courts and the administration had improved, and bribery had been largely extirpated in the last decade before the October Revolution; that later, while living in Europe and America, Russian immigrants observed much more widespread bribery than they had in Russia; that the bureaucracy achieved a high standard in some ministries, such as finance, under Witte, and agriculture; and that in general 'everywhere there were many officials who loved Russia and served it honestly' (Losskii 1957: pp. 48, 146–7). To know whether this version is correct or just another ideologization we need to suspend judgements derived from *belles-lettres*, drama, journalistic criticism, socio-philosophical writings and so on, and to direct our attention to less partial historical research.

Notes

1 According to P.N. Miliukov, Peter the Great's attempt to introduce professional education for the civil service failed because of the lack of suitable 'social material'. The nobility did not want to receive education and to work with people of non-noble origin. Even the introduction of jurisprudence into the programme of schools for the nobility did not induce nobles to take up this subject: in 1733, of 245 pupils at the recently opened Land-Military College only eleven studied law (Miliukov 1931: p. 742).

2 For more on this, see Chapters 2–4 in the present volume.

3 Chatskii (the hero of Griboedov's *Gore ot uma* [Woe from Wit], handwritten copies of which spread in 1824) asks Famusov what he would say if Chatskii proposed marriage to his daughter Sof'ia. Famusov replies that he would say: first, do not be eccentric; then, manage the estate properly; but — most important of all — enter the Service. It is at this point that Chatskii gives voice to his contempt for service.

4 Anon., 'Mysli vslukh ob istekshem tridtsatiletii Rossii' in *Golosa iz Rossii*, vypusk 1 (1856), pp. 83–4.

5 For example, the Principal of the gymnazium in Perm' complained in the aftermath of Alexander I's reform of 1804 that 'officials of higher ranks try to place their children in an official position as soon as possible, and doing this they think not so much about extra salary as about reaching the higher ranks earlier' (Miliukov 1931: p. 773).

6 The history of bureaucratic life between 1755 and 1855 has been reviewed by Walter Pintner (1980): although the social composition of the bureaucracy did not change significantly during this period, its levels of formal training did. The reforms of Alexander I also served to weaken the importance of family ties in state service and to undermine the strongly institutionalized link between military and civilian service. Note also the work of W. Bruce Lincoln (1982) on imperial Russia's mid-century 'enlightened bureaucrats'. The reforms planned and carried out by these men brought about important changes in several areas of officialdom — and perhaps nowhere more so than in the administration and practice of the law (Wagner 1994).

7 Thus, according to the same source, out of 333 graduates for the three previous years, only ninety-six joined the civil service (Miliukov 1931: p. 794).

8 For example, Alexander I based his reform of education in 1803 on the project by Condorcet submitted to the French National Assembly in 1792 (Miliukov 1931: p. 770).

9 After arrest, Decembrists were required to write answers on a standard questionnaire; the seventh (or sometimes fourth) question was: 'From what time and from where did you acquire your first free [*vol'nodumcheskie*] and liberal thoughts, for example, was it inspired by others, or by reading books; and in what way did opinions of that kind take root in your mind?' Many Decembrists said that it was due to the influence of their fellows; some pointed to real-life experiences, especially that of being abroad during the campaigns of 1812–15; those who cited the influence of books listed mainly Enlightenment authors (see the documents published in *Vosstanie dekabristov: Materialy*, 18 vols, Moscow, 1925–84). Some of the answers to questions about education have been cited by Raeff (1966b: pp. 44–57). See also the conclusion of the Investigatory Commission about the significance of education in the *Digest of the Testimony Concerning the Internal Conditions of the State Given by the Members of the Subversive Society* by A.D. Borovkov (Raeff 1966b: p. 33). For general information about the reading of the Decembrists, see the work of M. Nechkina (1955: p. 115).

10 Several social processes underlay the centrality of books in public life: the growth of literacy among the population; the expansion of the education system, which brought about a new readership (with new needs) for the broadening output of publishing; the establishment of mass magazines; the mass arrival of *raznochintsy* — people from the various lower strata — into public life in the 1850s–1860s, and so on.

11 *Voices from Russia* is a series of collections of anonymous articles/letters from Russia published in 1855–60 by Herzen and Ogarev in London.

12 Anon., 'Mysli vslukh ob istekshem tridtsatiletii Rossii' (see note 4 above), p. 86.

13 'Priiatel'skii razgovor' in *Golosa iz Rossii*, vypusk 1 (1856), chast' 2, p. 5.

14 For general information about the programme of the Union of Welfare and of the earlier Decembrist organizations see Nechkina 1955: pp. 163, 197–201; Raeff 1966b: pp. 71–5. See also the memoirs of the Decembrists in Fedorov 1981. The most famous example of practical activity undertaken in accordance with this programme was the service of I. Pushchin in the Court in Moscow.

15 It has been argued that the abstract, formal character of the Kantian notion of duty, which is detached from contingent events and needs and from social circumstances, predisposed it to provide a foundation for

the ethic of expertise in modern society (see McIntyre 1967, 1981; Bauman 1989). As McIntyre puts it, 'the agent does his duty in his immediate sphere without asking about the context within which he acts or the wider effects of his actions and of his responsibilities [...]. He is the outcome of all good bureaucrats, of those technical specialists such as Eichmann who boasted that they merely discharged their function in arranging for so much transport to be provided between point X and point Y. Whether the cargo was sheep or Jews, whether points X and Y were farm and butcher's slaughterhouse or ghetto and gas chamber, was no concern of theirs [...] the moral basis on which Eichmann claimed to have been educated was that of the categorical imperative' (McIntyre 1967: pp. 207–8).

16 An earlier similar interpretation was suggested by Lev Tolstoi: see his diaries for 1906 and 1907 (Tolstoi 1985: pp. 223, 233, 250).

17 B. Latour (1993) has challenged the idea that even the West was ever modern.

18 Thus, the annual salary of the chief constable (*starshii gorodovoi*) in Kazan′ in 1897 was 180 roubles, while the approximate budget of a moderate-spending middle-rank official (unmarried titular councillor [*tituliarnyi sovetnik*] 'Perchikov') in St Petersburg in 1857 was 318 roubles and sixty kopecks (P. Zaionchkovskii 1978: pp. 83, 89). Even if we assume that life in the capital in 1857 was more expensive than life in Kazan′ in 1897, the figures still show that the low- and middle-rank officials had to struggle to balance their budgets.

19 Kantor rests his account of Russian official life on Weber's classic concept of bureaucracy.

Bibliography

Bakunin, M. (1990), *Statism and Anarchy*, trans. M. Shatz, Cambridge.

Bauman, Z. (1989), *Modernity and the Holocaust*, Cambridge.

Bauman, Z. (1994), *Postmodern Ethics*, Oxford.

Berdiaev, N. (1946), *Russkaia ideia*, Paris.

Bulgakov, S. (1967), 'Na piru bogov. Pro i Contra: Sovremennye dialogi' in P. Struve et al. (eds), *Iz Glubiny: Sbornik statei o russkoi revoliutsii*, Paris.

Fedorov, V. (ed). (1981), *Memuary dekabristov*, Moscow

Fedotov, G. (1967), 'Tragediia intelligentsii' in Fedotov, *Litso Rossii: Sbornik statei 1918–1931*, Paris.

Frank, S. (1949), *Svet vo t′me: Opyt khristianskoi etiki i sotsial′noi filosofii*, Paris.

Frank, S. (1967), 'Etika nihilisma' in *Vekhi: Sbornik statei o russkoi intelligentsii*, Frankfurt.

Golosa iz Rossi: Sborniki A. Gerzena i N. Ogareva (1974), Moscow.

Griboedov, A. (1951), *Gore ot uma (The Mischief of Being Clever)*, trans. B. Pares, Oxford.

Il'in, I. (1956), 'O Russkoi idee' in Il'in, *Nashi zadachi (stat'I 1948–1956gg.)*, vol. 1, Paris.

Kantor, V. (1997), '... *Est' evropeiskaia derzhava'. Rossia: trudnyi put' k tsivilizatsii. Istoricheskie ocherki*, Moscow.

Kapnist, V. (1960), *Iabeda* in Kapnist, *Sobranie sochinenii v 2-kh tomakh*, vol. 1, Moscow and Leningrad.

Kropotkin, P. (1901), *Sovremennaia nauka i anarkhizm*, London.

Kropotkin, P. (1924), *Ethics: Origin and Development*, New York.

Latour, B. (1993), *We Have Never Been Modern*, trans. C. Porter, New York and London.

Lieven, D. (1989), *Russia's Rulers under the Old Regime*, New Haven, CT and London.

Lincoln, W.B. (1982), *In the Vanguard of Reform: Russia's Enlightened Bureaucrats 1825–1861*, DeKalb, IL.

Losskii, N. (1957), *Kharakter russkogo naroda*, Frankfurt.

Lotman, Iu. (1994), *Besedy o russkoi kul'ture: Byt i traditsii russkogo dvorianstva (XVIII–nachalo XIX veka)*, St Petersburg.

McIntyre, A. (1967), *A Short History of Ethics*, London.

McIntyre, A. (1981), *After Virtue: A Study of Moral Theory*, Notre Dame.

Miliukov, P. (1931), *Ocherki po istorii russkoi kul'tury*, vol. 2, parts 1–2, Paris.

Nechkina, M. (1955), *Dvizhenie dekabristov*, vol. 1, Moscow.

Pintner, W. (1980), 'The Evolution of Civil Officialdom, 1755–1855' in D. Rowney and W. Pintner (eds), *Russian Officialdom: The Bureaucratization of Russian Society from the Seventeenth to the Twentieth Century*, Chapel Hill, NC.

Raeff, M. (1957), *Michael Speransky: Statesman of Imperial Russia 1772–1839*, The Hague.

Raeff, M. (1966a), *Origins of the Russian Intelligentsia: The Eighteenth-Century Nobility*, San Diego, New York and London.

Raeff, M. (1966b), *The Decembrist Movement*, London.

Raeff, M. (1983), *The Well-Ordered Police State: Social and Institutional Change through Law in the Germanies and Russia 1600–1800*, New Haven, CT and London.

Serov, D. (1996), *Stroiteli imperii*, Novosibirsk.

Tolstoi, L. (1985), *Sobranie sochinenii v 22 tomakh*, vol. 22, Moscow.

Veidle, V. (1956), *Zadacha Rossii*, New York.

Wagner, W. (1994), *Marriage, Property and Law in Late Imperial Russia*, Oxford.

Zaionchkovskii, P. (1978), *Pravitel'stvennyi apparat samo-derzhavnoi Rossii v XIX veke*, Moscow.

7 The Representation of Bribery in Nineteenth-Century Russian Literature

Andrei Rogachevskii

One does not have to be a Russianist to realize that, however generous the space allocated for the present chapter, it is bound to be undersized. Therefore it seems only natural to impose certain restrictions before I proceed any further. First, as it is common knowledge that nineteenth-century Russian literature experienced two major climaxes, one in the 1820s to 1830s and another in the 1860s, my discussion will revolve primarily around them, with occasional forays into adjacent epochs. Secondly, I shall mainly concentrate on those literary genres which tended to dominate in Russia in the periods mentioned, that is, drama, sketch (*ocherk*) and novel, as well as on some examples of Russian poetry. Finally, since 'genres are stabilised by the minor' writers (Jensen 1997: p. 136), I am going to deal principally with less well-known names, although some internationally renowned authors will also be mentioned.

Perhaps the single most memorable work of art devoted to bribery in nineteenth-century Russian literature is Nikolai Gogol''s comedy *Revizor* (The Government Inspector, 1836), especially those several scenes in its fourth act where dignitaries in a provincial town line up before a rogue traveller, mistaken by them for an Inspector General, to 'lend' him various sums of money (see Gogol' 1926: pp. 73–82).[1] Gogol', however, was by no means the only figure in the literary tradition who sought to castigate bribe-takers and bribe-givers in Russia.

Let us briefly examine the satirical comedy in verse *Iabeda* (Chicanery, 1798) by Vasilii Kapnist (1758–1823), Gogol''s compatriot and predecessor in mocking bribery on stage.[2] Referring to the legal practice of the time, Kapnist explains why it is virtually impossible to purge Russia of this old and common sin:[3]

Один для давшего и для принявших суд,
Так чорт ли понесет кого-нибудь с доносом?
(For those who give and those who take the verdict is the same,
So why the devil should one wish to report?)
(Kapnist 1849: p. 77)[4]

Chicanery is loosely based on Kapnist's own experiences with the Russian judicial system (for more than a decade he had been involved in a legal battle with a landowner, Fekla Tarnovskaia, over his brother's estate).[5] A retired official called Pravolov (Dodgy) is eager to take possession of the estate of Lieutenant-Colonel Priamikov (Straightforward). With this in view, Pravolov bribes those in the Civil Court who could make the decision in his favour, among them the Chairman Krivosudov (Case-twister), the judges Bul'bul'kin (Drunkard), Atuev (Hunter; the Russian exclamation 'atu!' is similar to the English 'halloo!'), Parol'kin (Gambler; his name derives from a French term used in the game of cards) and the prosecutor Khvataiko (Grabber). Although Pravolov's strategy appears to be very successful, at the end of the play he is arrested on orders from the Senate and a criminal investigation against the corrupt judges is initiated. Priamikov retains his estate and marries Krivosudov's daughter.

With, as tradition dictated, vice punished and virtue rewarded, *Chicanery* would have remained merely a conventional classical play[6] had it not been for its unusually realistic depiction of immoral and cynical Russian legal eagles, inspired by Kapnist's intimate knowledge of the subject. In *Chicanery* there is a scene in which Prosecutor Khvataiko sings a song which expresses his credo:

Бери, большой тут нет науки;
Бери, что только можно взять.
На что ж привешены нам руки,
Как не на то, чтоб брать?
(Take, you'll learn the art with ease!
Take whatever you can seize!
God for this your hands did make,
That you may take!)
(Kapnist 1849, p. 101; translation taken from Wiener 1902: p. 400)[7]

A contemporary recalled that at one performance of *Chicanery*, in a provincial city, after this song the audience in the theatre began to applaud and, addressing a local prosecutor who happened to be there, cried out 'This is you! This is you!' (Bantysh-Kamenskii 1847: p. 67). It is hardly possible to suggest that the official in question could have served as a prototype for Kapnist's play. Such was the power of *Chicanery*'s realism, however, that this particular person was immediately recognized as a type.

The above-mentioned public reaction to *Chicanery* leads us to assume that the customs described in Kapnist's play were fairly typical, hence *Chicanery* can be very useful as a source of information about various forms of bribery, especially the non-monetary ones (that is, those types of bribes which try to conceal any direct connection with material gain and therefore pretend that they are anything but bribes). As a rule, the relevant characters in *Chicanery* are bribed in accordance with their hobbies and inclinations. Thus, Bul'bul'kin gets a cask of Hungarian wine and Atuev a pack of hounds (Kapnist 1849: p. 75). It is curious that even the Chairman's wife Fekla, possibly named after Kapnist's adversary in his lawsuit, receives a gift from Pravolov in the form of food, fabrics and beverages (see Kapnist 1849: pp. 40–4). This detail anticipates articles 401 and 405 in the 1845 *Ulozhenie* (Statute) which stated that: (a) not only money, but also 'things and whatever else [*veshchi ili chto by to ni bylo inoe*]' given to an official or a public servant should be treated as bribes; and (b) those who do not accept bribes personally, but do so by proxy, for example, through their relatives, should still be found guilty (see Chistiakov 1988: pp. 276, 278).

Kapnist's play successfully captures the status quo in the Russian judicial system. Yet the real encyclopedia of all types and forms of bribery in all spheres of Russian life in the late eighteenth and early nineteenth centuries was 'compiled' by the author Faddei Bulgarin (1789–1859), much despised by Russian literary critics for his allegedly flawed taste, vanity and connections with the Third Section (see, for example, Anninskii 1996: pp. 194–204; Kuzovkina 1995: pp. 35–46; Filin 1997: pp. 72–8).[8] Sometimes, however, he is sympathetically quoted by Western scholars because of his instinctive flair for the burning topics of the day and for the precious tiny details he provides on Russian *byt* (see, for example, Wortman 1976: pp. 46–7, 80). In *Ivan Vyzhigin* (1829), Bulgarin's fairly successful attempt at the genre of picaresque novel, the hero of the title starts off as a poor orphan and ends up as a wealthy prince while moving with relative ease in almost every imaginable social and ethnic sphere of the then Russian Empire, not excluding Polish, Jewish and Kirghiz circles. Although Bulgarin had had first-hand experience of standard operational procedures in Russian offices[9] (for years he had been in charge of his uncle's lawsuit concerning the ownership of 8,000 serfs; see Mocha 1974: pp. 98–9), a special exposé of bribery was clearly not his top priority in this novel.[10] All the more striking, then, is the fact that he mentions bribery in, on average, every other chapter. According to *Ivan Vyzhigin*, bribery is omnipresent. This becomes evident, first, from the fact that in Bulgarin's novel not only officers of the court, as in Kapnist's play, but people of all professions and standings in society appear to be involved in unscrupulous activities. A traveller bribes a stationmaster to speed up his journey, a smuggler bribes a customs officer to cross the border safely, visitors bribe the doorman at the house of a public prosecutor in order to gain admittance, and then grease the palm of the public prosecutor himself to persuade him to solve their problems (Bulgarin 1831: vol. 1, pp. 51–2, 69–71, 78, 81–2). In one rural district, everyone — landowners and peasants alike, as well as dangerous criminals at large — pays off the district chief of police, and he, in his turn, shares his dividends with the wife of a local prosecutor in exchange for her turning a blind eye to the escape of one of said criminals from prison (Bulgarin 1831: vol. 1, pp. 146–9, 150–1). Card-sharpers pay their partners in crime to keep their mouths shut. Merchants suborn the police and government officials. To ingratiate himself with his judges, a bankrupt treats them to lavish meals (at the expense of his creditors). Parents offer gifts and protection to the headteacher of a boarding school to improve their children's examination results. It is even said of a priest that he could have extorted 'donations' from his flock if only he had wanted to (Bulgarin 1831: vol. 1, pp. 108–9, 125; vol. 2, pp. 20, 144, 147, 165–6).[11] It is particularly remarkable that women (usually the wives or lovers of the more or less powerful) are bribed almost as often as men (Bulgarin 1831: vol. 1, pp. 151, 270–1; vol. 2, pp. 41, 166–7). Nor is a female bribe-giver a rarity, if *Ivan Vyzhigin* is anything to go by (Bulgarin 1831: vol. 1, pp. 269–71; vol. 2, pp. 41–2).

No less abundant in the novel are data on what can serve as a bribe. Money (including shares), of course, is the undisputed leader here. Meals, as well as food supplies and wine, seem to take second place (Bulgarin 1831: vol. 1, pp. 75, 144, 187; vol. 2, pp. 41–2, 82–3, 147).[12] Somewhat more exotic items include cashmere shawls, a Moscow-made sledge and a snuffbox full of pearls (Bulgarin 1831: vol. 1, pp. 151, 262–3, 270–1). To cut a long story short, a bribe can take any form.[13] If one were to sum up in one phrase the picture Bulgarin paints, perhaps it would not be a serious exaggeration to say that 'everybody bribes everyone with everything'. As far as the functions of different forms of bribery are concerned, all bribes seem to aim either for expediting the exercise of people's duties or for shutting their eyes to offences against the law.

It is not, in Bulgarin's view, that there are no honest people in Russia. He portrays one virtuous district chief of police and one incorruptible major-domo (Bulgarin 1831: vol. 1, pp. 259–60, 276; vol. 2, p. 164). These true heroes of the time, however, are hopelessly outnumbered by those who either take bribes openly, and even brag about this in front of each other,[14] or pretend to set moral examples while being utterly corrupt. From the latter group, the memorable figure of a superintendent of the market for bartering with the Kirghiz stands out:

> He passed for a very poor man all his life, and had received, on several occasions, pecuniary assistance from government, on account of his insufficient income; but after his death, when his property was sealed up, bank-receipts and bills were found for more than half a million of roubles. (Bulgarin 1831: vol. 1, p. 125).

A certain Akulina Semenovna, the wife of an influential provincial official, also belongs to the same group of brazen hypocrites, as the following comic scene testifies. An old, poorly dressed woman pays her a visit with the purpose of lodging a petition in favour of her grandson, whom the peasant community has marked out for recruitment:

> After falling down at her feet, the old woman gave Aquilina Semenovna a little box, adding, 'Take this, ma'am; if it does not suit you, it will do for your daughter.' Aquilina Semenovna, thinking that the old woman was giving her a snuff-box, fell into a passion, screamed out with all her might in order that the country gentlemen who were in the adjoining room might hear of her

> disinterestedness, and gave the old woman a box of another sort in return. The box fell on the ground, and the pearls were scattered on the floor. What a pucker she was in! There was Aquilina Semenovna sprawling on the floor, gathering up the pearls, and bawling out to her daughter Ashenka to come to her assistance. Ashenka flew to her from the other room, but forgot to shut the door, so that the gentlemen saw the whole farce. (Bulgarin 1831: vol. 1, pp. 270–1)

While revealing such practices and patterns of reciprocity, *Ivan Vyzhigin* features what could be termed 'the moral code of Russian bribers',[15] with a particular slant, first, on gifts which might look like bribes, although essentially they are not; and, secondly, on those types of bribe which in certain circumstances might be deemed permissible.[16] An example which falls into the first category is that of a policeman who comes to Vyzhigin to make an enquiry about a fraud involving two landowners and five card-sharpers. After the official business is over, the policeman, on Vyzhigin's invitation, relates how he has managed, through all his years in the force, to keep his conscience clear, albeit at the price of living near the poverty line. Vyzhigin is deeply touched and offers the policeman 100 roubles. The policeman declines with the following explanation: 'If I had not come to you upon business, I would have taken the money, but now I cannot. It is not according to the fitness of things, and your present would have the appearance of a bribe' (Bulgarin 1831: vol. 2, p. 171).

The second category includes, although not without ironic reservations, married officials who are excused from being castigated for taking bribes because they have families to feed (see Bulgarin 1831: vol. 2, pp. 268, 282–3). Moreover, when an official's salary proves to be insufficient to maintain him, 'the voluntary offerings of grateful people' are viewed as acceptable in such cases as the recovery of stolen property or the discovery of the concealed property of a debtor (Bulgarin 1831: vol. 2, p. 167).[17]

It is curious that a similar semi-justificatory approach to bribery was taken by some writers in the late 1850s to early 1860s, when the death of Nicholas I and the reforms of Alexander II triggered a massive public criticism of all spheres of Russian state and society. If we are to believe the satirical magazines of the period, the most radical critics of bribery were bribers themselves.[18] Moreover, the criticism of bribery in the 1860s had become so much the orthodoxy that it would make sense to pay more attention to those commentators who took a more independent (that is, more liberal and tolerant) stance. In 1860, Grigorii Danilevskii (1829–90), a career official and the author of many popular novels,[19] published a sketch 'Biudzhet odnogo vziatochnika' (The Budget of a Briber) apparently based on a genuine conversation between the narrator (possibly a disguised self-portrait of Danilevskii himself) and a certain Ivan Semenych, a senior police official in a provincial town in Ukraine. This official complains that he is practically forced to take bribes, because his salary (200 roubles a year) is fifteen times less than what he needs for the bare essentials of his household, which consists of his wife, their two children, his wife's sister, three servants, a horse and a dog. According to the policeman's calculations, 200 roubles a year is only enough to feed the horse, without which he could not indeed perform his duties. Ivan Semenych would like to be morally scrupulous, but he simply cannot afford it. 'One takes [bribes] because one really has to', he says (Danilevskii 1901: p. 204). Still, the policeman's family does not lead a life of luxury. His children, for instance, are even denied sweets (Danilevskii 1901: p. 209).

The issue of a married official caught between a rock and a hard place is thoroughly examined in Ostrovskii's *Dokhodnoe mesto* (A Profitable Vacancy, 1857). Zhadov, the idealistic nephew of a mighty and corrupt official, rejects the opportunity to fill a 'profitable' vacancy (that is, a position of influence, however small, which effectively ends one's dependence on one's salary alone) because of his praiseworthy but impractical belief that bribery should not be employed as a source of income. Another young official, Belogubov, is appointed instead. Zhadov and Belogubov marry the Kukushkin sisters. Before long a stark contrast in the lifestyles of the two families is revealed. Belogubov does not exactly overstrain himself at work, but his wife goes on a shopping spree every so often, whereas Zhadov's wife, paralysed with boredom, sits at home because she does not have any money to spare, although her husband works from dawn till dusk. As a result, Felisata, the mother of the Kukushkin sisters, accuses Zhadov of not taking proper care of his wife and, what is worse, Zhadov's wife threatens to leave him. Unable to withstand the pressure, Zhadov decides to do away with his principles, go to his uncle and ask him for a profitable vacancy. Upon his arrival at his uncle's house, Zhadov learns that his uncle has just been dismissed for malfeasance in office. This prompts Zhadov to change his mind again and reaffirms his faith in personal honesty.

Throughout the play, Ostrovskii manages to maintain a balanced view of the phenomenon of bribery. While not seeking to defend bribers, he nevertheless tries to be understanding and even compassionate. He knows all about the weakness of human nature and the irresistibility of temptation. He can see why it is so difficult to be a hero when the logic of your life is persistently pushing you in one, highly undesirable, direction.[20] Nor does Ostrovskii paint his bribers all black. Belogubov is always polite and good-mannered, he is rather jovial and not incapable of unfeigned gratitude to his superiors (in the best sense of these words). He is also genuinely well-disposed to his brother-in-law and does not mind sharing his prosperity with family and friends. (In comparison, Zhadov looks like an ill-bred bore who is hardly capable of anything other than moralistic tirades.) Nor could Belogubov's associates be called devils in the flesh. Paradoxically, in their unlawful and immoral deeds they appear to follow a certain moral code which they find it reprehensible to break. The bottom line of this code is disclosed in a scene when an official tells his colleagues about a clerk who made a false copy of a pending verdict, showed it to an interested party and was rewarded by a lump sum. When the real court session took place, however, the verdict turned out to be quite different and the hoax was exposed. Belogubov comments: 'Now this is a mean trick! [The clerk] should have been sacked for this'. The old and experienced administrator Iusov agrees: 'Sacked, indeed. Don't damage our reputation. If you take [a bribe], do business, not fraud. You should take in such a way that the petitioner is not offended and you are happy too' (Ostrovskii 1974: p. 77).

Such violations of the etiquette of give-and-take, not uncommon in the 1860s (as opposed to earlier epochs in Russian history),[21] would often lead to tragic notes in some representations of bribery in the second half of the nineteenth century. One of them is Nikolai Leskov's story 'Zhitie odnoi baby' (The Life of a Peasant Woman, 1863). Two peasants, Stepan and Nastia, unhappy in their respective marriages and madly in love with each other, are planning to elope. For this they need passports. Stepan and Nastia give twenty-five roubles — everything they own — to a clerk to issue the passports. The clerk accepts the bribe, but instead of issuing the required documents demands more cash. It becomes obvious that he simply cannot deliver his part of the deal. Nastia urges Stepan to argue with the clerk, but Stepan is afraid of being reported. The couple attempt to escape without passports and are captured. Stepan dies of typhus and Nastia goes insane (see Leskov 1956: pp. 358–9).[22]

Not only the lower classes were in danger of falling into traps devised by dishonest bribe-takers. Even for wealthy landowners, in a particularly hopeless case the ultimate price to pay could be just the same, namely all their possessions, and the stake could also amount to no less than their life. An apt example is Aleksandr Sukhovo-Kobylin (1817–1903), a rich aristocrat whose family was related to the Romanovs. From 1850 until 1857 he was under investigation as a prime suspect in the murder of his French lover, Louise Simon-Dimanche.[23] The case was dropped only after the direct intervention of the Empress. Before this intervention took place, Sukhovo-Kobylin exhausted all other possible means, including a bribe worth 10,000 silver roubles, given personally by the defendant to no less a person than the Chief Prosecutor of the Senate, Kastor Lebedev, in exchange for the promise of acquittal. No sooner had the relieved (in more than one sense) Sukhovo-Kobylin left the office of the Chief Prosecutor than he found out that Lebedev had lied to him and the acquittal was absolutely out of the question. The incensed aristocrat stormed back into Lebedev's office and threatened to expose him (prior to slipping his cheque into Lebedev's pocket, the far-sighted Sukhovo-Kobylin wrote down its number). In response, Lebedev took the cheque out of his pocket and swallowed it (see Otroshenko 1994: pp. 6–7).

To revenge himself on his tormentors for nearly bringing him to ruin, Sukhovo-Kobylin wrote a play called *Delo* (The Case, 1861; first published in 1869, first performed in 1882), the central part of his dramatic trilogy which also includes *Svad'ba Krechinskogo* (Krechinskii's Wedding, 1854) and *Smert' Tarelkina* (The Death of Tarelkin, 1869).[24] In its merciless portrayal of greedy extortioners who always gain the upper hand, *The Case* is yet unrivalled. It tells of the ageing landowner Muromskii, who reaches the end of his tether after five years of a criminal investigation which seeks to prove that his daughter Lidochka, together with her fiancé Krechinskii, plotted to steal his diamond pin, valued by a pawnbroker at 6,000 roubles. Dragged by the police and court officials through the ruthless routine of bribe-giving,[25] he is ready at last to wave goodbye to his whole estate just so as to close this unfounded case once and for all. To this end, he has to give one last bribe, worth 30,000 roubles, to the actual state councillor (*deistvitel'nyi statskii sovetnik*), Varravin, who allegedly has the final say in the matter. Muromskii is unaware of the fact that the powers above Varravin have already ruled that the investigation of this perplexing and convoluted affair should begin afresh. Varravin, however, is reluctant to let Muromskii out of his snare. He receives Muromskii at his office, takes the parcel with the money, promises to solve Muromskii's problem, and then, just before Muromskii leaves the building, officially announces that Muromskii tried to bribe him. The following scene ensues:

VARRAVIN:	I want to announce your crime here and now, like this, in front of witnesses.
MUROMSKY:	What is all this? (*Looks around*) A trap?!
VARRAVIN:	You wanted to buy me off, didn't you?
MUROMSKY:	(*utterly confused*) I'm afraid there's some misunderstanding here… forgive me… […]
VARRAVIN:	[…] I want you to understand that I do not take money! (*Throws the package on the floor in front of Muromsky*) Take it! And get out of here and take that *foul* case of yours with you! (Sukhovo-Kobylin 1995: pp. 139–40)

When the package is opened and the money is counted, there turns out to be only 1,350 roubles. The rest has been appropriated by Varravin, but this cannot be proved. The shattered Muromskii dies in his carriage on his way home.

The above episode is somewhat reminiscent of the scene with the snuffbox full of pearls in Bulgarin's *Ivan Vyzhigin*. In both incidents the bribers only pretend that they are incorruptible, Varravin with a hidden agenda in mind and Akulina Semenovna because of the assumption that the snuffbox was filled with mere tobacco and therefore had no real value. We have here a pattern of bribery which repeats itself within a period of thirty-odd years. It is remarkable, though, that what Bulgarin views as farce, Sukhovo-Kobylin pictures as genuine tragedy. He is convinced that, in comparison with the earlier, less bloodthirsty, as it were, period of

Russian history, in the second half of the nineteenth century bribery has completely got out of hand. Muromskii's manager, Razuvaev, characterizes the practices of contemporary bribers thus:

> Nowadays, you know, they don't stop at taking just their wages or what someone gives them besides out of gratitude for some favour or other — let them have this, it's not that we're arguing about — but instead they just wait for the chance to grab whatever they can so as to have plenty for themselves and enough left over to leave their brats. Well, as a result, the robbing and stealing has become enormous. (Sukhovo-Kobylin 1995: p. 109)

Such behaviour, of course, is rather distant from the moderate ambitions of Ostrovskii's proponents of old-fashioned reciprocity immortalized in *A Profitable Vacancy*. 'Many a pickle makes a mickle' is their principle (see Ostrovskii 1974: p. 77; and also Kurochkin's elegy 'Starichok v otstavke' [An Old Retiree, 1861] in Kravtsov and Morozov 1932: pp. 58–9). It is open to question, however, whether the difference in attitude detectable in Bulgarin's, Ostrovskii's and Sukhovo-Kobylin's descriptions of bribers reflects a wider literary dynamic and a real change in social practices. As Sukhovo-Kobylin's play was finished only four years after Ostrovskii's, and both playwrights therefore referred to more or less the same historical epoch, one might wonder whether Sukhovo-Kobylin, distraught by his exceptional circumstances (he was even imprisoned on more than one occasion), simply overstated his *Case*. Oddly enough, Sukhovo-Kobylin's point of view is supported by the memoirs of the statesman Filipp Vigel′ (1786–1856), although written about an earlier period of time (up to the late 1820s; first made public, in their censored version, in 1863–65) but pointing in the same direction with regard to the evolution of Russian bribery. Vigel′ describes the so-called old generation of bribe-takers (predominant in officialdom before the reforms of Alexander I) as one which would accept petitioners' 'gifts', however small, with gratitude. Moreover, they would never make use of these gifts before the end of a lawsuit, and would return such gifts if petitioners lost their cases. Vigel′ brands the officials in the times of Catherine II 'leeches sucking off the superfluous blood' (Vigel′ 1892: vol. 2, p. 27). A new generation of officials, victims of an increasing demand for luxury and the rapid fall of the currency exchange-rate (that is, of paper to silver roubles), in addition to the atheistic influence of the Enlightenment, has failed to control itself and 'so perfected the art of the unlawful procurement of money, that it could not apparently have been taken any further' (Vigel′ 1892: vol. 2, p. 28).[26]

On the surface, the technique of bribing in the second half of the nineteenth century largely remains the same, especially as far as the private, secretive, almost intimate nature of the transaction itself is concerned.[27] The circle of participants in give-and-take activities is still wide (thus, Danilevskii's policeman names merchants, thieves, Jews, alcohol-sellers and those not having a passport as potential bribe-givers: see Danilevskii 1901: p. 210; judges, district prosecutors, land surveyors and teachers in private schools are listed by the contemporary satirical journals *Iskra* and *Razvlechenie* among bribe-takers: see Kravtsov and Morozov 1932: pp. 109–10, 137, 179, 188). Not only money, but all other types of bribe seem to be welcome and acceptable,[28] including sugar, tea and sausages (see a poem, 'Uezdnyi gorodok' [The Chief Town of the District, not later than 1868], by Dmitrii Minaev [1835–89] in Kravtsov and Morozov 1932: p. 241), as well as coarse cloth for single officials, fine fabric for married officials and oats for those who keep horses (Ostrovskii 1974: p. 58). In an anonymous poem, 'Stanovoi' (The District Police Officer), published in the magazine *Osa* in 1864, the policeman of the title, while carrying out the distraint of an estate, does not balk at taking a tray from the owner of this estate, because that landowner 'was not provident' enough and did not have any cash on him (Kravtsov and Morozov 1932: p. 167). In compliance with the mercenary spirit of the time, however, one can observe a considerable reluctance to take payment in kind (in goods or natural produce) when there is money due. In *The Case*, the sergeant-at-arms Zhivets complains about his business with certain contractors:

> They've got all these places of theirs neatly sorted out, they have. Fine. Well, I come along and take a look, because it's my job to, and what do I see? They almost doubled their profits! Now is that good, I ask you? And what do you think they do then? Send me in a dozen peaches on a tray or raspberries for a holiday table. Well, you be the judge — I served in the army, what's a raspberry to me? I've got children, after all, what good's a raspberry to me?… What am I, a mammal or something? (Sukhovo-Kobylin 1995: p. 138; translation is slightly amended)

Another novelty which seems to emerge as a feature of Russian bribery mainly in the second half of the nineteenth century, in contrast with its first half, is buying favours by recourse to adultery. Let me adduce several examples demonstrating the whole range of attitudes to such action, from hostility to cynicism. In his unfinished novel *Prolog* (The Prologue) written in Siberian exile, Chernyshevskii refers to the end of the 1850s, when the preparation of the peasant reform was in full swing. A fairly liberal project for the liberation of the serfs has to be endorsed by the powerful Count Chaplin, an imaginary character in whom Chernyshevskii's contemporaries could recognize certain features of Count Mikhail Murav′ev (1796–1866), a member of the Chief Committee for Peasant Affairs. To make sure that the endorsement is granted, the author of the project, Savelov (another imaginary character, reminiscent of the Deputy Minister of Internal Affairs, Nikolai Miliutin, 1818–72), is trying to arrange a tryst between the lecherous Count and no other person than his own wife. Savelov's wife flirts with the repulsive Count unwillingly and finally rejects his indecent proposals. The deal is broken and the project is buried. In Kurochkin's poem 'Znaki prepinaniia' (Punctuation Marks, 1859) an old briber is saved from a criminal investigation by his wife and daughters, who were making advances to an unnamed powerful protector (see Kravtsov and Morozov 1932: pp. 50–1). In Chekhov's short story 'Nachal′nik stantsii' (The Stationmaster, 1883) an estate manager finds out that his wife is cheating on him with a stationmaster. Instead of challenging his rival to a duel or filing for a divorce, the estate manager asks the stationmaster to employ his nephew (Chekhov 1975: vol. 2, pp. 272–5). In a short story, 'Zhanr' (Genre), signed by the pseudonym 'Iks' and published in 1892 in *Strekoza* (the humourous magazine in which Chekhov's literary career had begun), a young man catches his wife on a sofa passionately kissing his boss. '"What is this?!" — exclaims the young man. — "What are you doing, wife?!" — "I am obtaining a vacancy in the province for you, my friend!" — answers the wife coldly, rising from the sofa and yawning' (Iks 1892: p. 3).[29]

It is interesting that, although formally satisfying the legal definition of bribery (a criminal offence is committed if the bribe-taker is an official and takes a bribe in return for an action that he has a duty to perform or can perform by the use of his official position: see Chistiakov 1988: p. 276), this particular kind of bribe, to the best of my knowledge, was never considered incriminating in the legal sense[30] but only deemed reprehensible from the moral point of view. This bring us to the question of the relationship of law and morals to bribery, and their methods of dealing with it, as reflected in nineteenth-century Russian literature.

The phenomenon of bribery has always belonged both to the domain of law and to that of morals. Moral judgements have acquired special significance because the law has often been ineffective in bringing bribers to justice. Even for the advanced civilizations of the twentieth century, the substantiation of bribery allegations in court frequently presents a serious problem. Besides, as a modern commentator notes, ‘the frontiers of bribery were always difficult to define: what about the congressman who accepts free hospitality, or the journalist who accepts caviar or free trips abroad? How could such social corruption ever be outlawed in a free society?’ (Sampson 1977: p. 284). For not-so-free societies, such as Russia, the situation was much worse. Whatever methods Russian authorities had tried in tackling bribery, from threatening bribers with the death penalty (Peter I: see Chalidze 1977: p. 231) to more or less leaving them alone (Catherine II: see Matsai 1958: pp. 40–1 and Clark 1993: p. 34), the ‘chronic Russian disease’ (Dmitriev 1869: p. 14) remained incurable. The aggravating circumstances lay in Russian people’s perpetual mistrust of the legal system as such (see Stepanov 1997: pp. 433, 438), in their ineradicable belief that laws in Russia were designed mostly to force people to break them, and then extort bribes from those who had done so for letting them get away with their misdemeanours.[31] Also, Russians found it difficult to appeal about the abuses of law to the perpetrators of these abuses themselves.[32] The candid crook Kandid Tarelkin explains why any complaint to his boss about Tarelkin’s wrongdoings does not stand a ghost of a chance: ‘he’ll simply hand over your petition along with all the others to a secretary. And he’ll say to him, Look them over and make a report [...] you understand [...]. And then the secretary will turn over everything to be checked — to me’ (Sukhovo-Kobylin 1995: p. 113).

This situation eventually led to the embedding of the dichotomy ‘mercy (*milost'*) versus justice (*spravedlivost'*)’ in the Russian collective consciousness. Here I am using Iurii Lotman’s terms as applied to Pushkin's *Kapitanskaia dochka* (The Captain's Daughter, 1836; see Lotman 1988: pp. 119–20). It is hardly coincidental that *The Captain's Daughter* has recently been analysed in the context of the Slavonic tradition of gift-giving (see Bethea 1996: pp. 132–49). According to this view of things, mercy (or *milost'*, for example, pardoning Grinev, who deserted his regiment and sought his enemy's assistance in order to save his fiancée and therefore is formally guilty of treason) is the ultimate (and 'fair') justice which is to be administered not only without any regard to the existing law but, on the contrary, by a direct infringement of it. The opposite action, namely going along with the law (for example, punishing Grinev), would be 'unfair' justice, or *spravedlivost'*. Taken to an extreme, this view resulted in Raskol'nikov's idea that transgression against the law (such as the murder of an old female money-lender) does not necessarily imply transgression against God's truth, but could rather be interpreted as an act of divine justice (see Thompson 1997: pp. 190–204). In effect, this line of reasoning helped to form the basis and the background for the representation of bribery in nineteenth-century Russian literature: if treason and even murder could in theory be justified on grounds which mattered more than the law itself, then why should one arm oneself against bribery?

In a situation where 'laws could not influence customs' (Bulgarin 1990: pp. 24–5), Russian literature was happy to assume the role of a forum for voicing people's opinions about the habitual and omnipresent practice of bribery, ideally with a view to doing away with it. Thus, Zhadov in Ostrovskii's *A Profitable Vacancy* says: 'I will wait for the time when a briber will be more afraid of public opinion than of criminal justice' (Ostrovskii 1974: p. 110). In practical terms, however, the standpoint of Russian literature towards bribery meant very little. Zhadov's uncle, Vyshnevskii, explains to his nephew why his position is unrealistic:

> We don't have a public opinion, my friend, and we cannot have it — not as you understand it, anyway. Here is our public opinion: if you are not caught [red-handed], no one may call you a thief. Society does not care where your earnings come from, as long as you lead a decent life and behave as respectable people should. (Ostrovskii 1974: p. 52)

Whether it was for the reason given by Vyshnevskii, or for some other reason (such as the incoherence of Russian writers' moral stand on the issue, reflecting the hesitancy of the Russian public as a whole), Russian literature did not succeed in uniting Russian society under the banner of war on bribery. In certain instances bribers even privately thanked journalists for their revelations: owing to them, petitioners now knew more about how to do business. In the late 1820s Bulgarin could still speculate in a Utopian reverie that the day would come when 'from the lowest to the highest tribunals, bribe-takers and mischief-makers will no longer prey upon the community' (Bulgarin 1831: vol. 2, p. 292). By the end of the century, however, the realization that bribery was something which one simply could not get rid of had been strengthened and had become unshakeable.[33]

This predicament, whether at the beginning of the nineteenth century or at its end, confronted Russian writers with three main choices: to take bribery in their stride, to shrug it off laughing, or to express their indignation at it. In reality, these choices would often overlap; for example, a philosophical acceptance of bribery and an ironic treatment of it could be combined in the following maxim by 'wise men from the East': 'Try to take from those who do not give, and give to those who do not take, and then you will always be successful in all your enterprises' (Miss Flora 1892: p. 6). Another example of mixed feelings about bribery, this time a combination of laughter and resentment, is *Chicanery* by Kapnist, the work with which I began my survey. It has been noted that the description of human vice in *Chicanery*, while retaining its comic qualities, at times also acquires a tragic angle (see Dmitriev 1869: p. 44).[34]

What seems to unite almost all artistic and semi-documentary images of bribery created between the reign of Paul I and that of Nicholas II, however, is their profound scepticism about the prospects for the moral improvement of Russian society. Although in the denouement of Kapnist's play all the crooks were awaiting punishment, an anonymous reviewer of *Chicanery* did not expect its audience to be particularly appreciative of Kapnist's message. His words, originally printed in 1805, appear to be applicable to the classical period of Russian literature in its entirety, as far as the representation of bribery is concerned:

> This is a mirror in which many people will see themselves if they only care to take a look. Whether it will do them any good is a different question. If only theatrical admonitions could improve our

customs, we would not have sinned at all. Alas, we are so sophisticated that we can easily distinguish dramatic fantasies from our real mission in the world. (Anon. 1805: pp. 374–5)

Notes

1 See, for instance: 'HLESTAKOV: Such a queer thing happened to me: I got regularly cleaned out on the journey. Could you perhaps lend me three hundred roubles? THE POSTMASTER: Certainly, I shall consider it an honour. Allow me, here. I am truly glad to be of service' (Gogol' 1926: pp. 75–6).

2 Some information on the life and work of Kapnist, a friend and a relative of Derzhavin and the father of two Decembrists, Semen and Aleksei, can be found, for example, in Babkin 1960: pp. 12–65; Byrd 1995: pp. 129–34; and Manning 1953: p. 65. See also Edgerton 1971: pp. 551–60; Gromova 1972: pp. 157–62; Lappo-Danilevskii 1989: pp. 49–56; Levin 1980: pp. 410–22; Makhrovskaia 1996: p. 252; Peter 1992; Petrova 1982: pp. 129–47; and Sandell 1974: pp. 19–22. Although first published (and performed on stage) at the end of the eighteenth century, *Chicanery* was banned (and its print run confiscated) by Paul I after the fourth show. The revival of the play was allowed only in 1805, which made it very much a nineteenth-century literary phenomenon. *Chicanery* remained fairly popular throughout that century, republished by A.F. Smirdin in 1849, by A.S. Suvorin in 1884, 1887 and 1889, and by F.A. Ioganson in 1893 (for more detail see Matsai 1958; *Chicanery* is examined from various angles in Drage 1978: pp. 92, 239; Fokht 1983: pp. 36–47; Grannes 1974; Istomin 1894: pp. 75–97; and Vsevolodskii-Gerngross 1955: pp. 423–9).

3 See articles 251 and 252 in chapter N of the 1782 *Ustav blagochiniia* (Code of Propriety), suggesting that bribe-giving, as well as bribe-taking, constitute a criminal offence (Indova 1987: p. 376). This practice had been reaffirmed by the 1845 *Ulozhenie o nakazaniiakh ugolovnykh i ispravitel'nykh* (Statute for Criminal and Correctional Punishment) and abolished only in 1866 (see Chistiakov 1988: pp. 280–1, 396). The 1782 *Ustav* does not specify what the punishment for the bribee should be, as opposed to the one for the briber. It is obvious from the 1845 *Ulozhenie*, however, that bribe-givers were treated more leniently (according to articles 407 and 412 of the *Ulozhenie*, the extortioner could be sentenced to up to eight years of penal servitude, whereas the bribe-giver could only be incarcerated for up to three years, depending on the circumstances). Exactly the opposite was true, at least for a while, of the Soviet legislation on bribery. According to the 1926 Criminal Code of the Russian

Federation, the imprisonment for offering a bribe could be longer than that for accepting one (see Chalidze 1977: p. 233).

4 This and all subsequent translations from Russian into English are mine, unless indicated otherwise.

5 See LeDonne 1984: p. 321; Levitskii 1991: p. 124; and Skalon 1891: p. 345.

6 Kapnist himself admitted that he modelled *Chicanery* on Jean Racine's comedy *Les Plaideurs* (1669) (see Gran 1881: p. 306). This disproves the statement that *Chicanery* 'has no foreign model' (Brown 1980: p. 358). It goes without saying, however, that *Chicanery*'s rather perfunctory 'happy ending' also reflects a typical strategy of Russian satire: one can be as critical as possible about most aspects of Russian life, as long as at the end the higher authorities intervene and put the situation to rights.

7 This song had become so popular that half a century later another prominent Russian playwright who exposed the corruption of Russian bureaucracy quoted it in his own play entitled *Dokhodnoe mesto* (A Profitable Vacancy, 1857; see Ostrovskii 1974: p. 99).

8 A long-awaited reassessment of Bulgarin in Russia has recently begun (see, for example, Reitblat 1990: pp. 73–101; Reitblat 1995–96: pp. 262–70; Rogachevskii 1996: pp. 85–103; for a balanced view of this controversial figure see also Błaszczyk 1980: pp. 15–43; Mocha 1974: pp. 60–209; Monas 1957: pp. 127–47; and Vaslef 1968: pp. 35–43).

9 In his *Mertvye dushi* (Dead Souls, 1842), Gogol′ gives an illuminating description of such a procedure. The transaction of a bribe from a customer (Chichikov) to a clerk (Ivan Antonovich) is conducted so casually and inconspicuously that it may serve as an instruction for generations to come: 'Chichikov, taking out a bank note, laid it down in front of Ivan Antonovich, which the latter failed utterly to notice and instantly covered with a ledger. Chichikov was about to draw his attention to it, but Ivan Antonovich intimated with a notion of his head that there was no need of pointing it out' (Gogol′ 1965: p. 180).

10 According to his foreword to *Ivan Vyzhigin* (in which he makes a respectful reference to Kapnist's *Chicanery*), Bulgarin simply meant to offer a broad and comprehensive picture of 'the current state of [human] vices and oddities and to point [...] at what should be followed and what should be avoided' (Bulgarin 1990: p. 25).

11 In Kapnist's *Chicanery* there is also mention of a priest who enjoys the reputation of being an arch-enemy of bribers while at the same time he is charging left, right and centre 'the living and the dead, for births, christenings, marriages and funeral services, for sins and for repentance'. It is curious that this passage appeared in the first edition

of the comedy but was censored in its 1849 printed version (see Kuntsevich 1906: p. 213).

12 So widespread was the tradition of gastronomic compensation for favours that the widow Felisata Kukushkina in Ostrovskii's *A Profitable Vacancy* had to argue that it was much wiser for an official (especially for a married one) to take cash rather than accept invitations to lunches and dinners, since 'he would return home sober and with the money too' (Ostrovskii 1974: p. 61).

13 With his penchant for the grotesque, Gogol' reduces this feature of Russian life to absurdity when in *The Government Inspector* he makes Osip, Khlestakov's servant, react as follows to the proposal of the provincial merchants who offer several sugar loaves and a basket of wine to Osip's master in hope that he will dismiss their mayor: 'It will all come in [handy] on a journey. Hand me over the sugar loaves and the basket. Give it here, it will all come in useful. What have you there? A cord? Give me the cord too — cord comes in handy on a journey too: if the chaise or anything else breaks down you can tie it up' (Gogol' 1926: p. 89).

14 Compare the following dialogue between Martynych, a lawyer, and Karp Karpych, a secretary in court, about their shady dealings with clients (their conversation takes place at a party; I have retained the 1831 transliteration of Russian names for its charming peculiarity): '"Marteeneetch! You deceived me, you wretch, and let the bear out of my toils. I would not forgive you for an age, if your wife were not my gossip." — "Don't get into a passion; you have given us quite enough of that; if you had had the skinning of the bear, you would not have left us a lock of the fleece. You cannot deny that you are a first-rate hand at gutting petitioners, Karp Karpeetch; at the same time you must not forget that I have also a wife and children to provide for." All the company laughed; "Nobody can deny Karp Karpeetch's skill in gutting", was echoed from all corners. The Secretary proudly turned about in his chair, stroked his head and paunch, and said, with an air of importance, "Why should an experienced tradesman flinch from his business[?]"' (Bulgarin 1831: vol. 1, p. 272).

15 Gogol', for his part, has contributed substantially to this picture. Thus, he pointed out the rule determining that one should extort strictly in accordance with one's rank. In *The Government Inspector*, the mayor tells a policeman off: 'And you mind, now! I know you; you are hand in glove with all sorts of people and slipping silver spoons into your boots — you had better look out, I have a sharp eye! What you have been up to with Tchernyaev, the draper, eh? He was giving you two yards of cloth for your uniform and you walked off with the whole piece! You'd better be careful! You take more than's due to your rank' (Gogol' 1926: p. 24). From *Dead Souls* we also learn that close friends

of the crooked officials do not necessarily have to pay for the services they require. When Chichikov comes to the Administrative Offices to execute his purchase deeds, the Chairman of the Offices suggests: 'And as for the clerks, don't give any of them anything — I beg of you, don't! Friends of mine must not pay' (Gogol′ 1965: p. 183).

16 Here Bulgarin's sarcasm almost gives way to what tends to be a philosophical attitude towards the unlawful procurement of (mis)deeds, common among his fellow countrymen. One of the characters in *Ivan Vyzhigin*, an old merchant, sees no other way of treating bribery than acceptance. He says: 'We must submit patiently to circumstances which we cannot avoid [...]! For instance, if the doors of the house are low, all that would enter, must stoop to avoid knocking their heads. If one spar on a bridge is higher than the rest, every carriage must be jolted on crossing it. Exactly so in some affairs of common life, there are continual abuses which arise from the facility of committing them: neither time, nor laws, nor force, can altogether eradicate them' (Bulgarin 1831: vol. 1, p. 264). Bulgarin's ambivalent feelings towards bribery could be explained, at least partly, by the fact that he himself was repeatedly accused of extorting 'gifts' from merchants for advertising their goods in his widely read newspaper, *Severnaia pchela* (established in 1825; for such allegations see, for example, Koni 1837: p. 81). Documentary evidence of such a practice (Bulgarin's letter to the tobacco merchant V.G. Zhukov of 12 March 1845) can be found in Rogachevskii 1995: p. 82. The following observation by Bulgarin might be viewed as a betraying slip of the tongue: 'No one can count the income of a briber, but everyone is surprised when an author is not begging on the streets' (Bulgarin 1990: p. 356; this passage is omitted in the 1831 English translation of *Ivan Vyzhigin*).

17 To complete the picture, it seems necessary to add that, according to Bulgarin, taking a bribe for supporting a legitimate cause in court in certain instances, paradoxically, was not regarded as an offence. A secretary in the court of law says to Vyzhigin of his rival in a legal row over one million roubles, Countess Nichtozhina: 'Neetchtozyeen offers me five-and-twenty thousand roubles — I confess I am a sinful mortal — I would have taken the money if her cause had been good — but to do wrong I will not take a kopeek [*sic*]. You are not yourself a rich man at present, but when God rewards you, perhaps you will recollect my children.' Vyzhigin comments: 'Although in strict justice much might be said against this sort of honesty, still, looking to things as they are, I was glad that I had met with such a good man' (Bulgarin 1831: vol. 2, p. 270).

18 See, for example, a poem by Vasilii Kurochkin (1831–75), 'Zhaloba chinovnika' (An Official's Complaint), published in the magazine *Iskra*

in 1859. Its lyrical hero, an official, maintains that 'those who wrote [derogatory] articles [for the so-called progressive periodicals], took [bribes] themselves' and hence they have no right to condemn anyone (Kravtsov and Morozov 1932: pp. 51–2). In 1863 the same magazine published a fictional dialogue between an applicant for the vacancy of a newspaper editor and a person in charge of making such appointments. The latter says to the former: 'To be a good editor one needs to be an experienced official first' (Kravtsov and Morozov 1932: p. 143).

19 On this rather neglected author see Gromov 1988: pp. 148–54; Klimova 1981: pp. 68–72; Levin 1890: pp. 154–70; Mikrut 1981: pp. 281–92; and Sviiasov 1981: pp. 170–9.

20 Ostrovskii admitted that he would not have written *A Profitable Vacancy* if he had not worked in court as an official on a six-roubles-a-month salary and had not watched bribery thrive among his colleagues (Ostrovskii 1974: p. 703).

21 To do justice to this issue, it is worth noting that already in *Chicanery* Pravolov laments that in the old times one could at least be sure that if the bribe was given the briber would keep his promises, whereas 'today everybody still takes [bribes] with both hands in the same old fashion, but [the bribe-taker] may go back on the deal if it causes him trouble, and he will pocket your cash anyway' (Kapnist 1849: p. 56). Pravolov's perception testifies to the fact that there is often a tendency to look back to a Golden Age when bureaucrats were allegedly humane and decent. Therefore one can never say for certain if the changing representations of bribery reflect actual social transformation. All one can do is to register such change of representations.

22 I am indebted to Dr Faith Wigzell for bringing my attention to this piece by Leskov.

23 For more on Sukhovo-Kobylin and his ordeals see, for example, Brodiansky 1946: pp. 11–21; Fortune 1982; Grossman 1987; Kleiner 1969; Rassadin 1989; and Rudnitskii 1957.

24 On Sukhovo-Kobylin the playwright see, for instance, Grossman 1940; Kleiner 1961; Koschmal 1993; and Kudriashov 1987.

25 The workings of the tricky mechanism of the worst type of extortion, when the bribe is taken but nothing is given in return, are described by the collegiate councillor Kandid Kastorovich Tarelkin, whose patronymic is meant to remind us of the real briber, the Chief Prosecutor Lebedev: 'First, [Muromskii] paid off through a third party; the third party snatched half of it for himself. Then he started to handle it himself, directly. It was even worse. Whoever he gives it to gets sick; then someone new crops up to take his place — and delivers another judgement' (Sukhovo-Kobylin 1995: p. 96).

26 Vigel' makes a curious note to this distinction between the generations of Russian bribers: 'I know about all that neither from rumours nor

from my own experiences, because I myself have never given anything to anybody and have not taken anything from anyone. One does not have to be too nosy to unfold these mysteries, which are open to everyone' (Vigel′ 1892: vol. 2, p. 27). Although this statement makes Vigel′ quite a partial witness, it should not necessarily discredit his social commentary altogether. Aleksandr Ostrovskii, in his capacity as an official in court, chose the same line of behaviour as Vigel′. He witnessed bribery rather than took part in it himself (see note 20 above), but his play *A Profitable Vacancy* has nevertheless been taken very seriously both by scholars and the public.

27 The following scene from *The Case* is vaguely reminiscent of the episode in *Dead Souls* quoted in note 9 above, since in place of direct statements about the imminent transaction of a bribe, both the briber and the bribee prefer to resort to hints and non-verbal signals. Muromskii's manager, Razuvaev, has to bribe the official Tarelkin for becoming a go-between; he wraps up the money in a piece of paper and says to Tarelkin: 'You dropped a little note, Excellency. TARELKIN (*surprised*): No. What note? RAZUVAYEV (*softly*): Just so, Sir — dropped it. I picked it up this minute. TARELKIN (*feeling about his pockets*): Not at all, my good man; I have no idea what note you're talking about. [...] RAZUVAYEV (*looking Tarelkin hard in the eyes*): What are you upset about, Sir? You dropped it, we picked it up, and (*with emphasis*) please take it! TARELKIN (*recollecting*): Ah — yes, yes, why of course! [...] (*puts the money in his pocket*) Well, with this one we can do business' (Sukhovo-Kobylin 1995: p. 91).

28 Sukhovo-Kobylin suggests the following classification of bribes in Russia: 'there is the *rural* bribe, so to speak, pastoral, arcadian. It is taken mainly in the form of agricultural products and from each according to his mug. [...] Then there is the *industrial* bribe, which is taken out of profit, a contract, or an inheritance, in short out of some acquisition. It is based on the axiom "love your neighbour as you do yourself"; he acquired something — let's divide it up. [...] There is the *criminal* or *snare* bribe. It is taken until there is nothing left to take, until a person is stripped bare! [...] It is carried out under the cover and shade of a dense forest of laws, with the help and by means of the snares, wolf pits, and rods of justice set everywhere throughout the field of human endeavour. And into these pits will fall the old and the young, the rich and the poor, without any regard for sex, or age, or profession, or wisdom or ignorance' (Sukhovo-Kobylin 1995: p. 75).

29 Practically the same plot (a woman starts an affair with her husband's boss because she wants her spouse to be promoted) is used in the short story 'Uzelok i bantik' (A Knot and a Bow) published in the same magazine in 1893 (see Karr 1893: pp. 7–8).

30 With the one possible exception of Soviet Russia in the 1920s. For the genuine debate of the time on whether sexual intercourse constituted a crime in cases of alleged bribery, see Chalidze 1977: pp. 237–8.

31 Compare the Russian proverbs '*Nepravdoiu sud stoit*' ('Courts are upheld by falsehood') and '*Za pravdu plati i za nepravdu plati*' ('You bribe if you're guilty and you bribe if you're not'), registered in Dal′ 1957: pp. 172–3. (Dal′'s collection includes a special four-page-long section called 'Court and extortion'.)

32 Compare the Russian proverb '*Ne boisia suda, boisia sud′i*' ('Don't be afraid of the court, be afraid of the judge'; Dal′ 1957: p. 172).

33 Literary depictions of people who have given up their fight against bribery are not infrequent in the 1850s to 1890s. Thus, in Chekhov's short story 'Prazdnichnye' (Holiday Bonus, 1885), General Bryndin says, when giving a tip to an extortioner: 'I used to struggle against this evil and suffered for it. [...] Evidently it is an invincible evil. Take [the money], take it!' (Chekhov 1975: vol. 3, p. 214). If literary characters stop taking bribes at all, they do so for non-obvious reasons. A satirical poem, 'Torzhestvo dobrodeteli' (The Triumph of Virtue), signed with the initials B.A. and published in the magazine *Razvlechenie* in 1860, tells us the story of a hardened briber who managed to kick his old habit only because he had once forgotten to share his acquisitions with his superiors who, when they found out, took disciplinary action (see Kravtsov and Morozov 1932: p. 178).

34 Vigel′ confesses that he does not understand why Kapnist called his play a comedy: 'both its action and dramatis personae are neither funny nor amusing, but only frightening' (Vigel′ 1892: vol. 3, p. 146).

Bibliography

Anninskii, L. (1996), 'Neistovyi Figliarin', *Novyi mir*, 2.

Anon. (1805), 'Iabeda, komediia v piati deistviiakh', *Severnyi vestnik*, 6.

Babkin, D.S. (1960), 'V.V. Kapnist: Kritiko-biograficheskii ocherk' in V.V. Kapnist, *Sobranie sochinenii v dvukh tomakh*, vol. 1, Moscow and Leningrad.

Bantysh-Kamenskii, D.N. (1847), *Slovar′ dostopamiatnykh liudei russkoi zemli*, part 2, St Petersburg.

Bethea, D.M. (1996), 'Slavianskoe darenie, poet v istorii i "Kapitanskaia dochka" Pushkina' in V.M. Markovich and W. Schmid (eds), *Avtor i tekst: Sbornik statei*, St Petersburg.

Błaszczyk, L.T. (1980), 'Ježovski and Bulgarin: A Case of Plagiarism or Collaboration?', *Polish Review*, 25, 2.

Brodiansky, N. (1946), 'Sukhovo-Kobylin (1817–1903)', *Slavonic and East European Review*, 24, 63.

Brown, W.E. (1980), *A History of 18th Century Russian Literature*, Ann Arbor, MI.
Bulgarin, T. (1831), *Ivan Vejeeghen, or Life in Russia*, trans. G. Ross, 2 vols, London and Edinburgh.
Bulgarin, F.V. (1990), *Sochineniia*, Moscow.
Byrd, C.L. (1995), 'Vasilii Vasil'evich Kapnist' in M.C. Levitt (ed.), *Early Modern Russian Writers, Late Seventeenth and Eighteenth Centuries*, Detroit, MI, Washington, DC and London.
Chalidze, V. (1977), *Ugolovnaia Rossiia*, New York.
Chekhov, A.P. (1975), *Polnoe sobranie sochinenii i pisem v tridtsati tomakh*, Moscow.
Chistiakov, O.I. (ed.) (1988), *Rossiiskoe zakonodatel'stvo X–XX vekov. Tom 6: Zakonodatel'stvo pervoi poloviny XIX veka*, Moscow.
Clark, W.A. (1993), *Crime and Punishment in Soviet Officialdom: Combating Corruption in the Political Elite, 1965–1990*, Armonk, NY and London.
Dal', V.I. (1957), *Poslovitsy russkogo naroda*, Moscow, 1862, reissued with corrections, Moscow.
Danilevskii, G.P. (1901), *Sochineniia v dvadtsati chetyrekh tomakh*, vol. 20, St Petersburg.
Dmitriev, M.A. (1869), *Melochi iz zapasa moei pamiati*, Moscow.
Drage, C.L. (1978), *Russian Literature in the Eighteenth Century*, London.
Edgerton, W.B. (1971), 'Laying a Legend to Rest: The Poet Kapnist and Ukraino-German Intrigue', *Slavic Review*, 30, 3.
Filin, M.D. (1997), *O Pushkine i okrest poeta*, Moscow.
Fokht, T.P. (1983), 'Fol'klorizm komedii V.V. Kapnista "Iabeda"' in D.N. Medrish (ed.), *Russkaia literatura i fol'klornaia traditsiia*, Volgograd.
Fortune, R. (1982), *Alexander Sukhovo-Kobylin*, Boston, MA.
Gogol', N. (1926), *The Government Inspector and Other Plays*, trans. C. Garnett, London.
Gogol', N.V. (1965), *Dead Souls*, trans. B.G. Guerney, New York.
Gran, K. (1881), 'Pis'mo Vasiliia Kapnista', *Rossiiskaia bibliografiia*, 90.
Grannes, A. (1974), *Prostorechnye i dialektnye elementy v iazyke russkoi komedii XVIII veka*, Bergen, Oslo and Tromsö.
Gromov, V.A. (1988), 'Nekrasov i istoriia publikatsii romana G.P. Danilevskogo "Deviatyi val" (1873)', *Nekrasovskii sbornik*, 9.
Gromova, T.N. (1972), 'Istoki dekabrizma i V.V. Kapnist', *Raduga*, 10.
Grossman, L. (1940), *Teatr Sukhovo-Kobylina*, Moscow and Leningrad.
Grossman, L. (1987), *Prestuplenie Sukhovo-Kobylina*, Jerusalem.
Iks (1892), 'Zhanr', *Strekoza*, 46.
Indova, E.I. (ed.) (1987), *Rossiiskoe zakonodatel'stvo X–XX vekov. Tom 5: Zakonodatel'stvo perioda rastsveta absoliutizma*, Moscow.

Istomin, V. (1894), 'Glavneishie osobennosti iazyka i sloga komedii V.V. Kapnista "Iabeda" (1757–1824)', *Russkii filologicheskii vestnik*, 4, part 2.
Jensen, P.A. (1997), 'Some Remarks on the Russian "Antinovel"' in K.A. Grimstad and I. Lunde (eds), *Celebrating Creativity*, Bergen.
Kapnist, V.V. (1849), *Sochineniia*, St Petersburg.
Karr, S. (1893), 'Uzelok i bantik', *Strekoza*, 13.
Kleiner, I. (1961), *Dramaturgiia Sukhovo-Kobylina*, Moscow.
Kleiner, I. (1969), *Sud'ba Sukhovo-Kobylina*, Moscow.
Klimova, L.Kh. (1981), 'Nravstvennoe i istoricheskoe v romane Danilevskogo "Kniazhna Tarakanova"', *Nauchnye doklady vysshei shkoly. Filologicheskie nauki*, 1.
Koni, F.A. (1837), *Tituliarnye sovetniki v domashnem bytu*, St Petersburg.
Koschmal, W. (1993), *Zur Poetik der Dramentrilogie: A.V. Suchovo-Kobylins "Bilder der Vergangenheit"*, Frankfurt am Main, Berlin, Bern, New York, Paris and Vienna.
Kravtsov, N. and Morozov, A. (eds) (1932), *Satira 60-kh godov*, Moscow and Leningrad.
Kudriashov, O.L. (1987), *Teatr A.V. Sukhovo-Kobylina*, Moscow.
Kuntsevich, G.Z. (1906). '"Iabeda", komediia V.V. Kapnista', *Izvestiia otdeleniia russkogo iazyka i slovesnosti imperatorskoi Akademii nauk*, 9, 3.
Kuzovkina, T. (1995), '"Rumianyi kritik moi...": K istorii vzaimootnoshenii Gogolia i Bulgarina', *Russkaia filologiia*, 6.
Lappo-Danilevskii, K.Iu. (1989), 'K voprosu o retseptsii sobytii Velikoi Frantsuzskoi Revoliutsii v Rossii 1790-kh godov: V.V. Kapnist i ego blizhaishee okruzhenie', *Russkaia literatura*, 3.
LeDonne, J.P. (1984), *Ruling Russia: Politics and Administration in the Age of Absolutism, 1762–96*, Princeton, NJ.
Leskov, N.S. (1956), *Sobranie sochinenii v odinnadtsati tomakh*, vol. 1, Moscow.
Levin, Iu.D. (1980), 'Poema Ossiana "Karton" v perelozhenii V.V. Kapnista', *Izvestiia AN SSSR. Seriia literatury i iazyka*, 39, 5.
Levin, S.S. (1890), 'Sovremennye literaturnye deiateli. I: G.P. Danilevskii', *Istoricheskii vestnik*, 4.
Levitskii, A.A. (1991), '"Iabeda" Kapnista: Sotsial'naia satira ili komediia nravov?', *Russkaia literatura*, 2.
Lotman, Iu.M. (1988), *V shkole poeticheskogo slova: Pushkin, Lermontov, Gogol'*, Moscow.
Manning, C.A. (1953), *Anthology of Eighteenth Century Russian Literature*, vol. 2, New York.
Makhrovskaia, N.N. (1996), 'Peterburgskii adres V.V. Kapnista', *XVIII vek*, 20.
Matsai, A.I. (1958), *"Iabeda" V.V. Kapnista*, Kiev.

Mikrut, L. (1981), 'Twórszość G. Danilewskiego: Stan i perspektywy badań', *Slavia Orientalis*, 3.
Miss Flora (1892), 'Izrecheniia vostochnykh filosofov', *Strekoza*, 18.
Mocha, F. (1974), 'Tadeusz Bułharyn (Faddej V. Bulgarin) 1789–1859: A Study in Literary Maneuver', *Antemurale*, 17.
Monas, S. (1957), 'Šiškov, Bulgarin, and the Russian Censorship', *Harvard Slavic Studies*, 4.
Ostrovskii, A.N. (1974), *Polnoe sobranie sochinenii v dvenadtsati tomakh*, vol. 2, Moscow.
Otroshenko, V.O. (1994), *Vedi menia, slepets: Povest' o Sukhovo-Kobyline*, Novocherkassk.
Peter, S. (1992), *Neue Wege in der russischen Literatur an der Wende zum 19. Jahrhundert: Das literarische Schaffen der Dichtergruppe G.R. Deržavin — V.V. Kapnist — N.A. L'vov — I.I. Chemnicer*, Halle (dissertation).
Petrova, Z.M. (1982), 'Epitety v lirike V.V. Kapnista' in Iu.S. Sorokin (ed.), *Literaturnyi iazyk XVIII veka: Problemy stilistiki*, Leningrad.
Rassadin, St. (1989), *Genii i zlodeistvo, ili Delo Sukhovo-Kobylina*, Moscow.
Reitblat, A.I. (1990), 'Vidok Figliarin: Istoriia odnoi literaturnoi reputatsii', *Voprosy literatury*, 3.
Reitblat, A.I. (1995–96), 'Bulgarin i Dubel't' in M.O. Chudakova (ed.), *Sed'mye Tynianovskie chteniia: Materialy dlia obsuzhdeniia*, Riga and Moscow.
Rogachevskii, A.B. (1995), '"Puchina razvrata": Derptskie studenty v dome Faddeia Bulgarina', *Slavic Almanach: The South African Year Book for Slavic, Central and East European Studies*, 3, 3–4.
Rogachevskii, A.B. (1996), '*Persona non grata* russkoi literatury', *Akmeologiia*, 2.
Rudnitskii, K. (1957), *A.V. Sukhovo-Kobylin: Ocherk zhizni i tvorchestva*, Moscow.
Sampson, A. (1977), *The Arms Bazaar. The Companies, the Dealers, the Bribes: From Vickers to Lockheed*, London.
Sandell, T. (1974), 'V.V. Kapnist's Role in Russo-Ukranian Culture', *Study Group on Eighteenth-Century Russia Newsletter*, 2.
Skalon, S.V. (1891), 'Vospominaniia', *Istoricheskii vestnik*, 5.
Stepanov, Iu.S. (1997), *Konstanty: Slovar' russkoi kul'tury*, Moscow.
Sukhovo-Kobylin, A.V. (1995), *The Death of Tarelkin and Other Plays*, ed. and trans. H.B. Segel, Amsterdam.
Sviiasov, E.V. (1981), 'G.P. Danilevskii v literaturnoi polemike nachala 1860-kh godov', *Russkaia literatura*, 4.

Thompson, D.O. (1997), 'The Problem of Conscience in *Crime and Punishment*' in K.A. Grimstad and I. Lunde (eds), *Celebrating Creativity*, Bergen.

Vaslef, N.P. (1968), 'Bulgarin and the Development of the Russian Utopian Genre', *Slavic and East European Journal*, 12, 1.

Vigel', F.F. (1892), *Zapiski*, Moscow.

Vsevolodskii-Gerngross, V.N. (1955), 'Pervye izdaniia komedii V.V. Kapnista "Iabeda" (1798)', *Ezhegodnik Instituta istorii iskusstv*, Moscow.

Wiener, L. (1902), *Anthology of Russian Literature from the Earliest Period to the Present Time*, part 1, New York and London.

Wortman, R.S. (1976), *The Development of a Russian Legal Consciousness*, Chicago, IL and London.

8 Reciprocity and the Soviet Cultural Revolution: The Literary Perspective

Stephen Lovell

Any researcher is grateful for literary sources when investigating the social and cultural history of unofficial and undocumented practices, especially those as stigmatized as bribery usually is. Even when the archives fall silent, novelists can usually be relied on to provide quotable descriptions of dubious goings-on or what will pass for sociological insights. Literature's status as a documentary source, however, should never be taken for granted: the relationship between works of literature and the practices they describe or allude to is by no means straightforward, and it may vary considerably from one period and location to another. Typically complex and variable is literature's interaction with those social norms that deem certain kinds of activity to be 'corrupt' or 'illegitimate'. What concerns me here is one area where new sets of social norms may be proposed, debated or debunked through the medium of literature: namely, social exchange in the context of tightening (or simply changing) legal regulation.

The importance of this theme — and in particular its cultural resonance — has already been recognized by many literary historians of the West. Industrial capitalism has been observed to bring a transformation in the way the human subject is viewed and human relationships are constructed. In much new historicist writing the term 'economy' has accordingly undergone significant

I am grateful to Julian Graffy, Jane Grayson and Catriona Kelly for reading drafts of this chapter.

expansion (or, perhaps more precisely, 'inflation'): it has infiltrated literary studies in the same way that 'politics' did in the 1970s.[1] The capitalist literary hero has been seen as a legal being enmeshed in a network of contractual obligations. The human subject under capitalism, so this argument runs, is caught up in a general shift from 'status' to 'contract', whereby 'traditional' forms of social exchange are brought into line with new notions of legality. Under capitalism, no areas of human activity are exempt from exchange, and all transactions have contractual markers. If capitalist society in theory corresponds to this ideal type, in practice, however, we usually have to deal with societies where old status-based practices and the emerging legal (or contractual) consciousness have a more complex and unresolved relationship; English literature can provide numerous illustrations of this point, from *The Merchant of Venice* to *The Mayor of Casterbridge*.[2]

In a sense, therefore, Soviet Russia in the 1920s encountered a problem that faces any modernizing society: to put social exchange on a sound legal footing and to draw a clear dividing line between 'corrupt' and 'legitimate' activities. But the Soviet case was particularly fraught with difficulties. Above all, this was cultural transformation on a scale and at a speed that no other society had ever had to contemplate. Moreover, the Soviet regime was not distinguished by its tolerance of traditional reciprocity in the period of transition: it was deeply hostile not only to the market, but also to all unregulated forms of exchange. This hostility was most famously expressed in Lenin's assessment of bribery as one of the three 'main enemies' facing Soviet society.

Not only was the Soviet regime confronted with a complex and unwanted legacy of unofficial reciprocal practices, it also had a highly ambivalent attitude to the law. One of the aims of the early Soviet cultural revolution was to instil a new legal consciousness that would inform people's social interaction. In *The State and Revolution*, Lenin argued that the state could wither away only 'when people have become so accustomed to observing the fundamental rules of social intercourse and when their labour becomes so productive that they will voluntarily work *according to their ability*' (Lenin 1992: pp. 86–7; italics in original). A little later in the same chapter, Lenin went into more detail on the ways in which the 'fundamental rules of social intercourse' would combat corruption:

> For when *all* have learned to administer [...] social production, independently keep accounts and exercise control over the idlers, the gentlefolk, the swindlers and other such 'guardians of the traditions of capitalism', then any escape from this popular accounting and control will inevitably become so incredibly difficult, such a rare exception, and will probably be accompanied by so swift and serious a punishment [...] that the *necessity* to observe the uncomplicated basic rules of all human intercourse will very soon become a habit. (Lenin 1992: p. 92)

It is highly characteristic of Lenin that the relationship between the coercive imposition of new social norms and their 'spontaneous' acquisition is here glossed over. Indeed, this slippage reflects a more general Bolshevik attitude to the law: Soviet citizens were to feel that they were legally obliged to behave decently (*kul'turno*), but they were contract-bound to the state, not to each other. Horizontal ties were to be replaced by vertical ones. This objective remained fundamental to Bolshevik legal policy through all the debates of the 1920s and was finally preserved in a weighted synthesis of two contending schools of thought. The first took an instrumental view of law and saw the codification of law as an important step towards the crystallization of central authority. The second held that the new socialist society could do without law altogether. Ultimately, of course, the former position came to dominate, but the influence of the latter did not disappear completely. It can be detected, for example, in the Bolsheviks' striving to create a justice system that was unbureaucratic, informal and accessible, had the authority conferred by legal 'objectivity' and 'fairness', yet remained heavily politicized. Law was to guarantee the stability of social and ethical norms, yet at the same time it was required to keep briskly in step with a rapidly changing political and socio-cultural agenda (Solomon 1996: pp. 1–77).

How, though, does literature relate to the interactions of reciprocity and legal consciousness in early Soviet Russia? There is certainly a relationship of some kind. It is always possible — and, I would argue, necessary — to investigate literature's relationship to the dominant ideologies of the period when it is created.[3] The works of literature that I will examine here vary significantly in their implied attitude to the new Soviet order, but they *all* engage with the prevailing ideological agenda — cultural revolution and the creation of a 'new man'. Indeed, they could hardly fail to do so.

The major preoccupations of cultural revolution — and in particular the cut-and-thrust between undesirable 'old' practices and 'new' legal and ethical norms — pervade early Soviet literature. Writers energetically set about the task of translating the ideology of *kul'turnost'* into a Soviet vernacular. In the process, they liberally dispensed advice and comment on subjects such as: how to square the demands of personal and public life; how to avoid the perils of *meshchanstvo*; what to do if one falls in love with an *intelligent* or *burzhui*.[4] Social exchange, or the politics and morality of giving and taking, was perhaps a less sensationalized theme than consumption and sexual morals, but it is central to several works written at the outset of the Soviet cultural revolution — and nowhere more so than in Aleksandr Tarasov-Rodionov's *Shokolad* (Chocolate, 1922).[5]

Tarasov-Rodionov (born in 1885) was an old Bolshevik with a particular interest in the new socialist legality: he worked as an examining magistrate in the Supreme Tribunal from 1921 to 1924. He enjoyed some success in his literary career in the mid-1920s, but by the end of the decade he had fallen out of favour and was duly 'repressed' in 1938. *Chocolate*, his best-known work, first appeared in the journal *Molodaia gvardiia* in 1922 and was reprinted several times in book form during the 1920s. Looking back from the vantage point of 1928, one critic commented that *Chocolate* was 'the first work of post-revolutionary literature that provoked a broad social and literary discussion' (El'sberg 1928: p. 231). It offers a more interesting commentary on the struggle for cultural revolution than any of Lenin's shrill pronouncements on corruption, because it problematizes the very concept of 'bribe'.

Corruption was one of the few areas where the Bolsheviks took a legal stand almost immediately after coming to power: as of mid-1919, the Bolshevik criminal law defined only 'political', 'service' (*dolzhnostnye*) and 'economic' crimes (Solomon 1996: p. 24). According to Bolshevik mythology, Party members in the Civil War remained fanatically devoted to an ethos of revolutionary self-denial and incorruptibility. The hero of *Chocolate*, Zudin, fits this model perfectly: he is a hard-working ascetic who refuses to ask for extra rations even when his own children are malnourished (and even though his duties in the Cheka entitle him to them). He aims for nothing less than ethical self-perfection, a striving which is reflected in his sententia 'The enemy is within us'.

The first episode of the story brings Zudin into contact with an ex-bourgeoise, the ballerina Elena Val′ts. This is the height of the Civil War, and Zudin is investigating a suspected White conspiracy. He eventually realizes that Val′ts is slow to provide evidence not because she herself is involved in the conspiracy, but because she is reluctant to enter into details of her love-life (she has had affairs with a couple of the main suspects). When she finally admits to being a 'fallen woman' and expresses the desire to earn a decent living, Zudin employs her to do some filing at the Cheka; Zudin is, after all, conducting a struggle for *all* those dispossessed by capitalist exploitation — even the dregs of the bourgeoisie.

Val′ts proves an efficient secretary, and rises somewhat in the esteem of Zudin. Moreover, she quickly finds herself on good terms with Zudin's wife. When Val′ts receives a substantial quantity of chocolate as a present from an long-standing English admirer of hers (who turns out to be a spy), she gives a couple of bars along with some stockings as a gift to Zudin's wife and children. This is done without Zudin's knowledge, and when he finds out he is dismayed, exclaiming that 'It looks like a bribe!' But while this is certainly not a wholly disinterested gift, neither is it a bribe: there is no question of any direct reciprocal arrangement. Zudin grudgingly lets it pass.

Shortly afterwards, however, Val′ts's operations become much more ambitious. She notices an old friend of hers on the list of those imprisoned by the Cheka awaiting sentencing. She visits his family and tries to extort twenty pounds of gold for his release. When she is found out and arrested, Zudin finds himself deeply implicated in all Val′ts's wrongdoings: it looks as if he has accepted bribes from his secretary and then abused his position by sending her to extort money from the families of those whose lives are in his hands. His position is rendered still less tenable by the semi-public (though unsuccessful) attempts Val′ts has made to seduce him. When Zudin is hauled in for questioning by his comrades, he has to admit that his experiment in social reconditioning has failed:

> I thought that an honest job would help to bring her to her feet as a human being, and would help her to shake off the cobweb of the despicable bourgeois mode of life. But apparently I made a mistake. Chocolate proved stronger. (Tarasov-Rodionov 1932: p. 196)

Zudin realizes the circumstantial evidence against him is strong, but attempts none the less to set the record straight at the revolutionary tribunal.

Before he does this, he is tormented by chocolate-related nightmares. In one, a peasant shares his last piece of bread with Zudin, but the bread does not fit in Zudin's pocket because it is already stuffed with an enormous piece of chocolate. In another, a riot in a capitalist chocolate factory ends with the workers forgetting their thoughts of revolution and fighting each other for pieces of chocolate. Finally, Zudin visits a cocoa plantation to encourage a slaves' rebellion against their masters. But the slaves too discover chocolate in Zudin's pocket, and he is lynched.

The conclusion, here drawn by the hero in an unconscious state, is clear: Zudin, despite his impeccable intentions, has compromised himself beyond repair — and this just at the time that Socialist Revolutionaries and Mensheviks are calling for the Cheka to be disbanded. His accusers are inclined to believe his story, but still sentence him to execution because of the exigencies of the moment. The oldest and wisest of them observes that the masses would be right to be outraged by Zudin's behaviour: 'Did he take the chocolate? He did! Now try and *prove* that it wasn't a bribe!' The accusation of bribery will always stick in people's minds 'because age-long want has made them suspicious about such things' (Tarasov-Rodionov 1932: pp. 259, 289).

Chocolate invites suspicion of all gifts — and especially those that seem to be free. Accepting a gift is an action that may be construed in ways entirely outside the recipient's control (especially when — as in the case of chocolate — that gift symbolizes just about everything that the recipient stands *against*). It is telling that, in *Chocolate*, bribery is linked to several other areas of cultural insecurity — notably sexual etiquette and *meshchanstvo* (petit-bourgeois mentality) — all of which were avidly explored by other Soviet writers of the 1920s.[6] Elena Val′ts could stand as the anti-hero of the cultural revolution: a female member of the 'bourgeoisie' with an uncontrollable sexual appetite, a taste for creature comforts and a penchant for extortion. Val′ts's gift of chocolate, along with its exceptionally undesirable cultural baggage, serves to remind us that all such 'transactions' are symbolically marked in some way.[7] Zudin epitomizes the Bolsheviks' desire to escape potentially contaminating traditional forms of exchange. For him, revolutionary 'purity' is quite literally dearer than human life.[8]

Chocolate had considerable impact in the first half of the 1920s. To a large extent this was for stylistic reasons: Tarasov-Rodionov was consciously trying to combine party-mindedness and civil-war subject matter with language and plot-manoeuvres more characteristic of the pre-revolutionary potboiler. The critic Aleksandr Voronskii was not alone in finding this too much to take: in his judgement, Tarasov-Rodionov's 'high-flown style[,] characteristic of a cheap novel', was 'quite unbearable' (Voronskii 1923: p. 303). I would suggest, however, that contemporary critics found Tarasov-Rodionov's style upsetting not because he was a particularly inadequate exponent of literary melodrama: it was rather the case that the crime novel/potboiler genre seemed somewhat incongruous when used to tell a story where legal and moral right and wrong are so ill-defined.

The moral haziness of the work was noted by contemporary critics. Most reviewers were dismayed by the extreme self-immolatory conclusion of *Chocolate*. To imply that a revolutionary had to act like a 'mystically inclined Jesuit [...] a kind of fanatical martyr' was, in the opinion of one commentator, to stretch a point (Pravdukhin 1923: p. 218).[9] Given that his ideals were at such variance with those of his party-minded literary peers, it is not surprising that Tarasov-Rodionov quickly became disillusioned with the course taken by the Soviet regime in the 1920s. He was not the only one, of course. Several works of the period expressed misgivings about the moral decline attendant upon the NEP. Il'ia Erenburg's early romanticized commitment to the revolutionary cause had wavered by the mid-1920s. In his novel *Rvach* (The Grabber, 1924) a cruel and ambitious young Bolshevik, Mikhail Lykov, is all too easily drawn into the world of corrupt trading operations. For all the narrator's efforts to disclaim his hero as an aberrant individual, Erenburg clearly intended Lykov to be representative of one part of his generation: those unscrupulous and upwardly-mobile young 'proletarians' for whom *spekuliatsiia* of various types was a natural and profitable career move after their early revolutionary activism. As Lykov admits to his brother Artem (who is an exemplary Bolshevik):

> We're all grabbers. That's the way our generation is, it's out for what it can get. Back in October 1917 we wanted to tear down the stars from the sky, there was 'the happiness of mankind' and all that. But it didn't work out, we had to make do with cash. (Erenburg 1964: p. 288)

Those characteristics — energy, willpower, directness — which in Zudin may seem admirable, lead the impulsive and self-serving Lykov inexorably into the high-living *demi-monde* of the NEP. Lykov was just one of many 'negative heroes' in the literature of the time. Erenburg was joined by Leonov, Aleksei Tolstoi and other 'loyal' (or semi-loyal) writers in exploring or bemoaning the social and psychological anomie of the time. It is even justified to speak of a whole 'literature of protest', concentrated mainly in the years 1925–27, which pointed out just how much work remained to be done in the cause of cultural revolution and in the forging of the 'new man'.[10]

The growing pains of *homo sovieticus* were nowhere more tellingly evoked that in the stories of Mikhail Zoshchenko. This writer, traditionally seen as a brilliant but primarily 'social' satirist, has been paid much more attention in recent scholarship as an explorer of human insecurity, as the 'poet of a mistrustful and hopeless quest for calm, protection, law, and order'.[11] Of course, as this last comment implies, the general phenomenon of human insecurity took very particular forms in early Soviet Russia. All interpretive schools — from the sociological to the psychoanalytical — have drawn attention to the concept of *(ne)kul'turnost'* in Zoshchenko's stories and the discomfort (even anguish) that it causes his protagonists. Zoshchenko's hero is typically unable to behave 'correctly', and hence stumbles into one embarrassing and painful social situation after another: he is a 'man who does not know how to live'.

Let us take a closer look at this *neumenie zhit'*. As any existentialist would argue, the 'authenticity' of the human subject always has to be compromised when that subject becomes a social actor. All human beings mould themselves according to the explicit or tacit rules of their social environment; correspondingly, all social situations require a particular set of skills, an etiquette. Social rules may on occasion, however, be hard both to identify and to assimilate. In Zoshchenko's stories of the 1920s, people constantly find themselves in situations where an old code of reciprocal obligation is no longer felt to be appropriate (or enforceable), but where no satisfactory new set of norms has replaced it. Several of Zoshchenko's narrators voice hostility to all forms of pre-revolutionary *uslovnost′* (conventions): in 'Meshchanstvo' (Petit-Bourgeois Mentality, 1925), for example, the lecherous narrator makes a self-serving argument in favour of free love; in 'Kitaiskaia tseremoniia' (A Chinese Ceremony, 1924) the ritual of handshaking is held up to scorn (but still found to be indispensable).[12] Other narrators and protagonists are caught between old norms and new habits. In 'Akter' (The Actor, 1925), the central character finds that a thief fails to observe the convention that creates and maintains a distinction between the theatre and real life. Theft (*vorovstvo*) — or the absolute negation of reciprocal *uslovnost′* — is the constant and overriding fear of Zoshchenko's protagonists.

But it is not only the absence of *uslovnost′* that causes trouble in Zoshchenko's stories. It is just as often the case that different and conflicting kinds of *uslovnost′* are recognized by the various parties in a social situation. In 'Ne nado imet′ rodstvennikov' (Having Relatives Is Not a Good Idea, 1924), a tram conductor finds that his duties prevent him from meeting his obligations to a relative (that is, from giving him a free ride). In a number of stories the cold light of economic profit and loss is shone on 'hospitality', an area of social activity where, according to Soviet self-mythologization, giving is always disinterested. The narrator of 'Stakan' (The Glass, 1925) unsuspectingly arrives at a memorial lunch for a recently deceased acquaintance; but when he cracks a glass the widow and the other guests raise such a scandal that he is forced to leave; subsequently he is made to pay for the glass by court order. In 'Gosti' (Guests, 1927) the hosts fear (with good reason) that their guests will steal food and household items. In 'Khozraschet' (Self-financing, 1927), the hosts openly begin totting up the cost of the food they are serving their guests; by the time they have finished their calculations, the guests have all got up and left.[13]

Many of Zoshchenko's characters worry about money, and not just because they are struggling to make ends meet. Money is the most fundamental symbol of norm-based (as opposed to custom-based) exchange. If the parties to an exchange can agree on what an object or a service should cost, they must have more in common than just a currency: they also understand how the currency operates and believe that it is underwritten by something more than the other party's word. The use of money makes any transaction less personal, but increases the individual freedom of each actor (Simmel 1990). Money has the effect of extending the scope of a good deal of human interaction and undermining microcosmic areas of human reciprocity, and by doing this it also threatens to objectify (or fetishize) human relations.[14]

For these very reasons, money is a source of profound insecurity for Zoshchenko's heroes: the opportunity to spend money freely leads the inexperienced Soviet shopper into unpromising transactions; and, since money is such an impersonal currency, there is no one from whom to seek retribution if the rate of exchange (of cash to goods or services) is found to be disappointing. In 'Beda' (A Misfortune, 1923) a peasant who has saved up for two years to buy a horse finds to his dismay that his new acquisition is 'worth' no more than one drinking spree on his way home to the village. In 'Aristokratka' (An Aristocratic Lady, 1923) the narrator does not understand that, in order to enjoy an evening out with a 'lady', one needs not only to procure theatre tickets, but also to pay for her to eat her fill of cake. In 'Priskorbnyi sluchai' (A Deplorable Incident, 1926) the drunk protagonist launches a vain attempt to recover his entry fee when ejected from a cinema. In 'Tsarskie sapogi' (Tsar's Boots, 1927) and 'Baretki' (A Pair of Women's Shoes, 1927) Soviet citizens have unhappy shopping experiences. Foma Kriukov (in 'Foma nevernyi' [A Doubting Thomas, 1924]) takes suspicion of money to an extreme: when he sees that a new five-rouble note does not have a picture of the Tsar, he cannot believe that it is not a forgery. But Zoshchenko's narrators would still have us believe that a world where money's role is ill-defined is better than one where everything — including civility — can be bought and sold. In 'Khamstvo' (Boorish Behaviour, 1928) a friend of the narrator cuts short a trip to Western Europe because he receives consistently hostile service in all hotels; he later discovers that he has been marked out for such treatment because of his reluctance to give tips.

In addition to these stories, which reveal the potential of money for causing humiliation and discomfort to those who do not understand how it functions, there are a number of others which suggest the destructive powers of money in general. Many of these stories were written and first published quite early in Zoshchenko's career, but they were revised and brought together in the first section of *Golubaia kniga* (A Skyblue Book, 1935). In this work Zoshchenko explicitly aims for more than a satirical portrayal of NEP society: instead, by combining episodes from world history with his own observations of Soviet society, he claims to be writing a 'history of human relations'. He divides his research into five main areas: 'Money', 'Love', 'Treachery', 'Failures' and 'Amazing Events'.

Together with his earlier stories, Zoshchenko's *A Skyblue Book* raises a question that is crucial for the present discussion. Namely: to what extent does his work simply offer withering (and witty) criticism of the existing state of affairs, and to what extent does it aim to suggest new norms by (albeit negative) example? Or alternatively: where does Zoshchenko's work stand relative to the Bolshevik cultural revolution? These questions may seem naive, but I hold that they are nevertheless necessary, because they draw attention to a tension between description, irony and prescription that is present in varying forms in all Soviet satire. There is no doubt that Zoshchenko quite genuinely detested the *nekul'turnost'* he so often evoked in his stories, but he was rather less consistent in implying that something could actually be done to eliminate it. In *A Skyblue Book*, the *skaz* narrator of so many of the earlier stories is largely replaced by an authorial and would-be didactic voice. At times, of course, this didacticism is severely undercut by the comic impact of the material, and by the suspicion that the author, by employing a more subtly marked form of speech than *skaz*, is satirizing 'authorial' discourse itself. But the ever-present hint of irony should not lead us to overlook another intonation persistently present in Zoshchenko's literary 'voice': a yearning for humanity to be better than it is at present.[15]

The *skaz* stories are rather different in the way they mix these intonations. Here we find not only satire of *nekul'turnost'* but also radical deformation of the discourse ('cultural revolution') that was intended to do battle with *nekul'turnost'*. Zoshchenko's heroes are truly 'new people' — their values and especially their language are quite different from anything we find in pre-revolutionary literature — but not at all in the sense intended by the Bolsheviks. The very characters who engage in undesirable social practices have internalized the rhetoric of cultural revolution. Perhaps the most famous case of this kind is the story 'Meshchanstvo' (mentioned above), but further striking illustrations can be found in stories pertaining directly to bribery. 'Slabaia tara' (Not Properly Sealed, 1932) begins with a number of strikingly upbeat assertions: we learn that 'these days people don't take bribes [*nynche vziatok ne berut*]', and that 'people's characters have taken a major turn for the better [*kharakter u liudei sil'no izmenilsia k luchshemu*]' (Zoshchenko 1989: p. 217). The rest of the story undermines these bold opening statements by revealing just how superficial the claimed improvements in human nature are.[16] An official at a rail station feigns outrage when a short-sighted citizen, misinterpreting a gesture he makes, brazenly (and automatically) offers him a bribe to accept a parcel even though it is 'not properly sealed'. After a lengthy and theatrical outburst, the official directs the miscreant to a man located just round the corner, who is conveniently equipped with hammer and nails for strengthening the packaging. When the narrator's turn to hand over his parcel comes, however, he discovers that the wielder of the hammer charges an extortionate fee for his services and shares the proceeds with the official.[17]

Zoshchenko's work is subversive of the Soviet cultural project not because it exposes 'abuses' within Soviet society, but because it reveals the problems facing *any* such willed transformation of long-standing values and practices. Even if they are aware of cultural imperatives from 'above', Zoshchenko's protagonists try (often unsuccessfully) to make their own rules in life and especially in language. This striving is particularly noticeable in stories that pertain to reciprocity, an area of social interaction which is highly symbolic and whose linguistic evaluation may vary enormously from one speaker to the next. Zoshchenko shows (sometimes, it would appear, in spite of himself) that the language of cultural revolution, far from introducing transparency into human relations, can make them even more confused. The word *vziatka* may not figure in the vocabulary of Soviet functionaries, but the practice to which it refers, far from disappearing, has merely been verbally and operatively repackaged.

It is clear enough that the major source of literary representations of bribery will be satire. But literary satire, as Zoshchenko's works have shown us, cannot be treated straightforwardly as an exposé of social malpractices informed by a sense of moral outrage, which is how the ancients would have it:

> Like the Senecan tragic mode, satire, in its historical origin as Roman *satura*, proceeds from a sense that the basis of social order, law, is eventually abandoned by that same order, leaving the expectant yet disillusioned citizen with hollowness at heart and rage in the brain. (Snyder 1991: p. 98)

Most modern readers would agree that current notions of satire have retained some common ground with this description. Over the past few centuries, however, notions of social 'order' have greatly diversified, as have the narrative means to criticize this order and the standpoints taken up by the satirist and his implied audience. Satire remains at some level a critique, but it is by no means guaranteed to affirm an alternative to an existing — flawed — state of affairs, or even to express any confidence that the aberrant present can be put right. The effect of satire is often to parody an authoritative discourse, without 'authorizing' a substitute discourse (Palmeri 1990: ch. 1). Rather than allegorically hinting at a fundamentally 'right' order of things, satire may simply luxuriate in irony for its own sake. The distinctive rhetoric of satire may be put to several different ends — inquiry, provocation, display and play — and not simply moral or social polemic (Griffin 1994).

These conclusions are further borne out by the most celebrated satirical novel of the Soviet period — Il'f and Petrov's *Dvenadtsat' stul'ev* (The Twelve Chairs, 1928). This novel, for all the roguishness of its main character, Ostap Bender, presents a surprisingly benevolent account both of his actions and of NEP society in general.[18] Indeed, recent research has suggested that the publication of *The Twelve Chairs* in the journal *30 dnei* in the first half of 1928 owed a great deal to the fact that, unlike so many other novels of the period, it did not present the moderately free market of the 1920s with deep foreboding. *The Twelve Chairs* was approved for publication in the pivotal year of 1927, at a time when Stalin and Bukharin were fighting against Trotskii and his Left Opposition. This novel proved, *pace* Trotskii, that there was no turning back to the past, and that the NEP was nothing to worry about.[19]

Perhaps it was these political considerations that gave Il'f and Petrov the freedom to compose what has often been called an encyclopedia of Soviet Russian life. They were further assisted in this endeavour by the particular mode of satire that they employed. *The Twelve Chairs* belongs to the subgenre of *plutovskoi roman* (a specifically Russian version of the picaresque novel), which by definition offers an unusually full and frank view of unofficial social practices. These insights are achieved thanks to the special position taken up by the main protagonist. The resident *plut* (approximately *picaro*) is spared the social and ethical responsibilites and scruples of his victims; he comes from outside the various groups with which he comes into contact. And, in fact, he may on occasion seem a good deal more sympathetic than these groups, in which case the *plutovskoi roman* gains an added satirical charge.[20]

In *The Twelve Chairs*, Bender's special extra-societal status makes him a penetrating (if sometimes unwitting) commentator on the shady practices that interest us here. His *kombinatsii* lay bare the workings of social exchange in a fictional microcosm of Soviet Russia, where reciprocities are shown to be a way of life. This is apparent not so much in actual descriptions of bribery and *blat* in action, but rather in the *expectations* of characters who engage in such practices. It is thanks to these expectations that Bender is able to be such a successful *moshennik* (swindler). Bribery and *blat* are regulated by largely tacit understandings, they are not underwritten by guarantees; if one of the parties wilfully fails to recognize their obligations, these obligations cannot be enforced. For example, the bureaucrat Korobeinikov unwisely neglects to take money up front for divulging to Bender information from the inventory of expropriated furniture to which he has monopolized access (Il′f and Petrov 1997: pp. 125–32). A few minutes later, *he* is the one who does not fulfil his obligations, as he charges the hapless Father Fedor fifty roubles for false information.

The various unofficial 'transactions' that are conducted in *The Twelve Chairs* (bribes, *blat*, deception, theft, blackmail)[21] are generally placed in some kind of legal context. As Bender insists to Vorob′ianinov: 'But let's have no criminality. We must observe the [Criminal] Code [*No i bez ugolovshchiny. Kodeks my dolzhny chtit′*]' (ibid., p. 251) Bender's reference to the text of the Criminal Code very accurately reflects his priorities: he is able to make use of the letter of the law without showing much concern for its spirit, to exploit the authority conferred by law without being burdened by any of its responsibilities. This is a topos of the *plutovskoi roman*; indeed, the literary *plut* may be defined as someone who continually gets something for nothing by manipulating the forms of social conduct (including legal relations) while failing to observe their content. The authority of an imposter is underpinned, first, by the permanently guilty conscience of those whom he encounters and, secondly, by the very vagueness of the law he is supposed to be representing. Bender is invariably able to seize the initiative in his dealings with people by identifying and homing in on their weaknesses. In the case of Al′khen, the deeply corrupt (and perpetually ashamed) head of Starsobes (the Stargorod social security office), Ostap is able to obtain a free lunch by means of a veiled threat to expose his host's nepotism. Later, when offered a ten-rouble note as he leaves, he reminds Al′khen that, according to the Criminal Code, it is an offence to offer a bribe to an official while he is carrying out his duties. But here, as elsewhere, Ostap is able to continue enjoying a bogus legal authority while retaining the option of ignoring the law: he takes the money.[22] Similarly, he tries to force the satirical writer Iznurenkov to acquiesce in the theft of his chair by invoking the law: 'The law must be observed! [*Zakon nado sobliudat′!*]' (ibid., p. 281). Iznurenkov has himself resisted an earlier attempt (by Vorob′ianinov) to steal the chair by claiming (unfounded) legal support for his actions: he maintains that, for a writer, a chair is a 'means of production' and hence not subject to requisition (ibid., p. 254).

Thus, in the world inhabited by Ostap Bender, the law is not a set of ground rules for human relations, but rather a store of useful formulas that can be selectively quoted or partially rewritten to suit any situation. The subordinate position of the law relative to the practical realities of social exchange is most strikingly suggested at the auction where the two treasure-hunters hope to claim all the remaining chairs at one fell swoop. Amongst the earlier lots are two matching bronze figures depicting justice (*pravosudie*); they go for a total of seventeen and a half roubles (ibid., pp. 229–30).

In Il′f and Petrov's follow-up novel, *Zolotoi telenok* (The Golden Calf, 1931), Ostap Bender retains both his respectful attitude to the Criminal Code and his determination to get rich quick. Now, however, these aims prove more often to be incompatible. Bender does not engage in quite so many small-scale deceptions, but rather devotes his energies to one major project — the blackmail of that rare creature, a Soviet millionaire. Whereas in *The Twelve Chairs* Ostap was able to prey on gullibility, rapaciousness, social insecurity and a host of other human weaknesses, in *The Golden Calf* he uncovers shady operations that the reader will more readily and unequivocally identify as 'corrupt'. Or, to put it another way, the situations described in *The Twelve Chairs*, however absurd or extreme they may be, are presented as profoundly 'normal' (in the sense that people will always be apprehensive of a visit from a *revizor*), while in *The Golden Calf* they represent deviations from ethical norms. For example, it is not 'normal' for state employees to embezzle money from their organizations in order to go on all-night drinking sprees (as they do in the provincial town of Arbatov);[23] it is also quite wrong for someone to exploit the catastrophic economic situation of the Civil War in order to make a fortune (as the millionaire Koreiko has).[24] As a more direct reminder of the Criminal Code, we learn that the members of Bender's entourage (the *antilopovtsy*) have all had brushes with the law. Abuses and malpractices which in *The Twelve Chairs* seemed amusing evidence of human weakness *en général* are here framed rather differently — as 'corrupt' activities (although they remain amusing). Dishonesty is now called a *dolzhnostnoe prestuplenie*; campaigns in the Soviet workplace aim to do away with the 'conspiracy of silence and backscratching [*zagovor molchaniia i krugovaia poruka*]' (Il'f and Petrov 1961: p. 51). Polykhaev, the most corrupt bureaucrat of all those featured in the novel, draws up a list of resolutions which includes 'an intensification of the struggle against bureaucracy, red tape, nepotism and toadying [*usilenie bor'by s biurokratizmom, volokitoi, kumovstvom i podkhalimstvom*]' (ibid., p. 222).[25] If in *The Twelve Chairs* corruption was *ad hoc* and faintly farcical, in *The Golden Calf* it has put down roots in institutions.

In a sense, therefore, *The Golden Calf* would appear to be a rather more orthodox piece of Soviet satire than its authors' earlier effort in this genre. The ending of the novel, where the new millionaire Bender finds that in Soviet society he can do nothing with his outrageous (and outrageously acquired) wealth, seems overtly to reinforce socialist values. Il'f and Petrov's selective mastery of the idiom of Soviet *zakonnost'* should not, however, lead us to conclude that their satire in *The Golden Calf* is narrowly focused on the corrupt 'enemies' of the First Five-Year Plan. Throughout the novel the authors maintain an ironic distance from the official language used to identify and categorize corruption. In particular, they demonstrate a characteristic literary sleight of hand by fudging the distinction between moral and Soviet normative categories, a technique which has the remarkable effect of making their work both ideologically sound and also extremely ambiguous. For example, the officials at Gerkules are about to be purged *and* (but not *because*) they embezzle funds and take bribes: the real reason is that their class allegiance (that is, family history) has come under suspicion. Another striking juxtaposition of this kind comes at the very beginning of the novel, when Ostap stumbles across a network of charlatans spread across the Soviet provinces, each pretending to be a son of the revolutionary hero Lieutenant Shmidt. The activities of this would-be *pluto*cracy are described in terms of a microcosmic labour market and are regulated by a special 'convention' according to which each 'son' gains his own territory; while the form of these operations is amusingly reminiscent of exploitative capitalist corporations, their content, however, is most definitely the nascent Soviet version of the age-old Russian *kumovstvo* (nepotism).

If *Chocolate* sets out the agenda of cultural revolution, and *The Golden Calf* offers an upbeat yet surprisingly ambiguous progress report, Bulgakov's *The Master and Margarita* provides a nice coda to the theme of reciprocity in early Soviet Russia. In *The Master and Margarita*, Woland and his entourage are generous in the gifts they bestow on official figures. These unofficial transactions are amusingly accompanied by nods in the direction of a legal culture: at every stage of the preparations for the Variety Theatre show contracts are signed and letters are sent. In the first such episode, the groggy director of the theatre, Stepa Likhodeev, is solicitously offered a shot of vodka and a few *zakuski* to get over a hangover. His mysterious visitor waves away his attempt to pay for the breakfast spread. A more striking example is the aggressive gift-giving of Korov'ev in the scene with Nikanor Ivanovich Bosoi of the Housing Committee. Bosoi, like any well-trained 1930s bureaucrat, is extremely nervous of not doing things strictly by the book. All his reservations are to no avail, however: he has money positively foisted on him. In a witty role-reversal, the bribee is persuaded by the briber that he 'deserves' a backhander; still more ironically, Korov'ev does this by referring to the norms of behaviour in the West, which always provided the *étalon* for Lenin's cultural revolution (and numerous earlier Russian attempts at behaviour regulation):[26] 'We don't do this sort of thing but foreigners do.' Bosoi is then unfairly branded a 'sly rogue' (*vyzhiga i plut*) by Woland and framed so cruelly that the phone call Korov'ev makes to inform on him prompts one of Bulgakov's striking narratorial interjections: 'And with that the scoundrel hung up' (Bulgakov 1967: pp. 117–18).

The fate of Bulgakov's bribee highlights one of the laws of reciprocity: exchanges with office-holders can function efficiently and invisibly in a stable environment, but the moment conditions change, they become extremely risky for both parties. The rules governing reciprocities in the 1930s were unstable and practically unknowable: many real-life bureaucrats must have felt as bewildered and defenceless as Bulgakov's Bosoi when they were accused of corruption.[27] These complexities were not registered in mainstream Soviet literature of the same period, which thoroughly re-inscribed human relations so as to eliminate conflict between public and private forms of exchange and stigmatize unregulated, non-'collective' reciprocity. Small social networks were depicted as conspiratorial. Transparency in human interaction was considered a quite attainable goal; opacity was reserved for villains.[28]

But the socialist realist tradition of the subsequent thirty years was by no means restricted to a single social philosophy: it veered from extreme egalitarianism to Prometheanism; if in one Five-Year Plan it would tend to give centre-stage to the politically conscious loner (or 'positive hero'), in the next it might accord greater prominence to idealized forms of social solidarity (the 'Great Family', or *Gemeinschaft* Stalin-style); it was capable of rapidly reorientating itself 'from a horizontal, undifferentiated ordering of reality to a vertical, hierarchical ordering' (Clark 1981: p. 136). Not only that, the socialist realist novel could on occasion register tension between instructions from above and local initiative. Vera Dunham, in her study of Soviet novels of the late 1940s, has argued that many of the literary products of late Stalinism reveal 'the dilemma [...] of a horizontal action challenging vertical controls' (Dunham 1976: p. 161). Activities that people engaged in within their collective and regarded as natural and necessary might conflict with instructions from further up the administrative hierarchy, or indeed with the law. Soviet writers of the 1940s were, of course, obliged to resolve this tension and to show that private initiative could be fully reconciled with the public good.[29] It is highly typical of the Russian cultural tradition that, when conflict was registered between bureaucracy and local practices, writers tended to come down in favour of the latter by accusing administrators and managers of 'formalism'.[30] In the 1940s the administrative fixer who knows how to fulfil the plan gains ever-greater literary prominence (relative to rule-bound bureaucrats and revolutionary 'idealists') until he becomes one of the main topics of discussion in the Thaw of the mid-1950s.

What socialist realism generally *failed* to recognize, however, was that conflict between vertical and horizontal planes of social life generally could not be resolved by the intervention of an enlightened Party worker, or by an improbably achieved consensus within a collective (or between collective and Party hierarchy). It was rather the case that categories drawn from the 'vertical' axis of social life could, when introduced along the 'horizontal', cause lasting misunderstanding, tension, conflict and unhappiness. This observation, and in particular its implications for forms of reciprocity in Soviet life, are explored in much post-socialist-realist literature, and they receive a particularly concentrated treatment in Trifonov's *Obmen* (The Exchange, 1969). This story is structured around the tension between two clans: the hero's own family (the Dmitrievs) and that of his wife (the Luk′ianovs). The Dmitriev grandfather is of good revolutionary stock (and, significantly, he received a pre-revolutionary legal education). His Old Bolshevik values are reflected in, for example, his horrified reaction when he hears that his grandson Vitia has offered a shop assistant a fifty-rouble bribe to put a radio to one side. Vitia's mother shares this disengagement from the world of practical give-and-take. She embodies (rather self-consciously) the ideal of selfless giving: disinterestedness (*beskorystie*) is the bedrock of her moral universe. The Luk′ianovs, on the other hand, are 'people of a different breed: they know how to live [*liudi drugoi porody — iz umeiushchikh zhit′*]'. Their *savoir-faire* encompasses all areas of the shortage economy: they know how to make the right contacts, and how subsequently to use those contacts; how to initiate and maintain the informal exchange of favours that is the only way of obtaining certain goods and services and of getting on in general.[31]

The meaning of Trifonov's story cannot be reduced to a polemic with either of the above ethoses (disinterestedness and *umenie zhit′*). In *The Exchange*, 'exchange' is not simply a question of *byt*, but rather a telling metaphor for the whole Soviet experience. This is a world where trust between people has broken down, where transactions too often have to be underwritten by human dignity. Emblematic in this respect is Ivan Vasil'evich Luk'ianov, the character most attuned to the reciprocal workings of Soviet society, whose high administrative position has been bought at the cost of one heart attack, constant aggravation and uncertainty in his career and a resultant deep distrust (*nedoverie*) of other people. *The Exchange* reminds us that, even in the 'mature' Soviet system, bribery and *blat* cannot be cheerfully relativized as 'things that everyone does'; these activities may not have a constant moral meaning, but they always have a moral context.

Conclusion

By dealing with other people we make ourselves vulnerable; but there is no other way to live. This general truth is particularly applicable to Russia, where human interaction has had to contend with vague, unstable or simply meaningless legal norms; 'knowing how to live' was a skill that by no means every Soviet citizen could straightforwardly and painlessly obtain. The cultural revolution of the 1920s tried to overcome this problem, not by using the law to protect Soviet citizens against official abuses and against each other, but rather by inculcating a new legal consciousness which would enable all Soviet citizens to identify certain activities as anti-social or corrupt, and hence to refrain from engaging in them. The ultimate aim was quite simply to introduce absolute transparency into human relations.

Literature of the early Soviet period engaged with this project by showing the new Soviet man striving to achieve such clarity in his dealings with other people. Cultural revolution was in this sense mapped onto literature — but the relationship between the two remained uncertain for all that. Even when literature is invoked as a normative force (as was the case, to varying degrees, with Tarasov-Rodionov, Zoshchenko and Il'f and Petrov), it may end up frustrating our desire for ethical certainties, drawing attention instead to the specific problems of each situation, to the complex meaning and moral content of human actions. Giving is an area of human activity to which meaning is especially likely to be ascribed, but which, in the absence of secure customs or legal regulation, is apt to generate a great deal of ambiguity. The hero of early Soviet literature is quite often unable to understand the intentions of his partners in various reciprocal transactions; and even when he does achieve this insight, he is unsure whether the transaction is right or wrong (or simply fails to ask such a question).

In the 1920s, the Soviet literary protagonist had to work much harder than subsequently to find a viable social ethos, and in the process he would on occasion do violence to the discourse of cultural revolution — by, for example, re-marking its key terms (*meshchanstvo*, *nepman*, *burzhui*, *vziatochnichestvo* and so on) to suit his own denotative or connotative purposes. In the 1930s, by contrast, the literary hero was able to set his sights on the *telos* of a social consciousness that harmoniously reconciled his life in the collective with 'higher' ideological principles and did not admit linguistic — or any other — ambiguity. For his Soviet literary predecessors, and for real Soviet people, 'knowing how to live' tended to come at a much higher price.

Notes

1 According to A.R. Veeser, one of new historicism's five central 'assumptions' is that 'new economics demand a new poetics' (Veeser 1992: p. 19).
2 Further examples can be sought in American literature, which registers a persistent conflict between 'the individual's need for freedom and society's need for order provided through rule by law' (Thomas 1987: p. 7). For the broader (3,000-year) context, see Noonan 1984.
3 This point holds only if we agree to think of 'ideology' not as 'a discursive superfluity that runs alongside literature but in a different and shallower channel', but rather as a set of 'complex and sensitive paradigms around and within which the priorities of a particular genre can be seen to be organized' (Simpson 1982: pp. xvi, xviii). For more reflections in this theoretical vein, see Thomas 1991: pp. 151–78.
4 These themes are treated at length in the following: Panteleimon Romanov's *Novaia skrizhal'* (The New Commandment, 1927) and *Tovarishch Kisliakov (Tri pary shelkovykh chulok)* (Comrade Kisliakov [Three Pairs of Silk Stockings], 1930) and Sergei Semenov's *Natal'ia Tarpova* (1928).
5 Tarasov-Rodionov himself defined the genre of *Chocolate* as *fantasticheskaia povest'*, a designation which is revealing both of the upheaval of literary norms in the 1920s and of the problematic nature of the work in question.

6 Ideologies that seek to regulate sexual behaviour and those that censure certain types of reciprocity often have a great deal in common, because they share notions of impurity and corruption (see Noonan 1984: pp. 700–2).
7 On the varying cultural acceptability of different forms of bribery, see Simmel 1990: pp. 384–9.
8 Although Zudin is tormented by thoughts of compromising confectionery, he expresses no remorse after ordering the summary execution of 100 prisoners.
9 When Tarasov-Rodionov's *povest'* was adapted for the Malyi Theatre in the 1960s, Feliks Dzerzhinskii was inserted as a *dramatis persona* in order to save Zudin from the firing squad. In this version, Zudin's death sentence was seen as an unqualified wrong that had to be righted (see Makliarskii 1968).
10 Besides Erenburg, note the following examples: S. Malashkin, *Luna s pravoi storony* (The Moon from the Right Side, 1926) and P. Romanov, *Bez cheremukhi* (Without Cherry Blossoms, 1926), both of which caused a minor sensation through their treatment of Soviet sexual morality; A.N. Tolstoi, 'Vasilii Suchkov (Kartiny nravov peterburgskoi storony)' (Vasilii Suchkov [Scenes of the Morals of the Petersburg Side], 1927), a lurid tale of psychological cruelty and wife murder; L. Leonov, *Vor* (The Thief, 1927), where the 'thief' of the title is a socially dislocated Bolshevik. For a detailed account of public discourse on sex as an expression of early Soviet cultural anxieties, see Naiman 1997.
11 A. Zholkovsky, 'Mikhail Zoshchenko's Shadow Operas' in C. Kelly and S. Lovell (eds), *Russian Literature, Modernism and the Visual Arts* (forthcoming from Cambridge University Press).
12 On the codes of reciprocal obligation underlying the practice of handshaking, see Brook Thomas, 'The Construction of Privacy in and around *The Bostonians*' in Veeser 1992: pp. 161–85.
13 A contrasting treatment of the same theme is 'Nashe gostepriimstvo' (Our Hospitality, 1932), where the unquestioning hospitality of a peasant family is regarded as inadequate compensation for the head of the household's wilful refusal to join the kolkhoz.
14 These problems were noted in early Soviet debates on money, which actually follow a similar pattern to the discussion of law: see Kurdiumov 1983: pp. 120–4. Resistance to 'fetishization' is of course central to Marxism and, before that, to Romanticism: here we find a telling example of the linkages that can exist between literary and socio-political 'ideologies' (for elaboration of this point, see Simpson 1982).

15 The extreme case of this kind is *Istoriia odnoi zhizni* (The Story of a Life, 1934), where a prisoner on the White Sea–Baltic Canal project comes to recognize the benefits of corrective labour.

16 The story was republished as part of *A Skyblue Book* (in the section 'Kovarstvo' [Treachery]), but here, significantly, the blithe opening remarks were omitted.

17 A similar example is 'S luny svalilsia' (Off Another Planet, also 1932), which purports to be a progress report on cultural revolution. In the first paragraph we learn that 'People don't steal much. And they don't take bribes at all. It looks as if the satirist will soon have to watch his pen go rusty [*Voruiut malo. I vziatok vovse ne berut. Priamo pero satirika skoro nebos' zarzhaveet*]'. In typical Zoshchenkovian style, the narrator immediately undercuts this bold statement: 'People don't take bribes, but they do on occasion accept money [*Vziatok ne berut, no den'gi v drugoi raz poluchaiut*]' (Zoshchenko 1989: p. 222). He then sets about explaining this fine distinction by telling two cautionary tales of his own experiences of booking into Soviet hotels.

18 The question of the precise attitude to NEP society taken by the authors of *The Twelve Chairs* has proved extremely controversial (see, for example, Kurdiumov 1983: pp. 9–34). For another work of the late 1920s which provides a commentary on social exchange under the NEP (and which also focuses on the circulation of furniture around the Russian provinces), see Boris Pil'niak's 'Krasnoe derevo' (Mahogany, 1929).

19 For more on the circumstances of the novel's initial publication, see M. Odesskii and D. Fel'dman's introduction to their new and 'complete' edition of *The Twelve Chairs* (Il'f and Petrov 1997). The novel's strangely muted initial critical reception is interpreted in Kurdiumov 1983: ch. 3.

20 For more on the *plutovskoi roman* and Bender's social 'non-involvedness' (*nevovlechennost'*), see Shcheglov 1990: pp. 34–49. Bender's uncanny ability to engage the reader's sympathies was registered with dismay by the first Soviet critics of *The Golden Calf* (see Kurdiumov 1983: pp. 112–13). For a valuable longer-term view of the Russian picaresque, see Jurij Striedter's study of the pre-Gogolian *plutovskoi roman* (Striedter 1961).

21 In *The Golden Calf* Ostap speaks of his 'four hundred relatively honest means of removal [of money] [*chetyresta sravnitel'no chestnykh sposobov ot"ema*]' (Il'f and Petrov 1961: p. 31).

22 For the episode in the headquarters of Starsobes, see Il'f and Petrov 1997: pp. 93–104. Of course, Ostap's familiarity with the Criminal Code hints at his own murky past.

23 Embezzlers were a much-loved subject of 1920s satirists: the best-known example is Valentin Kataev's *Rastratchiki* (The Embezzlers, 1926).
24 The theme of fortunes made illicitly during the period of revolution and civil war figures in other works of early Soviet literature, for example A.N. Tolstoi's *Pokhozhdeniia Nevzorova, ili Ibikus* (The Adventures of Nevzorov, or Ibikus, 1924) and L. Nikulin's *Vremia, prostranstvo, dvizhenie* (Time, Space, Motion, 1933) (see Shcheglov 1991: p. 439).
25 These phrases correspond closely to those used in the purges of cadres in 1929–30: see Shcheglov 1991: pp. 434–8, 507.
26 See C. Kelly, *Refining Russia: Gender and the Regulation of Behaviour from Catherine to Yeltsin* (forthcoming).
27 We have seen in *The Golden Calf* how widely and loosely the rhetoric of the anti-corruption campaign of 1929–30 could be applied.
28 The most telling illustrations of these points are to be found in novels which describe the transformation of deeply rooted social structures in the Soviet village: see, for example, the first part of Sholokhov's *Podniataia tselina* (Virgin Soil Upturned, 1960).
29 See for example Dunham's discussion of Galina Nikolaeva's novel *Zhatva* (The Harvest, 1947) (Dunham 1976: pp. 124–8).
30 See Irina Davydova's chapter in the present volume for more on the long-standing hostility to bureaucracy fostered by a Russian intellectual tradition that was highly influential in the Soviet period.
31 The works of Solzhenitsyn — especially *The First Circle* — are likewise a rich source of information on these networks of favours and contacts. For still later literary accounts of the *blat*-ridden Soviet system, see Vasilii Aksenov's *Bumazhnyi peizazh* (Paperscape, written in 1982 in emigration, set mainly in Moscow in 1973) and Il'ia Shtemler's *Univermag* (The Department Store, 1980).

Bibliography

Bulgakov, M. (1967), *The Master and Margarita*, trans. M. Glenny, London.

Clark, K. (1981), *The Soviet Novel: History as Ritual*, Chicago, IL and London.

Dunham, V. (1976), *In Stalin's Time*, Cambridge.

El'sberg, Zh. (1928), '*Fevral'* A. Tarasova-Rodionova', *Oktiabr'*, 5.

Erenburg, I. (1964), *Sobranie sochinenii v deviati tomakh*, vol. 2, Moscow.

Griffin, D. (1994), *Satire: A Critical Reintroduction*, Lexington, KY.

Il'f, I. and Petrov, E. (1961), *Sobranie sochinenii v piati tomakh*, vol. 2, Moscow.

Il'f, I. and Petrov, E. (1997), *Dvenadtsat' stul'ev*, Moscow.

Kurdiumov, A. (1983), *V kraiu nepuganykh idiotov: Kniga ob Il'fe i Petrove*, Paris.
Lenin, V.I. (1992), *The State and Revolution*, trans. R. Service, London.
Makliarskii, M. and Rapoport, K. (1968), *Vysshaia mera...*, Moscow.
Naiman, E. (1997), *Sex in Public: The Incarnation of Early Soviet Ideology*, Princeton, NJ.
Noonan, J.T. (1984), *Bribes*, New York.
Palmeri, F. (1990), *Satire in Narrative: Petronius, Swift, Gibbon, Melville, and Pynchon*, Austin, TX.
Pravdukhin, V. (1923), 'Literatura o revoliutsii i revoliutsionnaia literatura', *Sibirskie ogni*, 1–2.
Shcheglov, Iu. (1990), *Romany I. Il'fa i E. Petrova: Sputnik chitatelia*, vol. 1, *Wiener Slawistischer Almanach*, Sonderband 26, 1, Vienna.
Shcheglov, Iu. (1991), *Romany I. Il'fa i E. Petrova: Sputnik chitatelia*, vol. 2, *Wiener Slawistischer Almanach*, Sonderband 26, 2, Vienna.
Simmel, G. (1990), *The Philosophy of Money*, trans. T. Bottomore and D. Frisby, 2nd edn, London.
Simpson, D. (1982), *Fetishism and Imagination: Dickens, Melville, Conrad*, Baltimore, MD and London.
Snyder, J. (1991), *Prospects of Power: Tragedy, Satire, the Essay, and the Theory of Genre*, Lexington, KY.
Solomon, P.H. (1996), *Soviet Criminal Justice under Stalin*, Cambridge.
Striedter, J. (1961), *Der Schelmenroman in Russland: Ein Beitrag zur Geschichte des russischen Romans vor Gogol'*, Berlin.
Tarasov-Rodionov, A. (1932), *Chocolate*, trans. C. Malamuth, New York.
Thomas, B. (1987), *Cross-Examinations of Law and Literature*, Cambridge.
Thomas, B. (1991), *The New Historicism and Other Old-Fashioned Topics*, Princeton. NJ.
Veeser, H.A. (1994), *The New Historicism Reader*, New York and London.
Voronskii, A. (1923), 'Literaturnye zametki', *Krasnaia nov'*, 1.
Zoshchenko, M. (1989), *Izbrannoe*, Moscow.

9 *Blat* in Stalin's Time

Sheila Fitzpatrick

Blat is the Russian term for an unofficial system of exchange of goods and services based on principles of reciprocity and sociability. A subject of considerable interest to the sociologists of the 1950s Harvard Interview Project (Bauer, Inkeles and Kluckhorn 1959: ch. 8), *blat* re-emerged as a focus of scholarly attention in the Brezhnev period, when it became part of the discussion of corruption and the 'second economy' in the Soviet Union and other Communist systems (Grossman 1977; Millar 1985; Kornai 1992; Los 1990). Writing in the mid-1980s on China, with explicit comparative reference to the Soviet Union, the sociologist Andrew Walder noted the 'rich subculture of instrumental-personal ties through which individuals circumvent formal regulations to obtain official approvals, housing, and other public and private goods controlled by low-level officials' (Walder 1986: pp. 6–7). *Guanxi*, the Chinese equivalent of *blat*, is the subject of an important recent anthropological work by Mayfair Yang (1994). This was followed by Alena Ledeneva's (1998) pioneering sociological study of *blat* in late Soviet and post-Soviet Russia, based largely on interviews conducted in 1994–95.

In Ledeneva's formulation, 'blat should be considered as the "reverse side" of an overcontrolling centre, a reaction of ordinary people to structural constraints of the socialist system of distribution — a series of practices which enabled the Soviet system to function and made it tolerable, but also subverted it' (Ledeneva 1998: p. 3). Its origins, accordingly, lie in the Stalin period, specifically in the 'Great Break' at the end of the 1920s and early 1930s which established the new economic order and the institutional structure that remained more or less intact until the end of the Soviet era. It was with the 'Great Break' that the Soviet state became a quasi-monopolist in the distribution of goods and services. From the very beginning, the new official distribution system, based on central planning and bureaucracy, had its unofficial *Doppelgänger*, the *blat* system based on personalistic contacts and off-the-record deals.

As Janos Kornai points out, perpetual shortage was an endemic and systemic feature of Soviet-type systems (Kornai 1980, 1992). *Blat* was a function of chronic shortages: as one former Soviet citizen expressed it in the early 1950s, 'If there were adequate goods, there would not be any need for people to drink together and do things for each other. They do it because the amount of goods available is not adequate.'[1]

The Brezhnev-period discussions of the second economy usually linked *blat* practices with the furtive resurgence of an underground capitalist economy. Yet *blat* relationships were not really capitalist at all: they involved favours done for 'friendship', not for money; and their 'capital', as Ledeneva puts it, was the acquaintances 'accumulated throughout one's biography (family connections, school mates, army service and work colleagues, hobby partners, neighbours)'.[2] Even in 1994–95, with capitalism above ground and in some respects flourishing in post-Soviet Russia, Ledeneva reported that her respondents almost universally expressed great dislike of interpretations that portrayed *blat* in a purely commercial, instrumental light. They stressed that *blat* relations were based on friendship and a generous desire to help others. 'If the principles of blat were recorded in terms of participants', one Harvard Project respondent commented ironically, 'they would likely coincide with the Moral Code of the Communist, the most important principle of which was "One is a friend, comrade and brother to another"'.[3]

The present chapter is an essay in historical sociology on the *blat* practices of the pre-war Stalin period. The primary data come mainly from the bound volumes of Harvard Project interviews conducted with Soviet DPs and refugees in Germany and New York at the beginning of the 1950s.[4] In their standard interview, the Harvard researchers asked a series of questions designed to elicit information on *blat* and patronage practices. While Harvard Project respondents were even more skittish about *blat* than those in Ledeneva's study, tending to punctuate their responses with knowing smiles and giggles when they pronounced the risqué word, their answers provide a wealth of information on *blat* in pre-war

Soviet society that has not been systematically analysed, with the exception of Joseph Berliner's fine studies of *blat* and *tolkachestvo* in industry (Berliner 1954 and 1957). In contrast to Berliner, my main interest is in *blat* as an everyday-life practice and form of sociability.[5]

* * *

In 1940, a concerned citizen, Petr Georgievich Gattsuk of Novgorod, wrote to Andrei Vyshinskii, deputy chairman of the Council of People's Commissars, deploring the phenomenon of *blat*:[6]

> The word *blat* has appeared in the lexicon of the Russian language. I cannot literally translate that for you, since perhaps it comes from some kind of foreign word. But still in Russian I understand it well and can give an exact literal translation. In translation into the Russian language the word *blat* means swindling, cheating, stealing, speculation, slipshod practices, and so on. And what does it mean if we meet the expression: 'I have *blat*'[?] It means that I have a close connection with a swindler, speculator, thief, cheat, toady, and similar.

The citizen without *blat*, Gattsuk argued, was effectively disenfranchized.

> Not to have *blat*, that's the same thing as having no civil rights, the same as being deprived of all rights. [...] Come with a request, and they will all be deaf, blind, and dumb. If you need [...] to buy something in a shop — you need *blat*. If it's difficult or impossible for a passenger to get a railroad ticket, then it is simple and easy *po blatu* [by *blat*]. If you live without an apartment, don't ever go to the housing administration, to the procurator's, but better to use just a little *blat* and you will at once get your apartment.

Blat undermined planned distribution in the socialist economy and was 'alien and hostile to our society', Gattsuk concluded. Unfortunately at the moment it was not punishable by law. Gattsuk recommended that it be made a criminal offence with its own specific penalties. (Vyshinskii, a lawyer by training and inclination, or someone in his office, underlined this passage.)

Gattsuk was not alone in thinking that without *blat*, Soviet life was impossible. 'The key-word, the most important word in the language, was blat', wrote the British journalist Edward Crankshaw of the late Stalin period.

> It was impossible, without the necessary blat, to get a railway ticket from Kiev to Kharkov, to find accommodation in Moscow or Leningrad, to purchase a new valve for a wireless set, to find a man to mend a hole in the roof, to obtain an interview with a Government official [...]. For many years [*blat*] was the *only* way to get what was needed. (Crankshaw 1959: pp. 71–2)

Nor was Gattsuk unusual in treating *blat* as a pathology, something alien to the society, something that was essentially criminal. In 1935, the authoritative Soviet dictionary identified the word '*blat*' as 'thieves' jargon' for crime or theft, adding that the new colloquial vulgarism *po blatu* meant 'by illegal means' (*Tolkovyi slovar'* 1934). Respondents in the post-war Harvard Interview Project, distancing themselves as much as possible from both the word and the practice, described *blat* as 'a coarse Soviet term', 'a word that arose from the people and will never get into literature', 'a word that is derived from an abnormal way of life', and apologized for using it ('Excuse me, but I will have to use some Soviet jargon').[7] *Blat* was much the same thing as bribery, said some; *blat* was the same thing as *protektsiia* (protection, patronage).[8] Euphemisms for *blat* abounded: 'blat means acquaintances [*znakomstvo*]'; 'blat [...] in polite society was called "letter z" for "znakomye" [friends]'; *blat* is the same as 'Zis', which is short for *znakomstvo i sviazi* (acquaintances and connections).[9]

Blat may be defined as a system of reciprocal relationships involving goods and favours which, in contrast to patronage relationships, involve equals and are non-hierarchical.[10] As the participants perceive these relationships, their basis is friendship, even if money sometimes changes hands. Thus, from the participants' standpoint, the Russian proverb 'One hand washes the other' (*Ruka ruku moet*), which is the equivalent of our 'You scratch my back, I'll scratch yours', is a rather crude parody of the genuine personal regard and good feeling associated with *blat* transactions. A better representation (from the participants' standpoint) is another proverb reported by one of the Harvard Project respondents: 'As they say in the Soviet Union, "One must have not 100 rubles but 100 friends."'[11]

Involvement in *blat* was a necessity for almost everyone and almost a sport for some, writes Vladimir Andrle, one of the few social historians to have paid serious attention to the phenomenon.

> A sturdy pair of shoes, a meal in a restricted-access canteen, a holiday in a sanitorium, a place on a higher education course, a joyride in an official limousine, a jump forward in the housing queue — everything that was obtainable under administrative auspices was also obtainable, and generally believed to be often obtained, by the manipulation of personal contacts. It [was] difficult for a person who had some kind of official authority or a physical access to a scarce resource to refuse personal consideration of friends and acquaintances. [...] The belief that the world moved by personal string-pulling was widespread, and the incentives to try it strong [...]. (Andrle 1994: pp. 200–1)

Many Harvard Project respondents denied that they personally had *blat* dealings. But even those who made such categorical statements frequently related what were essentially *blat* episodes in their own lives (getting a job or a promotion through personal connections) in other parts of the interview,[12] remarked that life in the Soviet Union without *blat* was impossible, or repeated the aphorism '*Blat* is higher than Stalin' or '*Blat* is higher than Sovnarkom'.[13] The *blat* transactions that the Harvard respondents reported in their own lives (usually not calling them *blat*) had a multitude of purposes: for example, to get false identity documents[14] or residence papers;[15] to get into college;[16] to get a job or a better work assignment;[17] to get the materials to build a dacha.[18] Large numbers of reported *blat* transactions had to do with acquiring clothes and shoes ('I [...] had a friend who worked in a warehouse and I got clothing through her';[19] 'I knew someone working at a shoe factory, a friend of my wife's, and thus I managed to get shoes cheaply, and of good quality').[20] A Leningrad engineer reported that he had 'friends, contacts' in stores through whom he got furniture and other goods.[21] Another respondent reported that his family's *blat* connections were so extensive (his father worked in a co-operative and they had relatives in a kolkhoz) that 'we always had everything. The suits were expensive, although you could get some at government [that is, state, low] prices. We only had to stand in line for shoes, because we had no friends working in shoe stores.'[22]

Though *blat* was not generally considered a proper subject for public discussion, the humorous journal *Krokodil* published a number of cartoons on such topics as university admissions, medical certificates and getting places in good vacation resorts and restaurants. 'How come, friend, you are so often ill?' — 'I know a doctor', reads the caption of one cartoon.[23] Another cartoon shows a guest and a doctor talking on the balcony of a posh resort hotel: 'I have been on holiday here for a month and I still haven't once seen the director', says the guest. 'Do you really not know him? Then how did you get a room in the hotel?'[24] The *blat* theme is also present in a cartoon entitled 'Good acquaintanceship is a token of success', showing the writer Lev Tolstoi leaning out of the frame of his portrait to offer his novel *War and Peace* to some students. The caption explains: 'You may not resort to any acquaintanceship [that is, use any *blat*] to get into college, but you absolutely must make our acquaintance!'[25]

Respondents who admitted practising *blat* almost always used the language of friendship and stressed the human element in *blat* relations. 'Friends' were very important in the Soviet Union because they 'help' one another, said one woman who clearly had extensive *blat* relations. Answering a hypothetical question about what she would have done if she had a problem, she painted a picture of a warm, mutually supportive network of family, friends, and neighbours: 'My relatives [...] had friends who could have helped me [...]. One [...] was the head of a big trust. He often helped and if he needed help in turn, he would also come. He was our neighbor [...]. One relative was a chief engineer in a factory. He could always help people if he was asked.'[26]

A former engineer who became essentially a *blat* professional as procurements agent for a sugar trust used the word 'friend' constantly: 'I make friends easy and in Russia, without friends, you cannot do a thing. I had some important Communists as my friends. One of them advised me to go to Moscow where he had a friends [*sic*] who was just made head of the construction of new sugar plants [...]. I went to talk to him and, over the almighty glass of vodka, we became friends.' It was not only his bosses he made friends with, but also the supply officials out in the provinces with whom he dealt: 'I asked the manager to have dinner with me and filled him with vodka. We became good friends [...]. This ability of mine to make friends and get the necessary supplies was greatly appreciated by my boss'.[27]

Drinking was very important as part of the male *blat* relationship. With the respondent quoted above, drinking together and the establishment of friendship were inseparably linked; moreover, the drinking was clearly, at least sometimes, related to conversation 'from the heart', as in his first conversation with his future boss in the sugar trust, who felt out of his depth in his job and confided that 'only a couple of years ago, he did not even know what sugar was made of'.[28] True, this respondent sometimes described this drinking in more instrumental terms: 'usually it works', he noted in passing after describing one vodka-and-friendship session; 'after a few glasses of vodka, I talk him into [...]'.[29] Other respondents who were less involved in *blat* did the same, repeatedly saying that the way to get something or solve a problem was to take a bottle of vodka to someone who could help.[30] But the vodka was not just a gift, it had to be drunk together before the deal was cut — hence the term 'sharing a bottle' (*sobutyl'nichestvo*) applied to *blat* transactions.[31]

Vodka was not part of female *blat* transactions, which were usually conducted with other women, at least as reported by Harvard Project respondents. Many of these transactions involved direct contact with a woman friend whose husband had influence. Answering the question 'Did you have connections?', a woman gynaecologist said 'Yes, for example, the husband of the director of the gynaecological section was in the city department of health, and I managed to arrange several things for myself through her.'[32] Another respondent reported getting a job in an Institute 'only because the wife begged her husband [the Director] to give it to [me].'[33]

Family connections were often cited as sources of *blat*. 'I had friends in the Army who knew my family and they interceded for me';[34] 'I got into the Narkomat [People's Commissariat, that is, Ministry] of railroads [...] because my cousin was a director of an institute and he arranged it.'[35] A kulak's son got false documents through a chance meeting with a man who came from the same village as his parents.[36] This *blat* transaction, like many others, actually involved a chain rather than a direct connection: the man with whom the kulak's son had *blat* had, in his turn, *blat* with the president of a village soviet who could issue identity documents. Similarly, when a recent graduate from an agricultural college wished to get his job assignment changed, he did so through friends who were able to mobilize a relative working in the Commissariat of Agriculture.[37]

There was a fine line between *blat* and bribery. 'Bribe and blat are the same thing really', said one Harvard Project respondent, a peasant worker in his late twenties.[38] 'Look, blat and vziatka [a bribe] are not very different', said another respondent of similar age and social background. 'Blat means that we help each other out. Not simply that I pay you for it.' This same respondent drew a distinction between *blat* as a relationship and bribery as an act: 'Blat is a general and constant thing. Vziatka may be done just once but blat goes on continuously.'[39] Another drew the following distinction: 'Blat is the use of acquaintances, and a bribe you can give to someone whom you do not even know.' This respondent, however, a bookkeeper, noted that he had never encountered 'bribery in its open form' in the Soviet Union, only the kind of *blat* bribery that required an approach through acquaintances.[40]

Some respondents, former members of the Soviet élite, thought bribery was quite easily accomplished. A former trade and finance official said: 'You can do it quite easily if you have the money by inviting people to your home as guests, giving them something to drink and then talking about the case. Also a little package containing 100 ruble notes can be slipped under somebody's desk to great effect.'[41] 'It was nothing to pay a bribe of 42,000 rubles to secure an apartment in Moscow', claimed a newspaper photographer who had moved in high-society circles. 'I took bribes quite easily. Anything can be secured for money anywhere.'[42] (Yet this claim was undermined by the photographer's later admission that 'my lodgings were always very bad, always, despite money and connections. I was never able to find anything comfortable'.)

Other respondents emphasized the difficulty of giving a bribe. 'It was very dangerous to give a bribe because you had to be certain that the bribe would be accepted', a woman teacher said. 'You had to know to whom to give it, and how to give it, that is not directly.'[43] Another respondent confirmed that 'you had to give a bribe indirectly through a third person'.[44] In the opinion of a third respondent, senior officials could only be bribed by someone of comparable social status: a factory director or party secretary 'would not take a bribe from a lathe operator, but if he is an engineer or employee they would take it'.[45] A similar premise underlay the advice of one young worker on how to influence a judicial case: 'You must give money [...]. Not directly to the procurator but to a defense attorney and he will do it through the procurator.'[46]

Obviously *blat* had its dangers, especially when money changed hands and the transaction could be classified as bribery. 'It is very dangerous [...]. You may be tried in court for it', was a typical comment.[47] But even where cash was not involved, some people perceived *blat* dealings as risky. 'It was easy for me to go to the factory to get food or anything else', a former factory director told the interviewers, 'but this was dangerous. Once I were to get food from somebody it meant that I was selling myself to him. I would have to pay him back [...]. He could take advantage of this.'[48] A journalist noted danger of a different kind: 'If you have a friend, that's good, but if tomorrow he is arrested, that is bad. Because when your friend is arrested, you also get into difficult straits. The police are not only interested in him, but in his friends as well. When Yagoda was arrested, so were those with whom he had connections'.[49]

Blat professionals — later known as *blatmeisters*, though the term is anachronistic for the 1930s — played an important role in the informal system of distribution. You could solve a problem, one Harvard respondent said, if you were acquainted with some 'professional "blatniks"', 'persons who have contacts with higher persons and know the Soviet system. They know who can be bribed or presented with a gift, and what this gift should be.'[50] Such people were the subject of a humorous verse by the popular poet Vasilii Lebedev-Kumach, published in *Krokodil* in 1933 under the punning title '*Blat*-book'. The '*blat*-book' was the notebook in which you kept all the telephone numbers and addresses of your *blat* connections, plus cryptic notations: 'Peter's buddy (sanatorium)', 'Sergei (records, gramophone)', 'Nik. Nik. (about grub)'. This 'secret code' told you how to get expert help ('Just call — and in a minute you have "Nik. Nik.". He will get you everything you need'). The only problem, the poem concluded, was that contact with these shady characters might land you up at the Public Prosecutor's under interrogation.[51]

Harry Rosenberg, a Polish-Jewish observer pitchforked by the fortunes of war into exile in Kazakhstan as a young man, gives a fascinating fictionalized account of *blat* dealings in the industrial sphere as he encountered it in the 1940s. The many *blat* professionals in his stories — members, in the author's words, of 'an elusive underground network of people whose jobs provided them with the opportunity to exchange favours with the other members' — are almost invariably described in positive terms, not only because of their efficiency and boldness but for their lively, agreeable and generous personalities (Rosenberg 1994: p. 27).[52] When Rosenberg's young narrator, a *blat* apprentice, returns from his trip to Perm′ with, among other things, thick heels and soles for work boots, he notices that there are four spare sets. 'Don't they know know to count in Perm′?' he asks his mentor, Stepka, adding that 'They will be worth a fortune on the black market!'

Both these comments offended Stepka. The extras were sent as a gift by his '*very good friends*' (emphasis in the original). He would not think of selling them: 'Do you think I am some stupid black-marketeer? I would not dream of it. No. They will just sit here, and when one of my friends wants a pair of shoes repaired without an official order, well, I can help him' (Rosenberg 1994: p. 55).

One of the *blat* professionals among the Harvard respondents was the procurements agent for a sugar trust who has been quoted several times. Like many other professional *blatniki*, he enjoyed his work: 'I was happy in my job. It paid well, there was plenty of blat, I traveled throughout the Soviet Union — the per diems and traveling allowances came in handy — and besides I had the satisfaction of achievements, as I succeeded where others were failing.'[53] Pleasure in their métier was also characteristic of *blat* virtuosi, those non-professionals for whom *blat* was an avocation. One such virtuoso was an unusual character: an exile from Leningrad who worked as a kolkhoz bookkeeper, he was a jack of all trades (skilled at carpentry and box- and barrel-making) but also considered himself a member of the intelligentsia. In summer, in his house on the kolkhoz, his father took in paying guests (*dachniki*), and developed particularly friendly relations with the director of a big Leningrad garage, with whom he went hunting as well as maintaining regular *blat* relations (wood from the forest being exchanged for flour and sugar from the city). 'My father was esteemed', his son remembered. 'He worked well, and besides this, he could do very many things. He helped many people and he loved to arrange blat and knew how to do it.'[54]

How widely and deeply *blat* penetrated into Soviet society in the 1930s remains to some degree a matter of conjecture. 'Without blat, you could not live in the Soviet Union', said an accountant. But he added that 'blat is expensive — you need financial resources in order to use it'.[55] The point that *blat* was only available to persons of means and substance was emphasized by many Harvard Project respondents. A former merchant marine (obviously no stranger to *blat*) told his interviewer: 'You know, nobody would help a poor man. He has nothing to offer. Blat usually means that you have to do something for somebody in return.'[56] Another respondent (a veterinarian) was scornful of the interviewer's suggestion that a worker might have *blat* ('acquaintances'). 'What acquaintances could a simple worker have? If he had a good friend, he would not have been a worker in the first place'.[57]

The historical sociologist Vladimir Andrle, however, drawing on post-war interviews with Ukrainian working-class *émigrés* in the Hoover Archive, among other materials, concluded that most workers were routinely involved in *blat*, and those who held aloof from it were sometimes ostracized (Andrle 1988: pp. 54–7). This is confirmed by the life stories of many working-class and peasant respondents in the Harvard Project, including a number who denied personal involvement with *blat*. No doubt the contradictions are partly explained by the syndrome noted by Ledeneva among her respondents in the 1990s: 'If I do it, it is not blat.' (Ledeneva 1998: p. 60)

Nevertheless, it seems clear that there were people who had little or no personal involvement with *blat*, either because they lacked the social contacts or aptitude or because they were against it on principle. (This remained true in the 1990s, according to Ledeneva's data [1998: pp. 116–17].) A woman from the intelligentsia, a teacher by profession, professed ignorance of *blat*, but suggested that it might be more important in the village where 'people are closer to each other [...] and there still exist such close connections'.[58] A *kolkhoznitsa*, equally ignorant, thought *blat* and bribery was possible for party members, 'but if they get caught they will be arrested as Trotskyites and they may be shot. What a Trotskyite is I do not know.'[59]

Among workers, according to one of Andrle's informants, there was a generational difference in attitude to *blat*, with opposition to *blat* being associated with faithfulness to old revolutionary values:

> The old workers [...] did not use the *blat* as often as we did, I mean young workers. They were too proud, they used to say this was their factory. They really believed this during the *NEP* times, later on, they felt that they had been cheated. You know, after the revolution,

> the older workers could fight even the Party and the management through their trade unions. Later on, the power of the trade union was taken away from them. It was obvious that they felt deeply hurt and they still tried to strengthen the trade union. We younger workers, we saw that there was no use in it, therefore we jumped into the *blat* deals. (Andrle 1994: pp. 54–5)

* * *

One of *Krokodil*'s cartoons on *blat* captured the way in which Soviet informal distribution mechanisms tended to convert every formal bureaucratic transaction into a personal one. Headed 'A good upbringing', it shows a store manager talking politely to a customer, while the cashier and another woman look on. 'He's a courteous man, our store manager', says the cashier. 'When he sells cloth, he calls all the customers by name and patronymic.' — 'Does he really know all the customers?' — 'Of course. If he doesn't know someone, he doesn't sell to them.'[60]

The store manager was clearly guilty of violating the official rules of Soviet trade. From the state's standpoint, the essence of his offence was to allow the intrusion of the private into a domain subject to public regulation. From the standpoint of citizens who were *not* his acquaintances, he was implicitly flouting the popular principle that goods ought to be equally accessible to all. In Soviet reality, however, access to goods was never equal, since the state's own distribution practices produced a hierarchical system in which certain categories of the population had privileged access (see Osokina 1993). This lent force to the assumption of the manager's customers that, in giving them preferential access to goods via *blat*, he was correcting the injustices of an inequitable distribution system as well as showing that he was a good friend and a generous human being.

The affective nature of *blat* connections — their association with kindness, helpfulness, generosity and so on — was strongly emphasized both by Harvard Project respondents in the 1950s and by Ledeneva's respondents in the 1990s. Ledeneva calls this phenomenon 'misrecognition', after Bourdieu, which implies that the unacknowledged instrumental-economic meaning of *blat* was the real, fundamental one, while the affective meaning its practitioners attributed to it was a kind of self-deception or euphemism (Ledeneva 1998: pp. 58–72). This is a classic 'base and superstructure' formulation. But, Marxist premises aside, do we really have any grounds for assuming that the instrumental (economic) aspect of *blat* was more 'real' than its affective (social) aspect?

At heart, despite the 'misrecognition' formulation, Ledeneva accepts that there was a genuine affective component to *blat*, and Mayfair Yang draws the same conclusion on *guanxi*, its Chinese counterpart (Yang 1994). There can be no doubt of the enormous importance of *blat* as part of the informal system of Soviet distribution. Let us assume, however, that the respondents' assertions that *blat* relations were based on friendship are to be taken seriously, and see where it leads us.

It has long been a truism among Sovietologists that Stalinism was destructive of all forms of association — that, in Hannah Arendt's phrase, it tended to 'atomize' and fragment society (Arendt 1968: ch. 1). This is clearly accurate in many respects, despite anomalies like the unexpected strengthening of family ties discovered by the Harvard Project (Inkeles and Bauer 1968: pp. 211–16). But we have perhaps tended to understand 'association' too narrowly, thinking, like political scientists, in terms of institutions rather than, like anthropologists, in terms of social networks. If we understand networks as a form of association, the picture of association in Stalinist society changes quite radically. As this chapter has demonstrated, a web of *blat* networks pervaded Russian society in the Stalin period, and similar claims could also be made for patronage networks. The importance of these networks is underlined by the ceaseless stream of official condemnations of *semeistvennost′* and similar phenomena in the 1930s, not to mention the obsession with chains of association manifest in the interrogation practices of the NKVD during the Great Purges.

All of this suggests something very different from atomization. Moreover, the associative significance of the *blat* networks cannot be dismissed by describing them (in a favourite Soviet phrase) as mere survivals from the past. They were essentially not 'survivals' at all, for it appears that it was only in the Stalin period that such networks spread throughout society and became an important associational form. *Blat* was a product of the Stalinist distribution system itself, a compensatory function of the regime of chronic scarcity and elimination of the legal market introduced at the end of the 1920s. Thus Stalinism, which destroyed so many forms of association, engendered at least one of its own.

Very little attention has so far been paid to sociability in the Stalin era, or for that matter in the Soviet period as a whole. Perhaps thinking about *blat* as a form of sociability, as well as a form of economic exchange, will provide an entrée into this wider field of enquiry. The importance of friendship and small-group loyalties in Soviet (especially late Soviet) life was something well known, at an impressionistic and personal level, to several generations of Western Soviet scholars; yet for some reason this impressionistic knowledge was usually compartmentalized as 'field lore', not applicable to our theoretical understanding of how Soviet society worked. It is time to think more about the meaning of friendship in this society, the ubiquitous concept of 'one's own' (*svoi*) people, the importance of circles (*kruzhki*) of friends and networks of acquaintances and the relationship between the two, and the particular modes of sociability that characterized interactions in different Soviet contexts. *Blat* is a part of this story, but the story as a whole remains to be told.

Notes

1 Russian Research Center, Harvard University, 'Project on the Soviet Social System: Interview Records, "A" Schedule Protocols' (hereafter 'Project'), vol. 20, no. 407, p. 11.
2 Ibid., p. 63.
3 Ibid., p. 162.
4 For more detail on this project and its publications, see Inkeles and Bauer 1968. A full set of the bound volumes of 'Schedule A' interviews is in the Library of the Davis (formerly Russian Research) Center at Harvard. Thanks to Susan Gardos, the Center's librarian, for facilitating my research on these materials.
5 A shorter and earlier version of part of this chapter appears in my book *Everyday Stalinism. Ordinary Life in Extraordinary Times: Soviet Russia in the 1930s*, New York, 1999, ch. 2.
6 Gosudarstvennyi arkhiv Rossiiskoi Federatsii (GARF), f. 5446, op. 81a, d. 24, ll. 49–48.
7 'Project', vol. 20, no. 386, p. 24; vol. 1, no. 4, p. 36; vol. 21, no. 431, p. 7.
8 Ibid., vol. 21, no. 432, p. 16; vol. 26, no. 518, p. 29; vol. 19, no. 358, p. 18; vol. 20, no. 396, p. 12.

9 Ibid., vol. 20, no. 386, p. 24; vol. 38, no. 338, p. 8; Berliner 1954: p. 23.
10 But note that respondents in the Harvard Project (and in the J.K. Zawodny interviews of the same period, cited from the Hoover Archive in Andrle 1988: pp. 54–7) blurred the analytical distinction between vertical and horizontal connections, shifting back and forth between the terms *blat* and *protektsiia*.
11 'Project', vol. 13, no. 166, p. 44.
12 For example, ibid., vol. 1, no. 7, p. 23; vol. 1, no. 10, p. 6. In the latter case, the interviewer noted the discrepancy in his report.
13 See, for example, ibid., vol. 19, no. 381, p. 14; vol. 20, no. 387, p. 38; vol. 20, no. 399, p. 12; vol. 20, no. 415, p. 15; and Berliner 1954.
14 'Project', vol. 33, no. 338, p. 3; vol. 21, no. 416, pp. 3–4.
15 Ibid., vol. 19, no. 385, p. 99.
16 Ibid., vol. 34, no. 147, pp. 21, 30.
17 Ibid., vol. 1, no. 3, p. 5; vol. 30, no. 87, p. 8; vol. 20, no. 395, pp. 9–10.
18 Ibid., vol. 21, no. 431, pp. 28–9.
19 Ibid., vol. 7, no. 96, p. 18.
20 Ibid., vol. 26, no. 517, p. 36.
21 Ibid., vol. 14, no. 260, p. 6.
22 Ibid., vol. 20, no. 398, p. 31.
23 *Krokodil*, 1937, no. 8, p. 12.
24 Ibid., 1935, nos. 17–18, p. 11. For a similar joke on getting a place in a restaurant, see ibid., 1940, no. 14, p. 2.
25 Ibid., 1935, nos. 30–1, p. 18.
26 'Project', vol. 21, no. 421, pp. 17–18.
27 Ibid., vol. 33, no. 338, pp. 6–7.
28 Ibid., p. 6.
29 Ibid., pp. 6–7.
30 For example, ibid., vol. 20, no. 407, p. 11; vol. 19, no. 358, p. 13; vol. 1, no. 2, p. 16.
31 On *sobutyl'nichestvo*, see ibid., vol. 20, no. 407 , p. 11.
32 Ibid., vol. 16, no. 306, p. 13.
33 Interviewer's comment, in ibid., vol. 1, no. 3, p. 5.
34 Ibid., vol. 19, no. 359, p. 27.
35 Ibid., vol. 27, no. 526, p. 13.
36 Ibid., vol. 21, no. 416, pp. 3–4.
37 Ibid., vol. 26, no. 516, p. 17.
38 Ibid., vol. 21, no. 432, p. 16. See also vol. 28, no. 532, pp. 18–19.
39 Ibid., vol. 26, no. 516, p. 29.
40 Ibid., vol. 27, no. 527, p. 21.
41 Ibid., vol. 19, no. 381, p. 14.
42 Ibid., vol. 28, no. 534, p. 22.
43 Ibid., vol. 7, no. 91, p. 13.

44 Ibid., vol. 20, no. 407, p. 10.
45 Ibid., vol. 19, no. 381, p. 15.
46 Ibid., vol. 26, no. 521, p. 39. This is reminiscent of Mackenzie Wallace's story that the Western-influenced law reforms of the 1860s confused Russians, who could not see the difference between paying a defence attorney and bribing a judge (Wallace 1961: p. 88).
47 'Project', vol. 21, no. 419, p. 14.
48 Ibid., vol. 26, no. 516, p. 10.
49 Ibid., vol. 19, no. 359, p. 32.
50 Ibid., vol. 34, no. 147, pp. 6–7. The transcript of this interview gives the perplexing 'Slavchil' and 'Levkach' as synonyms for professional *blatnik*. Yuri Slezkine suggests that this is a mistranscription for '*slovchil*' and '*lovkach*', both derived from the verb *slovchit'/lovchit'*, meaning to pull off something in a clever way (personal communication to the author).
51 *Krokodil*, 1933, no. 3, p. 3. The Russian title is *Blat-not*, a play on the word *bloknot*, 'notebook'. Thanks to Yuri Slezkine for assistance translating the slang terms in this poem.
52 Thanks to T.H. Rigby for introducing me to this book.
53 'Project', vol. 33, no. 338, pp. 6–7.
54 Ibid., vol. 26, no. 518, p. 37.
55 Ibid., vol. 15, no. 302, p. 10. This respondent denied using *blat* himself, though admitting he had 'connections': 'I did not have enough money. I was only an ordinary accountant.'
56 Ibid., vol. 1, no. 7, p. 23.
57 Ibid., vol. 27, no. 528, pp. 16–17.
58 Ibid., no. 423, pp. 20–2.
59 Ibid., vol. 20, no. 394, p. 11.
60 *Krokodil*, 1935, no. 25, p. 13. The word used for 'sells' is *otpuskaet* (literally 'releases').

Bibliography

Andrle, V. (1988), *Workers in Stalin's Russia: Industrialization and Social Change in a Planned Economy*, New York.

Andrle, V. (1994), *A Social History of Twentieth-Century Russia*, London.

Arendt, H. (1968), *Totalitarianism*, New York and London.

Bauer, R., Inkeles, A. and Kluckhorn, C. (1959), *How the Soviet System Works*, Cambridge, MA.

Berliner, J. (1954), 'Blat Is Higher than Stalin', *Problems of Communism*, 3, 1.

Berliner, J. (1957), *Factory and Manager in the Soviet Union*, Cambridge.

Crankshaw, E. (1959), *Khrushchev's Russia*, Harmondsworth.

Grossman, G. (1977), 'The "Second Economy" of the USSR', *Problems of Communism*, 26, 5.
Inkeles, A. and Bauer, R. (1968), *The Soviet Citizen: Daily Life in a Totalitarian Society*, Cambridge, MA.
Kornai, J. (1980), *Economics of Shortage*, 2 vols, Amsterdam.
Kornai, J. (1992), *The Socialist System: The Political Economy of Communism*, Princeton, NJ.
Ledeneva, A. (1998), *Russia's Economy of Favours: Blat, Networking and Informal Exchanges*, Cambridge.
Los, M. (ed.) (1990), *The Second Economy in Marxist States*, London.
Millar, J. (1985), 'The Little Deal: Brezhnev's Contribution to Acquisitive Socialism', *Slavic Review*, 44, 4.
Osokina, E. (1993), *Ierarkhiia potrebleniia: O zhizni liudei v usloviiakh stalinskogo snabzheniia 1928–1935 gg.*, Moscow.
Rosenberg, H. (1994), *The Leica and other Stories*, Canberra.
Tolkovyi slovar' russkogo iazyka (1934), ed. D.N. Ushakov, vol. 1, Moscow.
Walder, A. (1986), *Communist Neo-Traditionalism: Work and Authority in Chinese Industry*, Berkeley, CA.
Wallace, D.M. (1961), *Russia on the Eve of War and Revolution*, ed. Cyril Black, New York.
Yang, M. (1994), *Gifts, Favors, and Banquets: The Art of Social Relationships in China*, Ithaca, NY.

10 Continuity and Change of *Blat* Practices in Soviet and Post-Soviet Russia

Alena Ledeneva

One of my respondents, a businessman, remarked: 'People used to say: if you don't drink, you aren't one of us [*ne p'esh' — ne nash*]. Now they say: if you don't take [bribes], you aren't one of us [*ne beresh' — ne nash*]'.[1] Problems which used to be 'drowned in vodka' are now becoming solvable, especially for those who can pay. It may also be suggested that the recent boom in bribery and corruption is simply a result of the monetarization of shadow, informal and personalized practices which used to permeate the 'command' economy. If we are to grasp the roots and nature of present-day corruption, we must analyse these practices and their implications for post-Soviet conditions.

I shall start with a brief discussion of the Soviet phenomenon of *blat* — which is bound up with the use of informal contacts and networks to obtain goods and services or to influence decision-making — and then move on to consider the implications of *blat* for the scale of corruption in post-Soviet Russia.

Soviet Blat

Given the multiplicity of its use-contexts, *blat* is not easy to define. '*Blat* seems an obvious word, it does not need definition', remarked one respondent. Interestingly, every Russian knows what *blat* is, but finds it difficult to define. One reason is that the term means different things in different contexts and is irreducible to some common ground. *Blat* is an acquaintance or friend through whom you can obtain some goods or services which are in short supply, cheaper, or of better quality than those available through the official system of distribution. Also, *blat* is a reciprocal relationship which people call '*Ty — mne, ia — tebe*' ('I help you, you help me'). *Blat* is about using informal contacts based on mutual sympathy and trust, that is, using friends, acquaintances, occasional contacts. *Blat* may also be employed to arrange a good job for another person, or to ensure that, other things being equal, the candidate who is known or recommended gets chosen. Sometimes *blat* means influence and protection, all kinds of 'umbrellas' (*kryshi*), the ability to drop the right names. Given this multiplicity of contexts in which *blat* is considered a relevant term, one faces the question: what are the shared characteristics of situations referred to as being solvable 'by *blat*'? The variation in regularity of favours, in the character of the relationship between the parties, in the type of need, in the nature of the reciprocity, and in the potential involvement of an intermediary, makes *blat* situations almost irreducible to any clear-cut classification. In what follows I shall explicate a range of features which may not be present in every particular *blat* situation but which together should be associated with *blat* practices.

First, *blat* is a distinctive form of non-monetary exchange, a kind of barter based on a personal relationship. It works where money does not. In the planned economy, money did not function as an equivalent in economic transactions; things were sorted out by mutual help, by barter. Apart from official rations and privileges allocated by the state distribution system to different occupational strata, every employee had a particular kind of access (*dostup*) which could be traded in *blat* relations. The relative unimportance of money in the command economy brought into being this specific form of exchange, lying somewhere between commodity exchange and gift-giving.[2]

The objects obtained in *blat* relationships were rarely exchanged in a straightforward manner. It should be emphasized that *blat* involved relationships and not merely goods. What was exchanged was neither objects for objects, nor the relative values people attached to those objects, but mutual regard and esteem. *Blat* was thus not a relationship for the sake of exchange but an exchange for the sake of a relationship. In gift exchange, inalienable objects of the same kind pass between people already bound together by social ties, whilst in commodity exchange alienable objects of different kinds pass between people acting as free agents. Gift exchange is concerned with social reproduction; commodity exchange establishes relations between things and ensures reproduction of the latter (Gregory 1982). Although *blat* certainly does transfer alienable objects (favours), it does so on the condition that social relationships already exist. 'The other' is not only functional but is regarded personally and in this sense is irreplaceable. *Blat* favours therefore bear a non-alienable character. They are marked by the personal stamp of the donor. This can best be imagined as the occasional lending or borrowing of a form of access (*dostup*), but the access itself is never alienable. Just as in gift exchange, where a debt cannot be paid by a different kind of gift, a received favour is never equivalent to that which the recipient can provide in return. The original favour leaves a 'memory', even if it has been returned in an 'unlike' form. Thus, access could be 'lent', 'borrowed' or 'exchanged'. In this sense *blat* is a 'favour of access' (*usluga dostupa*) which someone chooses to provide.

Favours of access became possible because they demanded no one's own resources and were perceived as 'sharing', 'helping out', 'friendly support', 'mutual care' and so on. Such help was provided not from one's own pocket, but rather at the expense of state property or someone formally entitled to this resource. Sharing access with friends and acquaintances became so routine that the difference between *blat* and friendly relations became blurred: one almost became consequent upon the other. The use of public resources for private (even if not selfish) purposes reflected a paradoxical feature of the Soviet regime: the character of state property. State property was declared to be public and supposed to be guarded by everyone: witness the common slogan 'Everyone must mount guard over public property! [*Vse — na okhranu obshchestvennoi sobstvennosti!*]'. But 'public' could also be interpreted as quasi-private, which was reflected in everyday sayings such as: '"public" means that part of it is mine', 'one gets what one guards [*kto okhraniaet — tot imeet*]'. The trickle-down of public property through the access provided by those who 'guarded' it to a wider circle of people was a common practice, either denied or sincerely 'misrecognized' by the rhetoric of mutual help used to speak of personal relationships.[3] Designating not just mutual help or friendly support but help given at the expense of the state or others, *blat* therefore referred to a wider system of possibilities and to one's position within it.

The functioning of informal contacts and connections was predicated upon the structural characteristics of the Soviet-type system. Soviet *blat* was similar to *guanxi* in China (Yang 1994) or *załatwić sprawy* in Poland (Wedel 1986), but had no direct analogy in the West. One reason for this was that the use of informal channels in Soviet-type society was not a matter of choice: rather, it was a practice necessitated by conditions of perpetual shortage. One could argue, however, that not every society characterized by scarcity and shortage generated *blat,* and this may be so. *Blat*-like phenomena result from a particular combination of shortages and — even if repressed — consumerism, from the paradox between an ideology of equality and the practice of differentiation through privileges and the closed distribution systems. In so far as *blat* enabled those who had no privileges in the state distribution system to bypass rationing and queuing, it had an equalizing as well as a stratifying effect.

In contrast to personal relations and simple barter, *blat* relations were not necessarily dyadic. *Blat* transactions could be circular: A provided a favour to B, B to C, C to D, and D (perhaps) to A. The important point is that there could be no immediate repayment — reciprocity was to be masked by the delayed return. Mediated favours were even more efficient for avoiding practical and social constraints against immediate repayment. Psychologically, mediation was very important because, in the words of one of my respondents, 'it was terribly difficult to ask on behalf of oneself. It was much easier to ask for a friend, or for an institution, just to put in a word for somebody'. It looked much more respectable when an intermediary asked to help somebody 'unselfishly', or when a donor helped an unknown person just for the sake of his or her relationship with the intermediary. Everyone acted 'unselfishly', but this efficient system of mutual help was called *blat* by outsiders.

In the Soviet period *blat* was less morally reprehensible and therefore more pervasive than other informal or 'corrupt' practices, such as informal economic activity or bribery. Being a specific form of social relationship embedded in personal (horizontal, non-hierarchical, compassionate and warm) networks, it became a socially grounded pattern of mentality and behaviour, a form of exchange based upon certain ethical and cultural codes. Let us now consider the changes that *blat* has undergone in post-Soviet conditions.

Blat *Today*

The expression 'by *blat*' is still known and understood today. Opinions differ, however, about the scope of its present-day applicability. Some argue that *blat* is still essential, even if its uses have changed, while others assert that it has been displaced by bribery and corruption. It is telling that the older generation, particularly those respondents not involved with new sectors of the economy, tend to emphasize the enduring significance of *blat* ('old connections'), even though they admit that it now meets new needs in new areas. In contrast, the younger generation of respondents tend to consider *blat* an out-of-date term, inappropriate to market conditions. 'The expression is falling out of use: teenagers do know it (though they do not use it), but those born since the late 1980s will not even understand', said a middle-aged businessman. Such a generational difference in usage of the term does not mean, however, that such a formerly pervasive phenomenon has disappeared completely. Rather, the forms *blat* now assumes extend beyond the areas to which the term was applied before. It is important to consider these changes, but also to see the continuity of *blat* — the ways in which non-monetary forms of exchange are adapting to new conditions.

The post-Soviet reforms were aimed at establishing a market economy and privatizing state property. These reforms undermined three basic parameters of the economic system that nurtured *blat*. First, functioning markets for goods and capital took over the economy of shortage, in which everything — foodstuffs, goods, services, places in hospitals and at cemeteries — had to be bartered for, with a concomitant reduction in the role of money in economic exchange. The point most frequently made in my interviews was that *blat* diminished because there was no longer a shortage of commodities for personal consumption:

> *Blat* was used to obtain commodities in short supply or to jump queues. As long as everything — decent shoes, a medicine, a car, an apartment — was in short supply, *blat* was vital. Now there is no shortage, and people have stopped talking about *blat* so much.

> Now everything for personal consumption can be bought, if you have money. Things are available and there is no point in 'obtaining' them. The former value of 'obtaining' has lost its significance. To obtain a piece of sausage, to book a place for a tourist trip (even if it is cheaper) is not valued so much when there are people who can simply buy these things. There is no need to use the channels of *blat* if one is buying shoes or clothes. High-quality medical services are available for money, and so is education. There are 'commercial' groups at the universities and educational courses can now be purchased. In areas which are still not commercialized — for example, army service — *blat* has been replaced by bribery. *Blat* in its previous forms has come to an end. Nothing is a problem these days if there is money.

Secondly, state property became increasingly privatized, which changed the customary attitude towards 'favours of access' and enhanced the economic interests of those in charge:

> the people responsible for rationing or distribution had access to resources which they were able to manipulate but which did not belong to them and which, therefore, they could dispose of without reluctance. This is not the case any more.

Thirdly, the system of socialist guarantees ceased to operate: the process of privatization in combination with the severe economic trends of the 1990s, such as the decline of industrial production, the investment crisis and the increase in mutual non-payments, ruled out previously dominant forms of solidarity and mutual help between industrial enterprises, weakened the social security system and welfare provision in organizations and launched a large-scale re-stratification of the population. The implications of this economic restructuring for *blat* are the following.

With the expansion of monetary exchange people say 'money became real', which means that they are now able to purchase goods, to differentiate between goods, to 'make' money and to invest it. As a consequence, money has become a 'shortage' and an overall need towards which *blat* connections became re-orientated. 'People use their contacts to obtain money: money for living expenses by making deposits in a bank where good contacts can ensure their safety; money for business by getting a loan on privileged conditions', summarized one of my respondents. At the very least, *blat* channels provide an opportunity to earn money or to arrange a 'good' job. It is not, however, the same *blatnaia* job as it used to be when only symbolic work was required for guaranteed salary and privileges. In places (normally commercial firms) where 'real' money is paid for 'real' work and effort, the *blatnye* are not necessarily the leading candidates.

More importantly, *blat* is often aimed at providing the basis for business and trading activities:

> In business, *blat* is most needed to provide access to bureaucratic decision-making and information, especially where bribery is impossible. Where bribes do not work, *blat* can still be effective. For example, to obtain a licence for the export of metals three people may be eager to give a bribe but the licence will be issued not to the one who provides the bigger bribe but to the one who has the most *blat*, who is the friend of the son of the head of the regional administration, for example.

The emergence of private business brought about a significant change in the division between public and private which allowed people's interests to shift towards the commercial sphere. Asked when *blat* is most significant today, respondents usually mentioned the needs of business: for instance, when starting business or attempting to run an existing business more efficiently. Personal interests have become business interests, and the ethics of *blat* have come into contradiction with a more impersonal and calculating business ethic. 'Finance, licences, privileged loans, access to business information are the "shortage" of today. The authorities for which *blat* contacts have become most important are thus those of tax, customs, banking and regional administration', as one respondent reported.

The spread of money has changed *blat* relations so much that *blat* has almost ceased to be a relevant term for the connections that characterize the new sectors of the economy. One businesswoman explained:

> the word '*blat*' is out of use now. I never hear that a bank loan is given 'by *blat*'. People still say 'by acquaintance' but this no longer refers to '*blat*' as it did before. There used to be no difference in the Soviet distribution system: there was a fixed state price for every product, and the alternative to obtaining it by *blat* at the state price was to buy it at a much inflated black market price. In the Soviet system one felt as if one had the right to buy goods at a shop for the state price (the black market [*barakholka*] was something people

> despised then). In return for providing access to products at the state price, a shop assistant would receive a non-monetary surplus (my indebtedness and, possibly, a potential favour). Roughly speaking, this non-monetary surplus was taken out of the state's pocket by substituting for the principle of equal access the principle of private access for 'people of the circle'. Nowadays, there are no fixed prices, there is no right to buy at a fixed price, and there is no *blat* in the Soviet sense. When I do an acquaintance a favour, for example, if I am a retailer and sell something at its wholesale price I violate the business code. I earn nothing and know the loss that I have suffered. The acquaintance is also aware of how much it cost me. Given this transparency, 'by *blat*' loses its meaning, its previous connotations have gone. It has become a dead metaphor.

In Soviet times 'helping out' by *blat* was often exercised at the expense of state property or by deploying the influence conferred by an institutional position. By helping out, people gave out not goods of their own, but benefits of which the other was deprived. These resources were to be distributed anyway, and in the rationing system the very fact of acquaintance could become crucial in determining who got what. The fact of a kindness granted to an acquaintance even bestowed some benefit on the donor, as it earned him or her gratitude and loyalty, and therefore nurtured a relationship which could result in reciprocation of favours granted and thus prove useful. *Blat* was a complicated, culturally grounded, 'social alchemy' for turning access to state property to one's own advantage but without stealing anything.

In private business, attitudes towards property and helping out are now quite different. Material calculations, rather than the fact of acquaintance, count foremost. In the current situation of instability, the fact of acquaintance does not necessarily ensure that favours will be returned. 'Market conditions have changed personal relationships and ruined many friendships. There is no room for *blat* as there used to be. It looks like *blat* won't be the same and the very word is going into oblivion'.

Can *blat* practices be found nowadays? Or have they disappeared completely in these radical changes? Although in post-Soviet conditions *blat* has ceased being a necessity for everyday life to the same extent as before (foodstuffs, goods and some of the services do not have to be 'obtained' any more), it is still needed to ensure a better life, a higher standard of living, convenience and comfort. Informal contacts still remain primary where money is not accepted as a means of exchange, that is, at the higher levels, which are riddled with corruption and nepotism; or at the very bottom level of society, where informal networks are used to tackle scarcity. Also, people routinely use their contacts to assist money-earning activities (especially in business) in the same way as they used to do for personal consumption, and this brings about an extraordinary rise in the scale of corruption. As one businessman noted:

> In the new distribution system, where land, raw materials and finance can be distributed in the same manner as sausages, cars and apartments, the effect of connections is a hundred times stronger. A friend of mine imported equipment and materials to construct a modern warehouse. If he could manage to locate it next to the market in the centre of the city, he would have enough income not to work for the rest of his life. The problem was to get a land lease. He got it through his friend in the regional administration, whom he worked with before or something. This could not be achieved by means of a bribe, but the acquaintance settled the problem.

The point about the scale of corrupt deals today was raised in another attempt to answer the 'continuity' question:

> The state system is changing, and *blat* like everything else in the social organism adapts to new conditions. There are continuities in this change. If one looks at the new bureaucracy (in administration and commerce and so on), they are usually the same people: former party leaders, directors and executives, who have migrated into the new 'élite niches'. One real problem is therefore that *blat* patterns rooted in parasitism towards the state still prevail in contexts which render them maladaptive. It used to be the case that instead of buying something in a shop or going straight to a doctor, a person chose (or was forced to choose) a roundabout way to acquire an object or service by *blat* (for example, circumventing the rationing system). The scale of dealings is different nowadays: in the legislature strings are pulled to enact laws in favour of private interests. The logic of action, however, remains similar: to get away with a bigger piece of the common pie.

One's slice could not be really big under socialism (because there was reticence about privileges), while now it can be huge. As was acutely concluded by one of the respondents, a journalist:

> there is a radical difference between getting an urgent medical service by providing a theatre ticket and getting financial support for one's own business. It is not relevant to speak of both as *blat* (the profit-making is not limited by personal consumption as *blat* was). The techniques are the same, however — using friendly contacts, sauna companions, 'constructive' drinking — and acquaintances are often drawn in too. In this sense we are not 'new Russians', we are 'old Soviets'.

It should be noted that *blat* subverted the Soviet economic system at the same time as it sustained it. In practice *blat* amplified personal relations (providing the possibility of 'mutual help'), but it also softened the rigid constraints of the command economy and the Soviet political system. It was well adapted to as well as restricted by Soviet morality. In the beginning of the transitional period after 1985, *blat* remained effective by contributing to the establishment of new forms of co-operation. Now, with the expansion of the market and the concomitant decline of Soviet norms and values, *blat* no longer follows customary rules, nor does it correspond to economic conditions. *Blat* practices stretched beyond their Soviet limits tend to be destructive of the national economy. Those patterns which were organically connected to and functional for the Soviet social and political system have been carried over into the post-Soviet era with no control of their corrupt aspects and no attention to their advantageous features. According to one of my respondents, in charge of combating corruption, the modification of *blat* patterns in the transitional period had serious implications:

> *Blat* prevalent in the Soviet Union was not a matter of material-financial significance. It was based on moral and ethical foundations. Together with these foundations *blat* was bound to change. The essence remained the same — the use of connections (family, friends, acquaintances) in solving all sorts of problems — but this form has been filled with new, material-financial content. Now, if some questions are to be solved 'by *blat*', via acquaintances, people imply, hint or even tell you directly how much it is going to cost. The deal, they say, has to be 'greened' [*nado pozelenit'* — referring to the colour of a US dollar bill]. Therefore, all the things that used to be done by *blat* now take the form of bribery, all sorts of bribery. Because bribery sounds unacceptable, it happens in the form of presents, gifts, payments for children's education, payments for holidays and 'business' trips

abroad, offers of jobs in commercial firms, banks and so on, that is, all forms of corruption. What used to be a matter of morals and ethics based on the modest norms of Soviet society and notions of kinship, friendship and other social ties, now — in the transitional stage of 'wild', as we call it, capitalism — involves material and financial capital. It is not surprising that the Anti-Corruption Law in Russia has slipped off the agenda. The spread of corruption is not dissimilar to the spread of *blat* in the Soviet era. The scale, however, is different. Even if *blat* — providing access to people of your circle at the expense of other citizens — meant a certain degree of relative deprivation, it was nothing in comparison to the degree of polarization of the population today.

An analysis of the implications of *blat* in the post-Soviet economy allows us to trace the roots of corruption and account for its recent upsurge. Let us now outline the main arenas of today's corruption resulting from the clash or intersection of the *blat* legacy of the past with new opportunities — the interpenetration of state nomenklatura and business, business and organized crime, criminal authorities and political institutions.

The Corrupt Implications of Blat

Nomenklatura and business

As has already been mentioned, *blat* operates most efficiently where limited resources are being distributed, and particularly where formal criteria are not sufficient to make a choice from several candidates with a claim on these resources. Formal criteria and procedures are in fact organized in such a way that they allow informal ones to creep in. Formal procedures are still routinely transgressed in the most significant affairs of the Russian economy: the distribution of the state budget and of state subsidies, the charging of export-import duties and the implementation of tax policy. 'Despite the changes in society which have reduced the role of *blat* in daily life and business activities, *blat* endures in the state sector, where the principles of distribution have not been changed radically', noted an ex-deputy of a local party committee. 'The psychological parameters of state management and control have remained the same', concluded the director of a large industrial complex. 'There are still niches of the state distribution system (collective farms, mines, large enterprises) where one can approach the director and arrange a personal deal.'

Blat often serves the needs of business in the spheres of the state budget and of state information. According to an expert involved with state auditing, the abuse of the budget is elaborate. There are no subsidies but rather state loans on privileged conditions or bearing no interest. They must be paid off, but, taking inflation into account, they still represent a subsidy:

> Nobody asks for bribes, but instead people ask for and propose discounts [*diskaunty*]. The term is foreign enough to be intelligible only to the 'initiated' and to euphemize the essence of the deal. 'To offer a discount' sounds Western, extremely up-to-date, but in its post-Soviet sense it is nothing but an all-too-familiar bribe.

The income of people in the bureaucracy in the Soviet period was not that high, but it was compensated for by the state system of privileges. Today privileges are nothing in comparison with what one can get for money. Commissions, percentages, securities and shares in businesses are now common forms of favour repayment. Money has become the most urgent need for everybody. Bureaucrats extort (*vykolachivaiut*) money by conjuring up obstacles:

> For a businessman today, giving a bribe is like buying cigarettes. It has simply become the norm. Nothing happens for free. This is understandable: if state officials helped every entrepreneur, the latter would benefit while the people making the decisions would stay where they are, with no cars, flats or incomes.

Just as it was not possible to get on without *blat* in Soviet everyday life, so it is impossible to run non-corrupt business activities in post-Soviet conditions:

> One has to hide one's money from the state and from racketeers. Everything needs a bribe — getting licences, reducing taxes or customs duties. Our taxes, theoretically, are up to 80 per cent. It would be impossible to operate a business like that. This country is not ready for civilized business. There are no laws, no principles, no traditions. (York 1995)

In such conditions one should not be surprised by the ruthlessness and crudeness of the class of businessmen. 'Now I understand', continues this twenty-eight-year-old banker, 'that Russia becomes a different country, the mentality of the people is different. Business here is very cynical. It's not quite the jungle, but it's close to it. How do you make money in this country? You kill somebody, you steal, you bribe' (York 1995). Even if this is too much of a generalization, it has its implications for the character of relations between businessmen and their treatment of bureaucrats.

The coexistence of state and commercial structures is often governed by horizontal contacts which create a niche for mutual favours. People have no formal mechanisms by which to press one another, so informal contacts are used to solve everyday problems:

> For example, the formal co-operation of the chairman of a state airport and the head of a commercial airline company allows each of them to exchange favours informally. This basically means that someone recommended by the chairman of the airport can fly with this airline without paying the full air-fare or without paying at all. The post-Soviet difference is that now these favours are calculated much more carefully at every link of the *blat* chain. People think twice before asking a favour and incurring an obligation.

So-called 'nomenklatura business', involving representatives of the upper echelons of the Soviet bureaucracy, is another form of interaction between nomenklatura and business. In the words of one experienced businessman:

> The 'old guard', the nomenklatura — directors of the enterprises and of regional, city, local administrations — kept their power and positions in the post-Soviet period. This power and position is now used for private deals. The nomenklatura used to be well connected and they still are. They know each other and are always in touch. Younger businessmen often have to find their own way while the 'old guard' decide things collectively. They are well informed and know the conditions of the market. It is no wonder that many firms established by the nomenklatura are flourishing. It is not a secret that some banks and large businesses were founded by the 'old guard'. They put 'their people' [*svoikh liudei*] on the boards of directors and provided starting capital, information and connections. An individual businessman running a firm has to make a fuss to obtain information, whereas nomenklatura who run businesses are supplied with access to regional economic statistics, data on supply and demand and information on foreign investment projects, not to mention moral and material support. This cannot be called *blat*, but the mechanisms are similar, just at a different, more organized level.

The dissolution of the Communist Party and attempts to reduce the influence of the former nomenklatura do not mean that this strong and well-connected apparatus has disappeared. A former deputy of a regional party committee argued that the nomenklatura is objectively more capable of handling management problems and that their personal qualities, their experience and their connections are needed in post-Soviet conditions.

> It is fair that they found jobs in line with their ability: the mayor is a former party leader and the local administration is formed by those who have experience in management. I am an expert on the previous system, as I worked at a state enterprise, in the Komsomol, in the Party and in the Soviets at their local, city and regional levels. I know every step of the nomenklatura career and I know how decisions were made, how directives were sent down and how the tasks were fulfilled. As I understand now, the core element of it all was the system of selection of personnel. You may call this 'connections' and you may say that the system worked because of informal contacts. Yes, these were important, say, 50 per cent important, but there was also responsibility and practical skills. These are still required.

Before *perestroika* the party apparatus was professionally engaged in regulating and sorting out the problems of the command economy. Maintaining informal contacts in order to loosen the rigid constraints of the system was part of their function. With such experience these people, particularly the Komsomol élite (sometimes called the 'young businessmen's club'), are objectively more adapted to and active in today's situation. Their starting conditions were immeasurably better than others'.

> Ex-party leaders and former Komsomol activists are comfortable in their places in the new system. Their positions are not bad, the big bosses have moved to governing bodies, to bank consultancies, and to the organization of large-scale corporations. Former state foreign-trade associations such as *Soiuzraznoexport* and *Mashimport*, through which all export-import contracts were enacted, were converted into joint-stock companies, headed by their former chairmen. They function now as private enterprises with the support of all their former connections.

Problems arise, however, when state property becomes involved with private business activities, and *blat* methods acquired in the Soviet system are transferred into the market economy. In order to get finance in the socialist system one had to arrange 'through party connections' that one's initiative would be included in the party decree or programme which was relevant and carried financial clout. 'For example, the tourist centre "Sibiriak" was included in the Decree of the Central Party Committee "On the Development of Oil and Gas Areas", even though Novosibirsk, where it is located, is far away from these areas. The criteria for distribution now are different. The nomenklatura has started trading their favours: they either want real money in return for favourable decisions or they launch their own businesses', remarked the head of a tourist firm. An example of the latter was reported by *Izvestiia*:

> The decision to register the firm 'Nord', which was organized by nine state organizations of St Petersburg, was signed by the first deputy of the chairman of the Executive Committee of the City. The governing body of this firm was headed by the same person, who afterwards also provided the starting capital: two buildings in the very centre of the city, on Nevskii Prospekt, and two more in a nice location near the park. In fact, these buildings were given to the firm: the seven-floor building was estimated at 174,000 roubles, at a time when the auction price of a single flat was above a million roubles.

That was the present the first deputy made from the state department of which he was in charge to the firm he was heading. Interestingly, these houses did not even belong to the Executive Committee but to the City Soviet, so usual is it to dispose of others' property. The operational activities of the firm, designed to develop foreign tourism, contained even more violations and after two years it was closed down by the Office of the State Prosecutor. But most of the VIPs involved evaded prosecution and, as the reporter concluded, '"Nord" will reappear under another name' (Solomenko 1995).

These corrupt tendencies spread over the new banking sector as well. 'In the Central bank, to get a licence for banking one has to pay "money on the side" [*levye den'gi*]. One has to have a good contact to be able to get it free of charge or on the cheap, or at least some contact to enquire why the decision is suspended and to find out how much has to be offered to whom', explained an expert in banking. Informal networks, networks of interests and networks of control, which ensure trust and risk-reduction, are in fact indispensable in today's Russia where, according to an expert in commercial law, 'it's crucial to remember that banks are not banks, money is not money, and insurance is not insurance'. It is not surprising that smaller banks form their clientele on an informal basis, selected entrepreneurs receive bank loans on privileged conditions, and the whole institution of 'people of one's own circle' (*svoi liudi*) functions no less effectively than *blat* networks did in the Soviet era. Similar as it may seem, the solidarity of informal networks nowadays is based on different principles and ethics. Having grown out of old *blat* ties and connections, corporate networks are now 'profit-orientated'.

Blat used to be the way to gain access to the state distribution of goods, services and honours. Now that the role of the state in the economy has been radically reduced, *blat* is found mostly at work in the distribution of information, which is mainly related to status or income. Information becomes both the channel and the filter of distribution of income in a 'market' society. Well-connected firms are able to build their marketing strategies on the basis of information about budget distribution. 'Having inside information, they offer their products to those possessing finance which is non-transferable to the next financial year', said an officer of a marketing department.

Blat always implied information obtained through contacts and exchanged within a certain circle of people. Yet the character of information nowadays has changed. 'It used to be information about what, where and how things could be obtained. Now it is information about money, business, laws and regulations, tax evasion and so on'. The privatization of enterprises through cheque-auctions has produced another sphere where information costs dear. 'Information about the variant of privatization to be chosen, about the administration of share sales and the intentions of the collective, about the position of the trade union and the possibilities of purchasing shares is in great demand. Most of the information required by foreign investors is inside information and cannot be obtained without good contacts', said the head of the Siberian centre for economic information.

Nomenklatura and privatization

The mixing of *blat* ways with the new opportunities provided by the market economy resulted in even more dubious activities, particularly to do with privatization. 'The process of privatization has gone out of control. Property is disposed of by the decisions of the nomenklatura. Not necessarily "big men", they are bureaucrats in local administrations, mayor's offices, housing authorities and so on', said Iurii Khachaturov, a deputy chairman of the Government Anti-Monopoly Committee:

> There are enough examples of this kind in Moscow. What is behind this? Hidden trade, huge bribes, the mafia? Difficult to say. One should suspect so if state property disappears or is transformed into private for only a symbolic price. There is no real control from the centre over the privatization process, and a lot of local manipulation and abuse as a consequence. Disagreement between Chubais, the Head of the State Property Committee, and Luzhkov, the mayor of Moscow, on this matter, for example, is not surprising in this context. The Moscow government opposes the Chubais programme of privatization and aims to follow their own line. This fact is telling. (*Elita* 1995: p. 91)

After a new chairman was appointed to the Committee for the Management of City Property in St Petersburg in 1991, he sacked 80 per cent of the employees; nevertheless, there have been five prosecutions of employees in this Committee and the Property Fund in the two years since that time. These included the deputy director of the Property Fund. Investigation prior to his arrest in 1993 had revealed a shortfall of 130 million roubles in vouchers and counterfeit privatization cheques, understatement of the value of property by 16 billion roubles, and understatement of the amount received from purchasers by 7.8 billion roubles. In addition the intimidation of bidders at auctions was rife. As the reporter for *Izvestiia* commented: 'our public auctions long ago turned into stage plays with roles assigned in advance. The directors are criminal "authorities" and corrupt bureaucrats.'[4] According to information from law-enforcement agencies, 'as much as 70 per cent of the real estate put up for sale at auctions winds up in the hands of individuals who are agreed on beforehand. Before a public auction begins, the information is conveyed to everyone that an "authority" is interested in this piece of property, and that if anyone takes the risk of competing for it, he shouldn't complain later that he wasn't warned'.[5]

Many such cases are reported in the mass media all over Russia, where enterprises, land and buildings are privatized in the interests of 'people of one's own circle'. 'The Tiumen oil and gas resources are being privatized. A former deputy gas industry minister Rem Viakhirev is now chairman of the privatized Russian gas monopoly Gazprom, conservatively estimated to be worth 170 billion pounds' (Meek 1995: p. 12). An investor by the name of Vasilii Timofeev bought 210 million 'Gazprom' shares, for which he had somehow made available 2 billion 100 million rubles. Fifty-one per cent of shares in the gigantic enterprise 'Uralmash' have been bought by one person.[6] On a smaller scale, those who were in charge of state property and had appropriate skills and connections managed to turn the privatization campaign to their advantage, whereas others given a share (*vaucher*) sold it cheap or lost it in the new financial structures (investment funds, commercial banks and so on). It also happened that workers were given a share but either not given the right to sell it under threat of dismissal or pushed to sell it by share-hunters.[7]

Business and organized crime

As used to be the case in *blat* deals, gaining introductions to useful people remains very important. Such a service is not necessarily included in contracts, but it tends to be paid for in one way or another. As one respondent explained:

> In critical cases, one has to find an intermediary, whose guarantee would be sufficient in the case concerned. This is a complicated matter. It does not mean looking for a good acquaintance or drinking partner or friend of the person to bribe. An intermediary must be willing to guarantee the reliability of the giver, on the one hand, and has to be tied by mutual obligations and dependence to the taker.

The search for an intermediary of this kind is extremely difficult. As a rule, it is carried out not by those in the higher administrative positions (if asked 'from above', one would feel reluctant to accede to the request, for fear of acquiring a reputation which might preclude subsequent promotion) but rather among those in parallel (often criminal) structures.

Organized crime and the so-called 'Russian mafia' have received a lot of attention in the literature (Zemtsov 1976; Chalidze 1977; Vaksberg 1991; Handelman 1994; Kampfner 1994; Follain

1995; Lloyd 1995), but one aspect seems to have been underestimated. Organized crime of the 1990s should also be viewed as an expanding network of recruits who did not receive any legacy from the Soviet past — no money, no power, no connections — and were forced to use violence to make money. As both an older respondent and a youngster suggested:

> The economic and social situation pushed many towards a criminal path. Bandits are just one of the traumatic consequences of the reforms. Just think of those who did not study, thinking it was pointless when easy money could be made; who did not have wealthy or influential parents able to back them up in the harsh post-Soviet reality; who did not acquire any profession, and who valued nothing but money. They wanted money at any price, and having no connections for a decent business turned into bandits.

> We'll have to deal with this for a long time. Half of my school graduates, for whom opportunities are closed, go to [...] a hairdresser's shop. They get a crew cut, buy 'Adidas' sportswear, a leather jacket, and later, if everything goes 'well', cashmere coats (in claret or emerald) and a BMW.

Bandits created their own solidarity, a net of connections they call '*bratva*' (brotherhood). They comply with their own, *blatnoi*, code. Their code, however, is not the same as a criminal *blatnoi* code. 'It is penetrated by the "economization" of relationships, they do "business". They have new ideals, they value wealth and comfort. In criminal circles money was always important, but these "new bandits" are different. They demonstrate their coolness [*krutost'*] publicly. The make of their cars (and their weapons) is normally a reliable indicator of their status. They know who is cool, and treat each other accordingly', says the head of the information office at the police department combating organized crime in Novosibirsk.

Acquaintances and connections with bandits are necessary for many businessmen. For example, all those who run kiosks have to face the extortion of payment 'for protection' (*za zashchitu*), to ensure that their kiosks are not attacked or burnt overnight. A person has either to pay or else to have contacts among bandits that enable him to avoid payment or cut down the sum. Other problems may also be solved by appeal to a bandit acquaintance. Bandits can be very useful in influencing official decisions by local authorities, for they establish their own contacts in the state structures. 'To receive the support of an influential bandit is, however, no easier than in any other place. It is all a matter of connections and recommendations again', complained a businessmen.

The rise of the 'mafia' is often linked to the inability of the state to provide protection, to secure a new system of property rights and to exercise the monopoly of legitimate violence: this brings a situation where everyone lives by their own laws while the laws of the state do not work or work selectively. The most recent data (provided by the St Petersburg Committee for the Struggle against Organized Crime in autumn 1996) indicate that the state police is becoming more and more able to re-establish the monopoly of state control. This is definitely happening in Moscow and will be starting to happen in other places. The increased efficiency of the tax police has also helped to strengthen the state. These tendencies do not necessarily mean that the police force itself is completely free of the legacy of *blat*. According to my respondents, however, businessmen would prefer to pay the police rather than bandits.

Criminal authorities and political institutions

According to specialists in departments combating organized crime, it is a fact that organized crime — rackets, banditism, criminal groups and groupings — does not exist without an 'umbrella', that is, without penetration into state institutions, without the involvement of state officials (including law-enforcement officials) in criminal activities. The deputy head of the St Petersburg department remarked that the interpenetration of criminal authorities and political institutions and its consequences is the reality they have to deal with:

> Even a common fact like the police force not being paid its salary for three to four months basically means that 'somebody' wants them to have an alternative source of income. As a result, there is often no legal way to deal with organized crime, as the criminals are well connected or even take posts themselves. According to our data, some LDPR deputies belong to the criminal world and entered election campaigns on 'dirty' money.

Another expert from the government anti-corruption committee confirms this gloomy diagnosis:

> The mafia is becoming blurred. It is now entering networks of control and back-up [*krugovaia poruka*], the most harmful and

> ineradicable legacy of the past, which provides protection and back-up for people of their circle. [...] deputies of the parliament are backed up by the administrative authorities. Administrative officials do not have the same legal immunity as deputies, but they are backed up by the security and police forces. Whenever cases are raised against high-up officials they are suspended or closed. Every administrator would back up his staff, because he knows if he does not do it, the day comes when he himself will have to rely on someone's support. This mechanism follows the same pattern as professional expertise in medicine or court — the inspection of complicated cases such as unfortunate surgery or prejudiced sentence consists of the same surgeons and judges who can find themselves in a similar situation. By providing back-up they ensure their own safety which they are bound to do in the context of lacking rights. This is an enforced practice, and its fundamental basis is fear.

The judiciary is yet another concern of the officials in charge of combating organized crime. Judges are protected by law, which seems a good principle, but looks different if a judge is 'bought'. At the moment it is virtually impossible to sack a judge (there is no legal stipulation for such cases), and this make them particular targets of corruption.

It follows that corruption derives from networks of control and support which can be based on fear as well as shared interests, co-operation or trust developed in *blat* networks. The environment of instability and short-term strategies in which fear is considered 'the best insurance' (*strakh — luchshee strakhovanie*) could not have been better for the spread of corruption.

Conclusion

Not only the Soviet past but also the unbalanced macro/micro reforms in Russia are to blame for the corrupt tendencies described in this chapter: targeted mainly at the 'state', at the privatization of its property and the marketization of the command economy, the reforms did not pay sufficient attention to customary law, civic responsibilities and civil justice. To quote the director of the research and analysis centre of the People's Party of Russia:

> A fully developed law and legal space have never existed in the Russian social order. The Orthodox mentality and the lack of rights have coexisted and intertwined, and have together helped to form

> that specific moral sensibility of the Russian soul alongside a complete lack of legal awareness. Isn't this a clue to the mysterious Russian soul and to that Russia which we allegedly 'can't comprehend by reason'? (*Elita* 1995: p. 199)

Changes which should have been considered in terms of civil society thus often had the familiar stamp of the state upon them. In his recent *The World after Communism*, Skidelsky describes the end of the 'age of collectivism' as a lapsing into a 'gangsters' capitalism and nomenklatura expropriation and rent-seeking' (Skidelsky 1995: p. 168). Pervasive bribery, corruption, the so-called 'nomenklatura businesses', a criminal 'second' society and the active interpenetration of big business and politics are all part of the criminalized legacy of the 'economy of favours' (Ledeneva 1998). The fundamental issue underlying these phenomena is how to deal with a society in which loyalty to one's connections means more than loyalty to the state and where unwritten codes and social conventions dominate the law. The outcome of the changes now under way in Russia will depend on whether the constructive and destructive effects of informal networks can be recognized as such and selectively integrated into a new Russian order.

Notes

1 The interviews cited in this article were mostly conducted during fieldwork in Russia in 1995 and autumn 1996. Some of this material has also appeared in my *Russia's Economy of Favours* (Ledeneva 1998): I am grateful to Cambridge University Press for permission to re-use it here.

2 Whereas Gregory (1982) counterposes gift and commodity as a binary pair, Sahlins (1972) places them at the opposite ends of a scale: from the positive altruism of what he confusingly calls 'generated reciprocity' to the 'unsociable extreme' of 'negative reciprocity'. According to Sahlins, reciprocity is 'not a single relation between incomings and outgoings, but a "continuum", a "spectrum", ranging from the pure gift […] to barter and theft which are each an attempt to get something for nothing with impunity. In between are those balanced reciprocities in which social conventions stipulate returns of commensurate worth or utility within a finite and a narrow period' (Sahlins 1972, pp. 185–96).

3 The theoretical concept of misrecognition is further elaborated in the Introduction to the present volume.

4 *Current Digest of the Post-Soviet Press*, 45, 1993, 51, p. 14.

5 Ibid., p. 15.
6 'The Goals of Privatization', *Radio i Televidenie* (Novosibirsk), no. 2, 24 January 1995.
7 Enterprise management is often involved in the purchase of shares through a third party.

Bibliography

Chalidze, V. (1977), *Criminal Russia*, New York.
Elita (1995), *Elita Rossii o nastoiashchem i budushchem strany: Interv'iu s predstaviteliami elitnykh grupp*, Moscow.
Follain, J. (1995), *A Dishonoured Society*, London.
Gregory, C.A. (1982), *Gifts and Commodities*, London.
Handelman, S. (1994), *Comrade Criminal: The Theft of the Second Russian Revolution*, London.
Kampfner, J. (1994), *Inside Yeltsin's Russia*, London.
Ledeneva, A. (1998), *An Economy of Favours in Russia: Blat, Networking and Informal Exchange*, Cambridge.
Lloyd, J. (1995), 'The Russians Are Coming', *London Review of Books*, 11 May.
Meek, J. (1995), 'Moscow Gold', *Guardian* (London), 20 September.
Sahlins, M. (1972), *Stone Age Economics*, New York and Chicago, IL.
Skidelsky, R. (1995), *The World After Communism*, London.
Solomenko, E. (1995), 'Operatsiia "Nord"', *Izvestiia*, 31 January.
Vaksberg, A. (1991), *The Soviet Mafia*, New York.
Wedel, J. (1986), *The Private Poland*, New York and Oxford.
Yang, M.M. (1994), *Gifts, Favours and Banquets: The Art of Social Relationships in China*, Ithaca, NY and London.
York, G. (1995), 'From Marx to Mammon', *The Globe and Mail* (Moscow Bureau), 27 May.
Zemtsov, I. (1976), *Partiia ili mafiia? Razvorovannaia respublika*, Paris.

11 Bribery as Reflected in the Russian Language

J.A. Dunn

The changes that have taken place in Russia since 1991 and, in particular, the replacement of a monolithic one-party system by a multi-party and parliamentary democracy, however flawed this may appear to many observers, have undoubtedly had far-reaching consequences for the ways in which the Russian language is used in the political process. These consequences are especially noticeable in certain genres new to the Russian mass media, such as political advertisements and party political broadcasts.

One individual television programme which appears to be exercising a particular influence on the relationship between language and politics is NTV's *Kukly* (Puppets).[1] In this programme, which would be immediately recognizable to British viewers as a Russian equivalent of ITV's *Spitting Image*, latex puppets representing prominent Russian politicians act out various scenarios which are intended to give a satirical gloss to current events.[2] Exactly how *Kukly* relates to the language of Russian politics is a question that the present writer has explored elsewhere,[3] but the point that is relevant to present purposes is that the scenarios often require various forms of slang and unconventional language to be put in the mouths of the politicians being represented.[4]

I am grateful to my colleague Andrei Rogachevskii for suggesting the original topic for this paper, as well as for a number of valuable comments on specific matters, including the suggestion of a Hebrew etymology for *kherek* (see note 10 below). Responsibility for any inadequacies in the treatment of the topic rests solely with the author.

So it was in an edition of *Kukly* entitled ‘O korruptsii’ (On Corruption), broadcast in the spring of 1996.[5] Dressed in Central Asian or Persian costume and sitting in the garden of what appears to be a *chaikhana* (tea-house), the puppet representations of various cronies and enemies of President Yeltsin discuss the alien phenomenon of corruption. Their collective conclusion is a comforting one:[6]

З: Это ведь у них там на западе кругом коррупция; а у нас на Востоке совсем другие традиции...
[...]
З: Не запад, слава Аллаху; у нас тут все по-людски: у нас тут калым...
Г: Хабар...
Ч: Свой интерес...
А: Попросту говоря, мзда...
Ж: Еще навар и подмазка, подмазка однозначно...
Г: И этот, как его, хапанец...
П: Не знал.
Г: Хапанца не знал?
П: Ну, не знал.
З: Это то же самое, что магарыч. Ну, вот, значит, калым, хабар, навар, мзда, хапанец, подмазка, магарыч, это все, конечно, при новой власти останется,
Л: А коррупция?
З: А коррупция, о наиострейший из слаборазвитых, коррупцию будем выжигать каленым железом.
(Z: It’s over there in the West that corruption is rife; here in the East we have totally different traditions…
[…]
Z: It’s not the West here, praise be to Allah; here we do things like normal people: we have *kalym*…
G: *Khabar*…
Ch: *Svoi interes*…
A: To put it simply, *mzda*…
Zh: There’s also *navar* and *podmazka*, definitely *podmazka*…
G: And the other one, what’s its name, *khapanets*…
P: I hadn’t heard of that one.
G: You’d not heard of *khapanets*?
P: No, I hadn’t.
Z: It’s the same as *magarych*. So there we are: *kalym*, *khabar*, *navar*, *mzda*, *khapanets*, *podmazka*, *magarych*;

all these things will stay, of course, when we get into power.

L: And corruption?

Z: Corruption, oh astutest of the not so highly developed, corruption will be expunged with burning irons.)

The terms *kalym*, *khabar*, *navar*, *mzda*, *khapanets*, *podmazka*, *magarych*, left untranslated here, are used to denote the familiar and normal human practices which are being contrasted with the alien *korruptsia*. As the reader will doubtless have realized, they are all words which are or can be used in Russian as synonyms for bribery or corruption.

What this episode displays can be considered an example of what may be termed Russian orientalism. Moreover it is an orientalism that works on two levels: the first level is the target of the satire in this extract, that is, the contemptuous rejection of all Western influence and the complacent acceptance of and indeed pride in what are taken to be 'Eastern' values. The second and less obvious level of orientalism is a view which appears to be endorsed by the scriptwriters, namely that bribery and corruption, of which they clearly disapprove, belong to the so-called 'Eastern' features of Russian life, imported through contact with Russia's eastern neighbours and with the oriental world in general.[7]

The question to what extent this orientalist view of Russian corruption is justified can be answered at least in part by an examination of the etymology of the words used in the *Kukly* episode. The word *kalym* is clearly of Tatar origin; its original meaning is 'dowry' (Fasmer 1986–87: vol. 2, p. 171; Shlyakhov and Adler 1995: p. 58). *Khabar* is also probably of Turkic origin: it is assumed to be connected with a word found in various Turkic languages meaning 'news' (Fasmer 1986–87: vol. 4, p. 213). This circumstance was the occasion of some amusement recently when a private television station opened in Kazakhstan under the name 'Khabar', not least because the owner of the station happened to be the daughter of President Nazarbaev. The etymology of this word, however, is not entirely certain, since the difference in meaning is not altogether easy to explain. This question is complicated further by what one source suggests is an additional meaning of a variant form of this word (*khabara*), namely 'prostitute' (*STLBZh*, 1992: p. 265).

Of the remaining terms there is one other which has an oriental origin: *magarych* comes from Arabic via Turkic, but this word is found in Old Russian from around 1500 and occurs in the other East Slavonic languages, so that it has had time to become well established (Fasmer 1986–87: vol. 2, p. 635). Perceived etymology often differs from scholarly etymology, and it would seem unlikely that this word is normally perceived as being in any way exotic.

As for the rest, their origins are clearly not oriental. *Mzda* is descended from Indo-European and is found in Old Church Slavonic (Fasmer 1986–87: vol. 2, p. 618). *Podmazka* has a transparent Russian etymology and can be compared to the English phrase 'to grease someone's palm'. Similarly, *navar* is from the Slavonic verb *varit′*, 'to boil'. Even the obscure *khapanets*, unknown to one of the participants and the only one of these words not found in any of the dictionaries consulted for this exercise,[8] can be derived from the verb *khapat′*, 'to take', now on the fringes of standard Russian but of undisputed Indo-European origin (Fasmer 1986–87: vol. 4, p. 222).[9] The final term, *svoi interes*, involves, just like the hated *korruptsiia*, a word borrowed from a Western language.

An etymological examination of the list of terms used by the *Kukly* characters thus gives at best only partial support to the orientalist proposition. This list is not, however, exhaustive, and it is interesting to compare it with the following list of synonyms of the word *vziatka*, 'to bribe', given in a dictionary of prison-camp slang:

> абиссинский налог, бакшиш, баран, барашек, вазелин, воздух, калым, курица, лапа, лапик, лапух, лопух, отмазка, панама, панты, погостный калым, подмазка, скуп, хабара, хала, химля, хэрек, шах-ход, швай, яса, ясак, ясырь (*STLBZh*: p. 317)

This list contains words which belong, or which can be regarded as belonging, to thieves' slang or *blatnoi zhargon*. Unlike the *Kukly* list, but not surprisingly in the context of this type of language, several of the words included here are of uncertain etymology: Fasmer (1986–87) does not include *panty*, *khimlia*, *kherek*, *shakh-khod* and *shvai*, though the penultimate of these is probably of Iranian origin.[10] Some of the remaining terms are Slavonic or Western words where the link with bribery is transparent (*vazelin* [cf. vaseline], *lapa*, 'paw', and its derivatives, *otmazka* [cf. *podmazka*], *skup* [cf. *kupit'*, 'to buy']), and the only words of clearly oriental origin are *bakshish, iasak, iasyr'* (Fasmer 1986–87: vol. 1, p. 111; ibid., vol. 4, pp. 564, 566), though the first (*bakshish*) is common in some Western languages (including English) and may, in fact, have entered Russian from that direction. Also to be mentioned here is the phrase *abissinskii nalog*, 'Abyssinian tax', which is a cultural, rather than etymological, orientalism; though the semantic and geographical equivalencies are not exact, its associations are analogous to the English phrase 'Egyptian P.T.', used in military slang to mean 'resting' or 'sleeping' (Brewer 1997: p. 172). The list published in *STLBZh* thus seems to confirm the conclusion suggested by the list in *Kukly*, which is that the linguistic evidence gives at best only partial support to the orientalist interpretation of Russian corruption.

Only three of the terms used in *Kukly* appear in the *STLBZh* list (and one of those is in a variant form), from which it may be inferred that the majority of the former are not part of *blatnoi zhargon*. The latter is, moreover, one of the shorter lists of synonyms to appear in that book: its twenty-seven items compare with 137 synonyms for *vorovat'*, 'to steal', seventy-nine for *nozh*, 'knife', 172 for *prostitutka*, 'prostitute', *zhenshchina legkogo povedeniia*, 'woman of easy virtue', and even thirty-nine for *chai*, 'tea', *chifir'*, 'strong tea used as a drug'. It would thus appear that the practice of bribery is relatively poorly represented in thieves' slang, while on the other hand there exist a number of synonymous terms to indicate this activity which do not belong to that particular layer of language. On this basis it is contended that the linguistic representation of bribery in Russian is different from that of other criminal activity and that this difference is a reflection of the peculiar nature of bribery as a crime. At the same time it is suggested that the use of the various orientalisms has little to do with the supposed or the genuine origin of the practice, but serves a rather different purpose.

There is a problem with bribery, as indeed with other activities which might be considered less than seemly, in that it is often desirable to refer to them in terms which introduce a certain opaqueness. This is not so much to hide the fact that the subject of conversation is when all is said and done criminal activity; that would have no point, since everyone is fully aware of what is going on. The real purpose is to make the transaction less undignified for the participants. In this context *korruptsiia* may sound like a nasty Western disease, but the word *vziatka* is awkwardly direct: the all too evident link with the verb *vziat'*, 'to take', gives the proceedings a crude transparency which is likely to be equally uncomfortable to giver and recipient alike. In this context it is interesting that the commentator Il'ia Zemtsov notes in connection with the late Soviet period that 'a taboo has been placed on the word *vziatka*' (Zemtsov 1989: p. 44).

Zemtsov (ibid.) suggests that the reason for this taboo is the working of a 'precautionary reflex' (*refleks predostorozhnosti*), caused by awareness of the fact that bribery is a serious crime. This may well be the case, but there is another possible reason for the peculiarities of the language used in relation to bribery and corruption. Assault or murder or robbery or card-sharping are, or tend to be, crimes perpetrated on innocent victims by criminals; in the Russian context it is precisely these crimes which are likely to involve fully signed-up members of the criminal fraternity. Bribery, on the other hand, is a transaction involving two people who are equally guilty, but who are in other respects likely to be perfectly respectable citizens. Indeed, one of them, the recipient, must almost by definition be a respectable citizen, since if this person is not in a position of influence, what is the point of paying the bribe?

In these circumstances it becomes understandable why there should be a desire to resort to language which is a little more indirect, more tactful or more soothing to the delicate sensibilities of both persons involved in the transaction, in a word, a euphemism. There exist for this purpose several expedients. One of these is to use a decently obscure word, if possible, one that is manifestly foreign. It is, after all, difficult to regard a practice as wrong if one is not quite sure of the meaning of the word used to describe it, and if suspicions do arise that something is untoward, the use of an exoticism or an obscure word lends the offence a remote dignity which is lacking in the direct term. In the context of the *Kukly* broadcast, *kalym*, *khabar* (exoticisms) and *khapanets* (apparently the most obscure of the terms used) belong to this category.

The second expedient is to use a term which is in itself respectable. The word *mzda*, for example, simply means 'financial reward'; there is ostensibly nothing inherently wrong with that. Equally, someone who says '*Ia sobliudaiu svoi interes*' (I am looking after my own interests) may not win any prizes for altruism, but is doing only what any prudent person would do. The word *podmazka* has the basic meaning of 'lubrication', and its respectability is enhanced by the diminutivizing prefix *pod-*. Its euphemistic force is indicated by two sayings in Dal′: *Bliny pekut″, tak″ podmazyvaiut″* (If you're going to make pancakes, you've got to grease the pan) and *Ne podmazano — ne katitsia* (If it's not greased, it won't roll), both of which refer to bribery (Dal′ 1978–80: vol. 3, p. 185). The word *navar* presents a more homely image: its basic meaning is the fat or grease which forms on the surface of certain types of soup. In financial contexts it can have the more innocent meaning of 'profit'.[11] It is true that the word *magarych* is perhaps slightly less respectable: the definitions in Dal′ suggest a link with horse-trading, but the most common meaning in modern Russian is a round of drinks consumed to celebrate the successful completion of a bargain, which, while unlikely to gain favour with the likes of Mikhail Gorbachev, is not inherently corrupt (Dal′ 1978–80: vol. 2, p. 288; *SRIa*: vol. 2, p. 213).

The third expedient is circumlocution. The use of a phrase which refers indirectly to the matter being described can be an effective form of euphemism, especially if the phrase contains terms which are themselves respectable. Although in general circumlocution does play some role in the forming of Russian euphemisms, as is shown by the terms *smorgonskii student*, 'bear' (literally 'Smorgon student'; Dal′ 1978–80: vol. 2, p. 311)[12] and, albeit disguised by the Russian liking for univerbation, *orgvyvody* (*organizatsionnye vyvody*, literally 'organizational conclusions', meaning 'dismissals of people from their jobs after a crisis') and *spetsmedsluzhba* ('special medical service', seen on vehicles used to transport 'patients' to sobering-up stations), it does not seem to figure prominently in relation to bribery. Of the terms found in the two lists only *abissinskii nalog* fits securely into this category.

The language of bribery and corruption as crime differs from that of other criminal activity. Because of its peculiar nature (and perhaps because the true *vor v zakone*[13] would not stoop to such actions?) the giving and taking of bribes does not figure prominently in the secret and essentially dysphemistic language of Russian criminals. Instead, bribery is largely represented in the Russian language by exoticisms and euphemisms, the purpose of which is to defuse the potential embarrassment of a situation in which otherwise respectable people are engaged in an illegal transaction.[14]

Notes

1 NTV is commercial television channel owned by the Media-Most group. It started broadcasting in October 1993 and rapidly acquired a reputation for independently minded news coverage and lively and innovative programming. More recently its reputation for independence has been tarnished somewhat by the open involvement of Igor′ Malashenko, the Director-General, in Yeltsin's campaign for re-election in 1996 and in 1997 by an increasing tendency to act as a mouthpiece for the commercial and political interests of the owner of Media-Most, Vladimir Gusinskii.

2 *Kukly* has been broadcast weekly since 1995, and the scripts of many of the early editions have been published in Shenderovich 1996. Though Shenderovich has written many (though not all) of the scripts, the idea for the programme seems to belong to Vasilii Grigor′ev (a.k.a. Basile Grigoriev), while the puppets are the responsibility of A. Drozdov and Alain Duverne. Grigor′ev's French links and the involvement of Duverne suggest that the main direct inspiration may be French programmes such as *Les Guignols de l'info*, rather than *Spitting Image* itself.

3 J.A. Dunn, '*Куклы* and the Russian Language', *Rusistika*, 18, September 1998, pp. 3–7.

4 The programme has been threatened with legal action on more than one occasion (see the episode entitled 'Ne tiani rezinu', Shenderovich 1996: pp. 145–51, and also Bogomolov 1995: p. 19). For what are therefore understandable tactical reasons Shenderovich in the published version of the scripts does not use the names of real politicians, but refers to the puppet 'characters' by nicknames, for example, Boriska (Yeltsin), Zhirik (Zhirinovskii), Andriusha-Kozyrek (Andrei Kozyrev), Tolik-Vaucher (Chubais) and Mishel′-Stavropol′skii (Gorbachev). He describes these nicknames as belonging to the kindergarten ('*tikhie detsadovskie imena*', Shenderovich 1996: p. 5), though some readers may take the view that they are equally redolent of the criminal world.

5 The videotape recording of this edition to which the present writer had access does not unfortunately indicate the precise date. The script for this edition, though written by Shenderovich, does not appear in his collection.

6 The various speakers are: 'Ziuganov' (Z), 'Grachev' (G), 'Chernomyrdin' (Ch), 'Anpilov' (A), 'Zhirinovskii' (Zh), 'Primakov'

(P), 'Lebed'' (L). Because of changes in the personnel of politics, not all these 'characters' have nicknames in the Shenderovich collection.

7 It is not among the purposes of the present chapter to identify the ideology of *Kukly*, if indeed such a thing exists, but it may be noted that an orientalism of the type discussed here does appear to be a recurrent theme of the programme. See, for example, the episodes entitled 'Tsar'-Sultan' (Shenderovich 1996: pp. 51–9) and 'Vostok — delo tonkoe' (based on the Soviet film *Beloe solntse pustyni* [The White Sun of the Desert, 1970], Shenderovich 1996: pp. 89–98, esp. p. 97).

8 In addition to those mentioned above these are: Dal' 1978–80; Ben-Iakov 1982; Kozlovskii 1983; Skachinskii 1983; *SVIa*; Bykov 1992; Dubiagin and Teplitskii, 1993; Elistratov 1994; Baldaev 1997.

9 Dal' (1978–80: vol. 4, p. 542) gives the meaning *brat' vziatki*, 'to take bribes', for this verb.

10 It is possible that *kherek* is connected with Romany *xara, hera* and associated adjective *xårakó* ('penny') (John Sampson, *The Dialect of the Gypsies of Wales,* Oxford, 1926, p. 178), although the nearest relevant words in the Demeters' dictionary is *kharkuma* ('*med'*') and *kharkuno* ('*mednyi*') (Demeter and Demeter 1990: p. 162). Another possible etymology for this word is the Hebrew noun *chérek* ('cut'; see Shachter 1961: vol. 1, p. 265).

11 As in the following example: '*Ne torguias', otvalil troiak (uchtite, chto nam, "prodavtsam", otpustili ekzempliar po dva s poltinoi, znachit, navar s gul'kin nos)*' ('Without bothering to haggle he threw down a three-rouble note (bear in mind that the "sales team" were getting the copies for two-and-a-half roubles each, so our profits amounted to peanuts)') (Vasiukhin 1992: p. 19).

12 There used to be a facility for training dancing bears in the Belarusian town of Smorgon.

13 Literally 'a thief within the law', that is, a sworn member of Russia's confraternity of criminals.

14 While preparing the original version of this chapter I was intrigued to read the following observation made by the journalist Simon Hoggart in the *Guardian* of 10 May 1997, shortly after a British general election campaign characterized by accusations of corruption: 'Wherever I went during the election, I met Tories who would say indulgently, "Well, at least we have less corruption here than in any other European country".' Perhaps those who are sceptical about Russian orientalism or about perennial Russian claims to uniqueness can take comfort from imagining a group of British politicians discussing the merits of their country: 'We do things properly: we may have masonic handshakes, the old school tie, favours for a friend, a little pot of money for my old age [*attrib.* Reginald Maudling, July 1969], cash in brown envelopes, but,

thank God, at least we have less corruption here than in any other European country.'

Bibliography

Baldaev, D.S. (1997), *Slovar' blatnogo zhargona v 2-x tomakh*, Moscow.

Ben-Iakov, B. (1982), *Slovar' argo GULaga*, Frankfurt-am-Main.

Bogomolov, I. (1995), '"Kuklam" na smekh', *Moskovskie novosti*, 48.

Brewer (1997), *Brewer's Dictionary of Twentieth-Century Phrase and Fable*, 3rd edn, London.

Bykov, V. (1992), *Russkaia fenia*, Munich.

Dal', V. (1978–80), *Tolkovyi slovar' zhivogo velikorusskogo iazyka*, 2nd edn, 4 vols, St Petersburg and Moscow, 1880–82, reprint, Moscow.

Demeter, R.S. and Demeter, P.S. (1990), *Tsygansko-russkii i russko-tsyganskii slovar' (kelderarskii dialekt)*, Moscow.

Dubiagin, Iu.P. and Teplitskii, E.A. (1993), *Kratkii anglo-russkii i russko-angliiskii slovar' ugolovnogo zhargona*, Moscow.

Elistratov, V.S. (1994), *Slovar' moskovskogo argo*, Moscow.

Fasmer [Vasmer], M. (1986–87), *Etimologicheskii slovar' russkogo iazyka*, 2nd edn, 4 vols, Moscow.

Kozlovskii, V. (1983), *Sobranie russkikh vorovskikh slovarei v chetyrekh tomakh*, New York.

Shachter, H. (1961), *The New Universal Hebrew–English Dictionary*, 2 vols, Tel-Aviv.

Shenderovich, V. (1996), *Kukly*, Moscow.

Shlyakhov, V. and Adler, E. (1995), *Russian Slang and Colloquial Expressions*, New York.

Skachinskii, A. (1983), *Slovar' blatnogo zhargona v SSSR*, New York.

SRIa, *Slovar' russkogo iazyka v chetyrekh tomakh*, Moscow, 1981–84.

STLBZh, *Slovar' tiuremno-lagerno-blatnogo zhargona*, ed. D.S. Baldaev, V.K. Belko and I.M. Iusupov, Moscow, 1992.

SVIa, *Slovar' vorovskogo iazyka: Slova, vyrazheniia, zhesty, tatuirovki*, Tiumen', n.d.

Vasiukhin, V. (1992), 'Kak ia prodaval "Sem' dnei"', *Sem' dnei*, 9.

Zemtsov, I. (1989), *Real'nost' i grani perestroiki*, London.

12 Rethinking Bribery in Contemporary Russia

Caroline Humphrey

Introduction

Bribery is commonly merged together with more general 'corruption' in studies of Russian society. Statements such as the following are commonplace: 'Less than six years after it began, the second great Russian revolution of this century is awash in corruption, opportunism, and crime. The government not only has failed to pursue the evidence of its predecessors' venality; it has been unable to hold in check the greed of its own ministers' (Handelman 1995: p. 3). This chapter attempts a more nuanced account of the specificity of bribery and its relations to certain other types of payments. It is not possible to document the incidence of bribery.[1] But, with the modesty appropriate to analysis of such a volatile epoch, we can try to explain what people think of bribery and whether this is changing.

It will be suggested that recent massive commercialization, together with lack of clear legal sanctions, has produced a myriad of new transactional 'grey areas', but that nevertheless ordinary people do make discriminations in how they ethically evaluate particular types of action. Bribery remains a morally condemned idea in Russian popular culture. It is, however, being re-thought in two ways since Soviet times: the scope of application of the idea of the bribe has shrunk, and the grounds for disapproval of bribery are changing and are sometimes challenged by different ethics. *Vziatka* (the bribe) as a representational category is applied unequivocally only to the public state sphere, and it is used with much less certainty with regard to unorthodox payments in private commercial life, which tend to be described in other ways, as 'additional fees', 'tariffs', 'subsidies', 'gratuities', 'discounts', 'premiums' and the like. Since 1991, as the formerly pervasive branches of the Soviet state have retreated, while private firms, cartels, crony networks and mafia-like organizations have burgeoned, the bribe may have increased numerically, but it has also retreated to a smaller arena of socio-economic life. Meanwhile, with regard to bribery itself attitudes seem to be diverging. We can begin to see links between different views and the economic situation of various categories of people. For the economically disadvantaged, bribery is abhorred and yet it is an essential survival strategy; for the radically impoverished, it is mostly out of reach and condemned as an unfair tactic of the better-off; and finally, among a small powerful élite, moral disapproval of bribery is swept aside in favour of a new ethic of commercial necessity.

The point here is that the torrent of analyses of corruption in the Western press, mirrored often in the Russian press, does not correspond to the differentiated practice and discourse of the people themselves. Journalistic harangues about generalized corruption cannot be helpful while they assume that all a-legal transactions are equally condemned and condemnable. Indeed, they risk a new orientalism whereby Russians appear as a thoroughly corrupted people. In my experience this is not at all the case. Certain transactions, like the bribe, are generally understood to be reprehensible, frequently even by the people practising them, while others, equally a-legal or even illegal, are thought to be morally good, and yet others are regarded as ethically neutral because they are forced by circumstances. It is this tangle that this chapter seeks to elucidate.

If we attend to Russian understandings it is possible to define the bribe (*vziatka*) by three features: it is a payment improperly accepted to influence public duties that are meant to be performed for free; it is intentionally and voluntarily taken/offered; and it creates a particular, usually short-lived, 'negative' social relation between the giver and the taker. The last feature is perhaps the most unfamiliar, but its social importance begins to be evident when one considers a statement made to me by several Russians: 'It is impossible to bribe a kinsman or a friend.' The statement brings to the fore three points made by Noonan (1984: pp. xii–xiii): that what counts as bribery differs in different cultures; that a tension often exists between laws on bribery and the actually applied moral views of a community; and that the seriousness with which bribery is condemned varies from society to society and historically within one country. The statement that one cannot bribe a relative or a friend means in effect that, in Russia today, inducements paid to such closely related people do not count as bribes but as something else.[2]

The Russian idea of the bribe focuses on the taking (*vziat'*, 'to take'), as opposed to the corrupting offer implied by the English word.[3] If the English abstract noun 'bribery' can connote generalized improper persuasion, the Russian *vziatochnichestvo* seems to refer simply to the presence of acts of bribing. In both languages, however, the definite noun (bribe or *vziatka*) refers to an exchange in a single time-span. Thus, although someone may repeatedly accept bribes, in each case the illegal favour is due for a particular payment taken. It is this feature of the *vziatka*, that it is essentially a one-off transaction, that serves to distinguish it sociologically from the reciprocal exchanges of favours within social networks of people in ongoing long-term relationships (*vzaimopomoshch'*) or the back-door version of this, *blat*. The 'presentness' of the return for the bribe lays bare the transactionality of the act and removes the possibility of seeing it in the warm light of 'giving' relationships. In other words, unlike the gift or the favour, the act of bribing cannot be seen as generous if its return is integral to the definition of the act. In part, the bribe's existence beyond the boundary of generosity also has to do with who can be bribed, because that person is always someone who has something specific to give. A warmly regarded relationship, on the other hand, seems to imply a richness of potential interactions, such that if you give something in that relationship you will not be sure of either when a return may be made or what precisely that return may consist of. Analytically, if *vzaimopomoshch'* or *blat* consist of multiple illicit favours given over time within such personal networks, the *vziatka* sets up specific, immediate deals outside them.

People prefer mutual reciprocity, as I shall show later. It follows from this that bribery is something to which people *resort*; in other words, bribery is practised when people do not have the necessary networks of friends. Thus, in everyday life for ordinary people bribery is something akin to other unpleasant economic necessities which are supposed to have disappeared with the previous regime (like queuing) and which are stigmatized partly because people with good connections do not have to engage in them.[4] Because of its relative impersonality and uncertainty, bribing often necessitates involving a mediator. The mediator provides information (for example, about who is dishonest enough to accept the bribe and yet reliable enough to perform the deed, how much should be paid, when is the right moment and so on) and becomes both a bridge and a buffer in what I shall suggest is the *essentially negative relation* of the briber and the bribed. Sometimes, as I shall show in a case-study in the next section of this chapter, mediators can form part of an ongoing structure, which persists while the individuals offering and taking bribes change.

The specificity of the *vziatka* can be seen if Russian practice is set against the types of bribery analysed by Reisman (1979: pp. 69–94). Reisman, referring mainly to America, suggests that there are three kinds of bribe: *transactional bribes* (payments to an official to expedite matters in one's favour, but not involving any illegal activity); *variance bribes* (payments made to secure deviance from the norm or the law); and *outright purchase* (when what is bought is not a particular service but a servant, an employee who appears to give full loyalty as an official while actually favouring the interests of the briber). In Russia the transactional type — the box of chocolates, flowers, bottle of vodka, envelope with a few roubles for the nurse, accountant, teacher and so on — is too much part of everyday necessity to be seen as a fully-fledged *vziatka.* Like a tip (*chaevye*), which is paid after rather than before a service, the transactional type of payment is seen as fundamentally innocuous, since after all no norm has been broken. The terms commonly used, *podmazat'* (to undergrease) and *dat' na lapu* (give to the paw), nevertheless suggest something slightly underhand, and the convention certainly is to be discreet about such matters. A telling point is that in this kind of minor payment, if money is handed over it is pocketed but not 'rudely' and openly counted. This practice indicates the existence of an unspoken convention that exactly how much is paid does not matter, though in fact this almost invariably masks what one man described to me as 'well-established local tariffs'. In such a situation uncertainty about how much to give can be a source of considerable anxiety and irritation. If someone is new to a place or lacks local knowledge they can never be sure that they have given 'enough' for the official actually to perform the service. In this respect people sometimes say they are glad about the rise of commercialism, because at least the new 'fees' are out in the open.[5] In contrast to common 'undergreasing', when a payment merits the more serious term 'bribe' (*vziatka*) the amount paid matters explicitly, is agreed by negotiation, and the transaction is definitely secret. There must be some overlap with 'giving to the paw', but in general the *vziatka* corresponds to what Reisman calls the 'variance bribe', when specific payments are made for definite violations of rules.

I would also suggest that the Russian idea of the 'bribe' does not extend to Reisman's third, 'most noxious', type, the outright purchase (Reisman 1979: pp. 88–93). Such a case turns a public office-holder into someone who is also a secret employee. The maintenance of the organization has precedence over particular acts, so the sporadic nature of the bribe is replaced by the regularity of wages. As the case-study shows, there are ambiguous cases here too, for example, when a customs officer is regularly paid bribes for each consignment he allows through. But the fully bought person (*kuplennyi*), who cannot refuse a trick and who remains a member of the illicit organization even after being dismissed from the official post, is no longer seen as taking bribes but rather as being 'kept' (*na soderzhanii*). Particularly prevalent in 'mafia'-organized activity, the relation is often underpinned by threat of violence, so the bought person is more afraid of reprisals from underworld bosses than of discovery by police (Konstantinov 1997: p. 235). This situation removes an essential aspect of the bribe, which is that it is generally understood to be a voluntary act which might in principle be refused. Thus regular payments made to police or racketeers (for example, by traders and kiosk-holders) are also not counted as bribes but as 'tribute' (*dan'*), given under duress.

In some ways, attitudes towards bribery today continue those of Soviet times, but in others they diverge from them. The Soviet state created countless situations in which services were 'free' and 'equal', and yet could hardly be obtained without paying bribes. Whatever they actually did, people on the whole admired the Communist ethic of honesty and accepted the public socialist ideology of unpaid, egalitarian distribution. The idea that housing, social services, transport, education and so forth might be paid for at the cost of producing them never entered people's heads, if only because there was no way to know how much this cost was. Bribery therefore was doubly illegitimate, because it not only went against the public rules of probity and honesty, but also because the very idea that there might be a financial cost to the state's provisions (for example, the idea that 'time equals money') was absent. So persons offering and taking bribes could not see themselves as employing money to pay for something, only as personally and duplicitously depriving others of their due. People might well feel that 'stealing' (usually known by some other term, such as 'lifting') from the state at the workplace was almost their right, because they were badly paid and it was the state's duty to supply its workforce. But I have been told of a different feeling about bribery. Unlike 'lifting', bribery could not be seen just as a relation between yourself and publicly owned objects lying around; first, to bribe was to provoke the venality of *someone*, and secondly it was a degrading use of money to divert the just allocation of resources away from its due recipients, one's comrades.[6] And from the point of view of the official, 'taking' can be like stealing from an individual.[7] Bribery was practised, but was rhetorically repudiated by both ordinary people and high officials. A woman, describing a bribe she had given, said to me, 'I hated myself for "buying" Valia and I hated the regime for putting me in the situation where I had to do it.' Soviet officials accused of bribery, even while sitting in prison as a result of their own alleged confessions, like Usmankhodzhaev, former First Secretary of Uzbekistan (Karaulov 1993: pp. 116–32), or Churbanov, former first deputy in the Ministry of Internal Affairs of the USSR and son-in-law of Brezhnev (Karaulov 1990: p. 372), resolutely refused to admit that they had taken bribes, insisting that the accusations and confessions were fabricated.

Of course, it must be admitted that there were other, more cynical ways of talking, where the officials of the state were pictured as an anonymous 'they'. Enquiring about whether a friend's son was accepted into an institute, someone might ask, '*Dal?*' (Did you give?) to which the laconic reply would be '*Dal*' (I gave). In such discourse, assuming a rotten regime, reference to bribery could take on the overtones almost of resistance, that is, refusing the whole oily, sanctimonious, spuriously 'personal' relations between officialdom and the people, and treating 'them' as no more than obstacles to be paid off. Today such late-Soviet attitudes are diverging into two uncertain streams. On the one hand, bribery is pictured tiredly and cynically as an inevitable aspect of commerce and capitalism. On the other, there are new perceptions that state and city officials, like everyone else in a commercial world, should be accountable. Either they should not take bribes, or they should give a receipt (!) — and in the latter case, the representation begins to shift, so the payment ceases to be a bribe and becomes a tariff (*taksa*) or an additional charge (*nadbavka*). 'Everything and everyone has their price', people now say — but with a hint of uncertainty, as if they are aware that in the new circumstances things should not be like this. Outflanked by tariffs and discounts, the bribe has almost become an insult from the past. But nevertheless it lurks still, being applicable to hidden, illicit agreements in those spheres where public probity continues to be expected. But this is not entirely a survival from Soviet times and the situation now is complex and many-layered. Radical income differentiation has raised the stakes, creating both more reliance on bribery for survival as well as louder condemnation of it. To earlier moral bases for such judgements — Christian ethics, the ideal of the just, allocatory state, and one's role as a deserving citizen in it — is added a new post-Soviet one: the idea that people wielding cold money rather than their common humanity are taking advantage of the weakness of the state.

An important aspect of the new situation is that bribery can now be talked and written about openly. Accusations fly around concerning other people and the press is likewise eager to publish stories concerning named businessmen and officials. This suggests a heated moral temperature around the subject akin to that of witchcraft accusations in other societies, a point discussed at length in Noonan (1984). The topic of the personal and political vendettas pursued by bribery accusations is an important one, but in this short chapter I shall confine myself to involvements in bribery itself. The fact is that people rarely use the term *vziatka* about their own activities.

There are two aspects to the misrecognition of one's own bribes, which overlap although they can be analytically distinguished. The overt disguising of an act as 'not a bribe' is to be expected when it contravenes public norms and is no different from the various masking tactics intended to deceive the outside world that may accompany any illegal act. In the case of bribery, however, there may also be self-deception. It is suggested here that this relates to the personal nature of the negative emotions most frequently associated with the bribe: shame and humiliation. As Simmel has argued (1978: p. 384), in all European cultures even small bribery is abhorred as the purchase of a person ('purchase' being used here not in the sense of hiring an employee, as in Reisman, but to suggest the idea of buying something which should not be bought, a personality). Indeed, the small bribe is somehow more shameful than a very large one, suggesting as it does that the person is willing to sell themselves for a paltry amount. Simmel argues that a huge transaction, just like an expensively 'kept' person such as a millionaire's mistress, escapes entirely from the slur of bribery. The person in question may even be admired as worthy of the expenditure of tremendous sums (Simmel 1978: p. 388). As we shall see, this applies also in contemporary Russian, where *vziatka* tends not to be used in such cases and the word is somehow confined to smallish amounts handed over in person.

Specific emotions spring to life in the bribe encounter, when the domination and 'hold' of one side over another is negotiated by subtle signs. So the disguise which cloaks the act of bribery is not just an issue of the extent to which people accept public norms, but is also tied to the equivocality of *facing the accomplice*. The act itself, of 'handing over' and 'taking', has the potential of putting out on the table, as it were, the price of the persons of the participants. As the case-study shows, even in criminal circles the discomfort this engenders gives rise to characteristic approach tactics, displacements, 'non-meetings' and evasions. So in discussing bribery we are not dealing simply with a moralizing public discourse about declining social standards that floats separately over cynical private habits. The arena of the bribe itself is a space full of ethical discriminations, and it is in the physical actions and etiquettes of displacement that we can see the evidence that moralizing and practice meet.

Anthropology has paid attention mostly to positive relations in society, especially those that are ongoing and self-reproducing. Negative, disavowed relations have received relatively little comment. Bribery is one of such relations. Although, as pointed out earlier, the bribe sets up what is in principle a short-lived, even instantaneous, relation, in fact its negative charge lives on afterwards. Each side has entrusted to the other the possibility of disclosure and shame. I have suggested that in Russia the potential scenarios in which such feelings might arise have diminished drastically in the past few years, having been overtaken and swamped by relations conceived in other ways and with other ethics. They still exist, however, as will be documented below.

In what follows I provide a case-study of bribery to illustrate some of the points just made. The argument then broadens out to indicate how the bribe is distinguished from other types of relation now current in everyday life.

A Case-Study of Bribery

The case concerns bribery of customs officials on the Russian borders with Lithuania and Latvia in the mid-1990s, based on the work of Konstantinov (1997). Starting around 1992, various firms in St Petersburg realized they could make huge profits by buying up metals cheaply from ailing state factories and selling them abroad. To do this, they had to pass through the customs at the border with the Baltic states, whence the goods were exported by other firms to Poland, Sweden, Holland or Germany.

To exit from Russia each container-load of metals had to be accompanied by a Goods Customs Declaration, which was filled out at the customs office in St Petersburg and then confirmed by inspection officers at the border itself. This set of circumstances gave ample opportunity for bribery.[8]

The best-laid plans are liable to failure. In September 1992, five lorries carrying nickel and copper belonging to the firm Trans-Oktavian were stopped at the Brusnichnoe post near Vyborg and turned back. They had been delayed en route and therefore missed the rota of the bribed officials waiting for them. Forced to improvise, the firm attempted to rush the customs into letting them through: the trucks lurched out of the forest fifteen minutes before the post was due to close and the armed guards with the convey threatened to report the inspectors if they did not 'perform their duties in working time' and make a double-quick check. But an official spotted an irregularity in the documents, phoned the St Petersburg customs office, and discovered another thicket of bribery there — at the truck inspection workshop called 'the pit'. Here there was huge pressure of work and a constantly changing staff, yet in such a place an officer could learn the secrets of preparing false documents (*fuflia*). The unsuccessful venture of Trans-Oktavian provides us with two significant incidents that shed light on bribery more generally.

The customs man had spotted that there was something wrong with the stamp used on the documents. Now this stamp (number 181) belonged to a girl called Lena working in the St Petersburg office, and she had carelessly left it lying around.[9] While she was away for a few days, her brother Sergei, who worked in 'the pit', had filched the stamp in order to use it 'to pay back a large loan' he had obtained from Artem, an employee of Trans-Oktanvian. Artem asked for the customs stamp for one day, telling Sergei that he would use it to formalize a customs declaration for some dollars he intended to export. Sergei, having accepted the 'loan', gave him the stamp knowing really that it would be used for something far greater than a few dollars. Meanwhile, Sergei was too ashamed to admit to his sister Lena that he had taken the stamp. He encouraged her to think that it was 'lost' and that he had had a new one made for her, exactly the same as the old one, so that she would not get into trouble. He gave her the 'new' stamp, but when she looked carefully she understood that it was the old one and that her brother was deceiving her (Konstantinov 1997: pp. 309–13).

In this episode we can see the characteristic misrecognition and displacement of the bribe. Evidently Sergei was bribed by Artem, but neither of them admitted it. What is interesting is that their disguises were not addressed to the public (that is, were not a matter of putting the law off the scent) but were addressed to themselves and their close kin. Artem and Sergei pretended that the money paid was a loan and that the hand-over of the stamp was for a small personal transaction, thus avoiding ever having to use the word bribe. Sergei meanwhile elaborated a story to try to convince his sister that he had not taken a bribe and not filched the stamp.

This is an example of what we can see as the dual mechanism of the negation of the bribe by the people concerned. On the one hand, Konstantinov documents negative moments such as the tearing-up of a written bribe agreement (ibid.: p. 154), the non-meeting when the bribe is left on the back seat of a parked car to be collected later by the accomplice (ibid.: p. 137), or the silent offer, when a policeman hands a note to a girl reporting a theft, 'All that interests me is *baksy* [dollars]', a note she tore into tiny pieces having handed over $100 (ibid.: p. 202), all of which can be seen as cover-ups to hinder investigation. But, at the same time, all of these acts are also more phenomenal repudiations of bribery itself, acts of destruction and deflection that cancel out what is denied by the honest self. Even bribed customs officials at the border do the same: they keep two seals, a false one for goods they know to be contraband, and a genuine one for ordinary work, and Konstantinov remarks that they *do not even look at* the counterfeit documents they stamp (ibid.: p. 317).

Now the second incident connected with Trans-Oktavain is the history of how Artem came to work for the firm. It turns out that he too had previously been a customs official in 'the pit', but had been dismissed for refusing to name mates involved in a drunken brawl. Former customs officials are hot property in smuggling circles, because they know the changing formulas whereby counterfeit documents can be made to look genuine. All the same, Artem might have remained without a job were it not that he was helped to find work 'according to his profession' by Oleg, a customs worker who 'took' from Trans-Oktavian. Oleg suggested to the firm that they employ Artem to prepare false documents. Here we can begin to perceive the structure surrounding bribery along the 'channel' leading from Russia to the rest of Europe.

Most common was for a particular customs official on the rota to be bribed for a given load at a particular date and time. Konstantinov describes an example: on 30 November 1993 the chief inspector at the tiny post of Torfianovka, Vladimir Ivanovich, took $2,000 for passing two containers of copper, and he subsequently took money for two further loads on 12 and 28 December. Then he refused to take any further bribes, but the smugglers persuaded the head of the executive department, Sergei Evgen′evich, to take $1,500 for two further loads. He then also gave up, and it became the turn of a third official, Iurii Vasil′evich, to take the bribes, this time for only $1,000. There are two sides to the pattern thus revealed. On the one side, that of the customs, one must realize that the officials came from a small desolate village, which did not even have its own school, where the customs zone was an area of wealth, movement and excitement, with its own glittering shop. All the villagers were insiders (*svoi*) and mostly related by kinship. The chance to 'earn' by bribery was passed among them. Seniority was respected in the amounts demanded, and individuals moved in and out of the system (Konstantinov 1997: pp. 420–1).

On the other side, that of the smugglers, it is evident that correctly arranging the bribe was a matter of considerable organizational complexity. They had to calculate the speed of the convoy and align it with the coming on duty of the bought team, as well as ensuring that viligant overseers and extraneous lorries were out of the way. Konstantinov estimates that around 20 per cent of the customs officials took bribes, and then perhaps only for a time (ibid.: p. 301). Smuggling firms tried to have a permanent employee on the customs staff (like Oleg, mentioned above in the Trans-Oktavian case, who was based in St Petersburg), but at the border itself they always operated with someone called a 'controller', who lived near the post and could monitor movements. Their controller was an independent operator, who informed the firm of 'windows' (*okna*), the times when bribed officials came on duty. The firm would attempt to use each of the windows, paying the controller a percentage of the profit on each successful transit (ibid.: pp. 412–14). The bribed officials were paid a lump sum by the controller for each load, while an 'employee', who was a full member of the firm, was paid $3,000–4,000 a month (ibid.: p. 415). The structure thus comprised the smugglers themselves, an employee who worked 'on both sides of the barricade', some private entrepreneurs of information like the controllers, and a changing array of bribed officers on duty.

The controller in this scenario is the classic mediator, who negotiates the potentially awkward matter of the actual bribing. Konstantinov writes that the most successful controller on the Vyborg border, Arkadii Degurevich, achieved his numerous 'windows' by means of his café. Once upon a time, he had persuaded the customs administration that their officers had 'difficult material conditions', and he was thus able to open a café right inside the customs zone. Providing dinners and drinks at absurdly low prices, Arkadii was able to be present in the zone at any time he liked, while luring whole teams of customs men to his tables. He began by asking for the occasional 'friend's' truck to be examined separately (*vne ocheredi*). Soon many criminal bosses frequented the café too and Arkadii became the main controller for gangs all over north Russia, until an attempt was made on his life and he was forced out of business (ibid.: pp. 418–19).

Arkadii's café may suggest a certain sociality to this whole operation, but it should be remembered that most customs officials did not take bribes, that others refused offers after a few tricks, and that the ambience in this case was clearly one of danger and violence. Below I shall argue that the relations understood as bribery are essentially different from relations understood as reciprocity.

Bribery and Networks of Reciprocity

Personalized relations of reciprocity and rendering of favours have been, and are, extraordinarily widespread in Russia and other formerly state-planned countries (Pawlik 1992; Wedel 1992; Firlit and Chlopecki 1992; Lonkila 1997; Ledeneva 1996; Bruno 1997). The use of personal connections (*blat*) to bypass the regulations and obtain benefits was so common that we must agree with all those writers who have argued that it was integral to state-planned economies, being the way that they could be made (more or less) to work. Although *perestroika* saw the condemnation of *blat* by higher authorities,[10] the system was deeply embedded in social relations, including kinship, neighbourhood, ethnicity and common religion. Sometimes, as reported for the Polish *środowisko* (Pawlik 1992), reciprocity was experienced as a negative pressure, for example when an unwanted costly gift required the recipient to make a return at great expense. But more commonly the web of mutuality was felt as a welcome and supportive communality. Maternal networks are an example of this. Shchepanskaia (1996: p. 266) writes:

> The maternal tradition is not only an informational network for pregnant women, it also has a well-developed set of customs, in particular of mutual help. [...] The majority of things for my first child were donated by friends, close relatives and even distant acquaintances. Indeed, this has a ritual significance. There is a popular belief that a pregnant woman should not sew or knit or buy the baby things herself: if she does the baby may be still-born or not live long. Buying baby things in a shop, therefore, is treated almost as a lack of respect for the custom.

Bribery, it is argued, was excluded from this morality. Like buying the baby clothes in a shop, it was rather a step out of 'community' and into an asocial, monetized world.

It is a legitimate question to ask whether the distinction between bribery and networks of reciprocity has been eroded by the dramatic commercialization of recent years. Recent evidence suggests that the cultural systems of networks remain in place, and that bribery continues to be excluded from them. This can be seen from a recent study comparing informal exchange relations in St Petersburg and Helsinki (Lonkila 1997). Data collected in 1993–94 among groups of teachers in both cities indicate a far greater prevalence of informal reciprocities in St Petersburg and monetary purchases in Helsinki. The Russian teachers' diaries include such items as a loan of money, roughly equivalent to one week's wages, to Anton, 'a neighbour whom we often meet; we help one another', or meeting 'an old childhood friend who asks for help in placing her child in Alla's school' (Lonkila 1997: 4.2, 5.2). It is significant that the services offered give the teachers access not only to the personal resources of their exchange partners, but also to the resources of their work organizations (for example, an employee of a shoe factory who offers boots that are either better or cheaper than those obtainable in a department store, ibid.: 6.2). Illicit access to products through an employee is in principle a characteristic site of the bribe, but the St Petersburg teachers operate instead entirely with the notion of *vzaimopomoshch'* of friends, in which 'instrumental and altruistic aspects of social relations are intertwined to the extent that they seem impossible to separate' (ibid.: 6.3). The teachers devote much care to these friendships, for which ritual and sentimental occasions, such as birthdays, are important times of sociality.[11]

Similar attitudes are present also in the world of commerce. This can be seen from Bruno's perceptive work (1997) on gender and the culture of entrepreneurship in Moscow. Bruno finds the emergence of a strong counter-culture of resistance to market relations, which are seen as 'fraudulent' because the prices asked for goods are no longer set according to a consensual notion of fairness but according to monetary market laws.[12] This reactive culture is based mostly among women, including traders, who try to do everything *po znakomstvu*: through and for the sake of acquaintance. Increasingly, Bruno writes, money's buying power is seen as wiping out individuals' reliance on personal interaction and the ability to construct networks (Bruno 1997: pp. 69–70). In this situation, bribery is associated with market culture and the huge, disturbing shift it seems to presage: the notion that value may be expressed through monetary prices. As Bruno notes (ibid.: p. 68), this 'threatens to undermine all the intricate webs of personal relations by offering the option of paying for something'.

Bribery is condemned not just among the general public but by market traders themselves, and here it is linked to a self-perception of weakness and lack of knowledge. Traders at the huge Gariunai market in Lithuania (Hohnen 1997) are ashamed of having to trade at all, as street trading is still regarded as a makeshift strategy for those who do not have proper employment. They pay bribes of at least two kinds — to policemen at the market, who might pick them up for not having the necessary permits, and to custom officials at the Polish border to avoid having to pay large, erratic sums in VAT. Collective payment somewhat assuages the awkwardness and shame of bribing. One trader said, 'So money is collected from all traders in the bus to bribe the custom officals in order to avoid problems. But if I was sure that I could pay the same or less by going by the rules, of course I would rather pay the government, but I don't know. I have nowhere to phone and ask about the rules and tell about the corruption at the borders' (Hohnen 1997: p. 80). Better connected traders, this man implied, would have friends among the police and be able to make some stable arrangement at the border.

There may be some inclination to convert a bribery relation into a longer-term one of mutual help. One could conceive of this happening where the bribe itself takes the form of a rather long-lasting service. In one such case, in Ulan-Ude in Siberia, working on a doctor's vegetable plot was offered in order to obtain an operation for a child. This arrangement did not, however, lead to an ongoing friendship. The man who did the gardening had agreed to work for one season only, for a single benefit (the operation), and he did not conceive of carrying on digging in the future for the open-ended possible benefit of future medical services. The doctor, for his part, might have appreciated having a worker on tap, but the fact was that he did not want to enter into a relation of sociality and equality with the person who did the gardening. In short, this was a bribe, and sociality between the two would have had to have been far broader for it to transform itself into a friendship. Indeed, the understanding that this was a bribe, even if it was never openly stated, would work against the development of friendship. People said to me that if in some case a long-term relation had in fact been initiated by a payment, that payment or service not only would never be called a bribe, it would not even be thought of as a bribe. For that would be to insult one's own friendship. Here what is at issue is not only the intentionality of the act, but also the social capacity in which the participants are acting. We are dealing here with multiple aspects of the person. Precisely because a bribe does evoke the professional person of 'the doctor', the doctor must separate acting as a friend, a positive ethical act, from the equivocal matter of selling his services, which was justified by him in this case by his low salary and overburden of work.

It is therefore interesting that the presence of such discriminations is recognized in the practice, if not the letter, of the Russian law. People prosecuted for taking bribes may successfully use the defence that the payment was not a bribe but bound up in close personal reciprocities. In 1994 a certain Colonel Bukaev, a policeman, was prosecuted in St Petersburg for obtaining bribes in the form of apartments for his wife and mistress in return for casting a blind eye over the affairs of a huge building firm he had been assigned to monitor on a regular basis. Though elaborate subterfuge was certainly going on in order to give the impression that the flat was an above-board transfer to an employee — Bukaev had divorced his wife, while continuing to live with her, and she had registered as a cleaner with the building firm, though never once appearing with mop and pail — Bukaev was vindicated at his trial. He was set free by the court, on the grounds that the flats received could not be called bribes, because a series of familial links, including those with the wife and mistress, were involved with the head of the building firm, and Bukaev himself 'had acted in the capacity of a private person, not as a policeman' (Konstantinov 1997: pp. 207–23).

The journalist Konstantinov clearly implies that the court judge had been got at by the firm. Nevertheless, he asks:

> Can we regard the mutual 'indebtedness' of officials and entrepreneurs as corruption? If in society such 'indebtedness' is the only method for the normal conduct of business, and for the overcoming of the obstacles of an incomplete law and tax system, then there is a real possibility of their becoming a basic part of the national mentality. [...] People practising such mutual debts will be very surprised if they are accused of dishonesty. (Konstaninov 1997: p. 224)

Here we see the tendency of the rhetoric, even the practice, of mutual help to wipe out that of bribery.[13] Bukaev may have recognized that what he was doing was taking bribes, as is suggested by his subterfuges, but it was in the interests of both himself and the building firm to represent their activities as a different kind of relation — because 'helping a friend' continues to have great positive resonance.

Bribery and the New Commercialism

In general, cultural representations regarding transactions for profit may differ markedly from one region of Russia to another, and they may also change with new economic conditions.[14] How, therefore, are we to understand the following report, recently sent to me by an anthropologist from the city of Derbent in Dagestan?

> Pervasive venality has become increasingly clear. There seems to be almost no access to public services without some kind of extra payment or present. For example, admission to the kindergarten requires flowers, a box of chocolates, and US$20 for the kindergarten director, in addition to the regular monthly fee. Although every employee pays monthly into an obligatory health insurance, every single service in the hospital has to be paid for separately. Private and public institutions of education require substantial payments (several thousands dollars) for admission. For employment, the applicant requires a close relationship with the decision-taker and/or a large payment. If the applicant cannot pay in advance, he usually agrees that the decision-taker keeps the first year's salary. Many of these practices are not particularly new for local people, although they seem to have inflated since perestroika. (Leonhardt 1998)

The situation described might be one of ubiquitous bribery, or the pervasive use of personal connections, or the appearance of a new kind of 'tribute' — or a mixture of all three. Clearly the report indicates a massive monetization of public life, but we cannot understand what is going on in such situations unless we can penetrate the cultural context of local judgements.

Let me turn briefly to Ulan-Ude, where I have some confidence of understanding the context. Although not as pervasively as in Derbent, here too extra payments are made for access on a range of fronts (higher education, trading licences, hospital beds, desirable jobs and so on). The operative moral distinction people try to apply here is between public and private institutions. An extra payment made to someone in charge of a public service is far more likely to be called a bribe than one made in the private sphere. The issue is not one of ownership, because in many cases ownership is unclear or has a mixed or collective form. The matter seems to have more to do with traditions of public (formerly state) allocation, in contrast to services which people now understand to be 'bought'. Thus, an extra payment for a university place made when the institution has been established for generations is more condemned than an extra 'fee' paid to a newly established school.

The whole situation is obscured, however, by the fact that all institutions these days, including state ones, are expected to balance their budgets and almost all are disastrously lacking in money. This means that now, unlike in Soviet times, some people see that their 'extra payments' may be necessary. Parents often willingly pay odd sums (for food, clothing and so on) to schools and they sympathize with teachers whose wages are delayed for months. The 'extra payments' can enter organized systems for the upkeep of the institution itself. This includes the distribution of incoming sums to teachers for their personal use. At the same time, some people at least are coming to think that extra payments to ensure admission are justifiable 'in this commercial world'. In other words, we are seeing here a situation where 'bribery' is being *institutionalized.* Reisman (1979: p. 85) notes that variance bribes become institutionalized when (a) they enjoy overt or tacit support at the pinnacle of power; (b) the volume of variance business is large; and (c) when a bureaucracy develops to process the volume. These conditions may be in the making in parts of Russia for certain types of variance bribes, which are now coming to be regarded as more or less legitimate fees. As a result, the bribe *per se* is left in other, more limited, fields. It is difficult at this stage to be precise about what these are, but my impression from talking to people in Ulan-Ude is that the term 'bribe' is restricted to individually pocketed sums paid for variance services to public officials who do actually receive reasonable salaries.

Meanwhile the Derbent account raises several questions not yet addressed. What about the large payments made to get employment? Let us recall that the entire first year's salary is foregone if the applicant cannot pay in advance. Here we must turn to the relation between the bribe and 'tribute' (tribute being understood here as a payment made in respect of power subordination and political protection, rather than for any economic return).

Bribery and 'Tribute'/Racket Payments

Russians might comment that the world of business is the wrong place to look for bribery. 'Where do you find bribery? Where the state is, there will be bribes', several people have said to me. Here again, however, we must do some clarifying work. Bribes to officials, it will be argued, are not the same as regular illicit payments (tribute) made to them.

In the Soviet period it is well documented that in certain regions money and presents flowed upwards to state officials, a process known as *vykolachivat' dan'* ('extorting tribute'). How did this work? Zemtsov, who worked as a sociologist for the First Secretary of the Azerbaijan Communist Party, describes (1976) the machinations in great detail. Briefly, the state-owned company produced more than stated in the plan, sold the extra products on the side, and used the illicit profits to line the pockets of the managers as well as to pay upwards to higher authorities.[15] Bribery was used along the way; for example, a paint-producing firm would use a small bribe to obtain from a supply company cheaper or less good quality components but in twice the planned amount. The distribution of the profits, however, to all those involved in the subterfuge — the head of the paint workshop, the storeman, accountant, the manager and salespeople of the paint shop, and the director of the firm himself — was not thought of as a matter of bribery (Zemtsov 1976: pp. 22–3). One cannot bribe oneself, and all these people were in it together.[16]

The crucial payments upwards through the party and administration were also not seen as bribes. The rationale holding this vertical system together was quite simply the threat of losing one's own privileges at whatever level these were held. The honest director, who did not sell on the side and made no payments, would be called up and threatened, though no reference would be made to the real reason. Precisely because these illicit payments were expected and the whole system was protected from above, official posts were sold. In Azerbaijan in 1969, a police chief inspectorship cost 50,000 roubles and a district procuratorship cost 30,000 roubles (Zemtsov 1976: p. 26).

The issue here is the distinction between the illegitimate selling of access, which is acknowledged to be bribery, and payments made under threat, that is, for little other reason than that the payee is in a position of power and wants to be paid. A lowly, but extremely widespread, example of the latter is the activities of the GAI (State Automobile Inspectorate). In Almaty today, I am informed, the classic action is as follows: the motorist is flagged down, he comes over to the traffic policeman (*gaishnik*), bows and offers a cigarette, the *gaishnik* invents some minor infringement, states what the 'fine' is, and the motorist pays up.[17] This is often loosely called a bribe by foreigners, but it is more often known as *dan'* by locals.[18] It would only be a bribe if the motorist were really infringing a rule for which he/she could expect prosecution. In other words, the motorist would be getting something back from the deal. Usually, however, the payment is just 'tribute', an acknowledgement of who rules the streets.

The same distinction holds for the payments made by stallholders to racketeers controlling markets, or payments made to police for ostensibly protecting them from rackets. Sometimes racketeers and/or police provide a real service of protection, but very often they are simply engaged in extortion. The latter, being a regular payment under explicit threat of physical retribution, is tribute in naked form. The distinction between extortion and bribery is recognized in Russian law and is often used in defence by people accused of offering bribes.[19]

Tribute-paying, even the erratic street variety, seems to involve a different kind of sociality from that of the bribe. A prostitute, for example, when asked about rackets and whether everyone around was not 'bought' (*kupleno*, that is, bribed) by them, replied, 'No, they are not bought, but put on a regular basis [*postavleno na osnovu*]. It's the same everywhere. Their own girls, their own waitresses […] they prefer to have dealings with people they know and not strangers' (Karaulov 1993: p. 181). This sociality, however, is not an affair of equal friends or relations, as in the networks of reciprocity, but skewed by the underlying threat. The prostitute said she was terribly afraid of the racket. In this situation, people play on gender, ethnicity, their humble poverty and any links they might have to mask and humanize the situation (Humphrey 1997). Bruno, for example, writes of how women traders in Moscow try to appeal to the racketeers' gallantry in order to limit their dues to the 'mafia' (Bruno 1997: p. 72).

This need to present a front, in order to counteract the underlying threat, differentiates the tribute relation from ordinary reciprocity. At the same time, it is the absence of any specific return which differentiates tribute from bribery.

Finally, it should be noted that there is one important scenario where 'tribute' turns mass bribery to its own purpose. The privatization of state assets by bureaucrats has created enormous opportunities for bribery. Rather than condemning this, certain reformers justify it by what looks like the tribute rationale masked as economic realism. For example, Gavriil Popov, then mayor of Moscow and engaged in privatizing city real estate, was asked in 1991 to explain why he had written that bureaucrats have a right to take bribes. He replied:

> The situation is as follows. Here is a bureaucrat. He has under his command, let's say, various shops and firms. What should we ask of him? That he organizes privatization by giving out everything he has got and leaving himself naked as a bird, so he has to go out to work himself as a hired man in one of his own shops? [...] You should understand, as long as there are departments allocating [privatized flats] for free, there will always be the danger that someone will do it for a suitable reward. Everything that happens today is covert participation in this system. Ideally it would be different, and Ivan Ivanovich would simply give the contract to the best project. But we are realists. I know one thing: in our country these days, any privatization is a step ahead — at any price! Do you expect us to acquire capital and protect our virginity at the same time? (Karaulov 1993: pp. 406–7, 410).

This is bribery that looks much like tribute, and for this reason it too may become accustomed, embedded and part of the scenery, though no one who is not himself a top bureaucrat is likely to justify it quite like this. Yet words seem to fail before the huge sums acquired by figures of national importance, which no one knows how to describe; '*vziatka*', at least, seems inadequate, almost irrelevant, as Simmel predicted.

Conclusion

The short account of bribery on the Baltic frontier showed in camera some processes which I attempted to describe in more general terms at the beginning of the chapter. Bribery is surrounded on all sides by other kinds of relations, with which it partially overlaps, and yet it is sufficiently distinct to generate characteristic behaviours. On the one hand, we saw how the customs men of the village of Torfianovka distinguished the taking of bribes, which they did for a time, from the handing on of the bribe-opportunity to their co-villagers, which was part of 'mutual help'. Thus, both inside the micro-arena of the bribe itself and in society more generally, bribery tends to be distinguished from personal reciprocity. On the other hand, the case-study showed that *vziatki* are also differentiated from either regular wages paid by smuggling firms or payment for information given to a privateer. Arkadii, the 'controller', was not thought of as bribed because he was not in a public post. He was the archetypal mediator (between criminal firms and bribed officials) and with his café he created a border space — inside the zone and yet penetrable, a space where bribery could be hinted at, prepared and set in train. As this chapter has tried to show, bribery is differentiated from commercial payments in a double sense: it is both illegal and it is ethically negative. Mediators are often employed precisely because of the combination of secrecy, cunning and moral discomfort involved in bribing.

This chapter has shown how, despite commercialization, which has pushed people into rethinking bribery in some spheres, the concept remains alive in its classic arena — the gateways of the state. Here Konstantinov made a highly significant observation. He noticed that among the customs officials the sum demanded varied strictly according to the rank of the officer. The higher the official, the larger the bribe, even though the task to be accomplished through the 'window' was exactly the same in each case (Konstantinov 1997: pp. 429–31). In other words, the bribe is not in essence just a payment for a commodity or service but is also a recognition of socio-political, non-market status. This idea may provide a starting-point for us to rethink bribery too, seeing it not so much as 'corruption' and more as providing insight into the articulation of socio-political hierarchies of the people who make up 'the state'. Such a social perspective also reveals how the process of privatization is resulting in the institutionalization of bribery in some spheres. Nevertheless, although bribery may be socially systemic, we should not forget that it can be pushed this way or that by the conscience of individual people.

Notes

1 As Noonan (1984) points out, because of the secrecy of bribery it is always impossible to document how much of it exists.
2 Another way to put this is that bonds of loyalty to close relations outweigh those to organizations, the state or the social system itself (Reisman 1979: p. 136).
3 The contemporary English connotations of bribery may have changed historically from a form closer to the Russian, since the Middle English *briben*, 'to purloin or steal', derives from the Old French *briber*, *brimber*, 'to beg'.
4 Hohnen (1997) describes how in contemporary Lithuania selling at the open market at Gariunai is regarded as shameful and traders hide from friends and relatives if they see them coming. People say, 'The ones who trade are those without influential aunts and uncles.' Bribery similarly is something done only if no other avenue is available.
5 It is more 'easeful to the soul' (*spokoino na dushe*) to pay an open 'fee' than to worry about how much to give undercover, one woman said to me.
6 See the distinction made by Firlit and Chlopecki (1992: pp. 97–100), referring to Poland in the late 1980s–early 1990s, between 'theft', which was highly stigmatized because it was conceived as an action against an individual, and 'lifting' from one's place of work, which was regarded as morally tolerable because the bearer of the loss was abstract and unknown.
7 Pawlik (1992: p. 80) describes a similar ethic for Poland. Quoting a mechanic, Pawlik writes 'If you can't steal, then you can take bribes. Even the director who doesn't trouble himelf with production, steals; he "arranges" something for someone, "takes" from him in return and this is really stealing from him. Maybe that is really a worse crime than stealing from society, since society as a whole gets robbed [by the Communist state]. But that director robs an individual.'
8 At this period (1991–95) the smuggling out of unsanctioned strategic raw materials was counted as an administrative rather than a criminal offence, and therefore the KGB was not involved in following up cases. Until 1993, furthermore, there was no external frontier between Russia and the Baltic states, so for one-and-a-half years, between 1991 and 1993, Russian firms experienced a 'golden period' of export during which they had to breach only one border (that of the former USSR). The smugglers were inadvertently aided by the activities of 'Soviet nationalists', who burnt down the first customs posts established with the Baltic countries (Konstantinov 1997: pp. 307–8).

9 Lena's stamp was accredited to the wrong department, which was noticed by the customs official but not by Artem, the smuggler (Konstantinov 1997: p. 310).

10 In one of his speeches Gorbachev deplored the practice of *blat* and said that the government must improve the situation in the country so that *blat*, along with the verb *dostavat'* (to procure, obtain something with difficulty or through manipulation) would disappear from the Russian language (Corten 1992: p. 30).

11 The study found that in Russia birthdays are celebrated much more widely and frequently (a person often has several birthday parties) and at far greater cost than in Helsinki (Lonkila 1997: 6.4, 6.5).

12 The intense desire for Western goods has come to be counteracted by a retroactive condemnation of them which goes together with a new positive discourse about Russian goods as 'familiar', 'pure' and 'solid'.

13 In her recent study of seven large businesses (1997), Hertz demonstrates that Russian firms do rely above all on personal relations, often those established over many years and set up in Soviet times. Only two of the seven firms were beginning to look for new suppliers on the basis of price and quality, as opposed to using old links. Contracts are so open-ended that they are subject to endless re-negotiation, while debts between firms are very rarely pursued in the courts. In the frequent cases of non-payment between companies, 'friendly discussion' is preferred over any other option, and the firm owed money may even help the debtor firm sell its goods in order to keep the whole network afloat (Hertz 1997: p. 114). In such a business environment, it is evident that shifting mutual indebtedness over rather long periods is the norm and bribery is not only difficult to prove but may be less common than is generally supposed.

14 As Putnam (1993) noted in his study of civic traditions in different regions of Italy, customary practices and discourses regarding illegality can reach back for centuries.

15 'Everything I have described on the model of one producer should be translated into the scale of the entire country — thousands and thousands of workshops and factories — and then you will get an almost realistic picture of a gigantic organized subterranean business. The goods, geography, technology of production, all may change, but the structure of the crime remains the same — the substitution of costly components by cheap ones or the secret disposal of non-accounted materials, or both at the same time. [...] The main problem was how to render discovery impossible, or at least unlikely' (Zemtsov 1976: pp. 24–5).

16 Hertz (1997: p. 144) writes that in the mid-1990s one major reason why foreign investors and shareholders in Russian companies try to oust previous directors and insert their own man is to try to cut out the

long-standing practice of selling on the side and distributing the proceeds upwards.

17 Ruth Mandel, personal information.

18 In more official language this is known as *vymogatel'stvo* (extortion). In the courts, the distinction between bribery and extortion is often made according to whether the receiver of the payment is an official (bribery) or not (extortion) (Konstantinov 1997: p. 139), but ordinary Russians admit the idea of extortion by state officials too.

19 For example, see Konstantinov's account of one such case, when a bureaucrat accused of taking a bribe tried to argue that he took the money only because the briber showed him photographs of his children and threatened that they would suffer if he did not comply (Konstantinov 1997: p. 189).

Bibliography

Bruno, M. (1997), 'Women and the Culture of Entrepreneurship' in M. Buckley (ed.), *Post-Soviet Women: From the Baltic to Central Asia*, Cambridge.

Corten, I. (1992), *Vocabulary of Soviet Society and Culture*, Durham, NC and London.

Firlit, E. and Chlopecki, J. (1992), 'When Theft Is Not Theft' in J. Wedel (ed.), *The Unplanned Society: Poland during and after Socialism*, New York.

Handelman, S. (1995), *Comrade Criminal* (2nd edn), New Haven, CT and London.

Hertz, N. (1997), *Russian Business Relationships in the Wake of Reform*, London.

Hohnen, P. (1997), 'A Market Out of Place? Remaking Economic, Social and Symbolic Boundaries in Post-Communist Lithuania', unpublished PhD dissertation, Institute of Anthropology, University of Copenhagen.

Humphrey, C. (1997), 'Culture, Justice and Racketeering in Russia', in J. Heyman (ed.), *States and Illegal Networks*, London (forthcoming; paper originally written in 1997).

Karaulov, A. (1990), *Vokrug Kremlia: Kniga politicheskikh dialogov*, vol. 1, Moscow.

Karaulov, A. (1993), *Vokrug Kremlia: Kniga politicheskikh dialogov*, vol. 2, Moscow.

Konstantinov, A. et. al. (1997), *Korrumpirovannyi Peterburg*, St Petersburg.

Ledeneva, A. (1996), 'Formal Institutions and Informal Networks in Russia: A Study of Blat', unpublished PhD dissertation, University of Cambridge.

Leonhardt, M. (1998), 'Report on Fieldwork in Derbent, Dagestan, November 1997', unpublished MS.

Lonkila, M. (1997), 'Informal Exchange Relations in Post-Soviet Russia: A Comparative Perspective', *Sociological Research Online*, vol. 2, no. 2 (available on the internet at the following address: www.socresonline.org.uk/socresonline/2/2/9.html).

Noonan, J.T. (1984), *Bribes*, New York and London.

Pawlik, W. (1992), 'Intimate Commerce' in J. Wedel (ed.), *The Unplanned Society: Poland during and after Socialism*, New York.

Putnam, R.D. (1993), *Making Democracy Work: Civic Traditions in Modern Italy*, Princeton, NJ.

Reisman, W.M. (1979), *Folded Lies: Bribery, Crusades and Reforms*, New York and London.

Shchepanskaia, T. (1996), 'The Body Encoded: Notes on the Folklore of Pregnancy' in H. Pilkington (ed.), *Gender, Generation and Identity in Contemporary Russia*, London and New York.

Simmel, G. (1978), *The Philosophy of Money*, trans. T. Bottomore and D. Frisby, London.

Wedel, J. (1992), 'Introduction' in Wedel (ed.), *The Unplanned Society: Poland during and after Socialism*, New York.

Zemtsov, I. (1976), *Partiia ili mafiia: Razvorovannaia respublika*, Paris.

Zemtsov, I. (1991), *Encyclopedia of Soviet Life*, New Brunswick, NJ and London.

13 Attitudes to Bribery and *Blat* in Contemporary Russian Society: The Psychologist's View

Vladimir Spiridonov

Bribery is an area of human interaction that repays psychological analysis. Economic, historical, sociological and literary methods of investigation certainly yield a whole range of interesting results, but I will here argue that experimental psychology can offer useful additional insights into the attitudes of individual human subjects to the various unofficial forms of giving. Rather like Freud's unconscious, psychological aspects of bribery and *blat* are not available for direct research. And the resemblance does not end there: just like the contents of the unconscious — fear, aggression, sexuality — bribery provokes a strongly emotional reaction in people. The aim of the experimental research described below is to go beyond the widespread — and extremely negative — declarative assessments of bribery and *blat*, and to gain a more nuanced understanding of the place of these phenomena in contemporary Russian life.

If we are to believe the contemporary Russian mass media, bribery must be marked out as an unqualified evil. In press and television reports anti-corruption rhetoric sounds much as it did in Soviet times: it is time, we are often told, to 'bring this phenomenon under control' (*obuzdat' eto iavlenie*), to 'put an end to a shameful practice' (*polozhit' konets pozornoi praktike*), to 'root out corruption completely' (*vykorchevat' s kornem korruptsiiu*). On the level of public discourse, bribery is unreservedly condemned and pushed to the periphery of social life (Petrovskaia 1996; Babichenko 1997a, 1997b; Zhdakaev 1997).

But is the position of bribery in the social consciousness of contemporary Russia as marginalized as the mass media suggest? My professional experience as psychological consultant for various organizations (among them universities, banks and trading and consulting firms) led me to hypothesize that people's underlying attitudes are a good deal more ambivalent than they would care to admit, and that bribery is not actually dismissed outright as a morally reprehensible practice but rather accommodated in interesting ways within people's value systems. This working hypothesis was only strengthened when I was able to observe the audience reaction at the conference from which the present volume emerged. British academics responded with great animation to accounts of corrupt practices in Russia over the centuries: they were shocked, dismayed and amused by turn. Delegates from Russia, on the other hand, listened to the same accounts with apparent equanimity: their attitude was remarkably neutral by comparison.

The psychological experiment that we conducted in Moscow aimed to test (in a much less impressionistic way) the hypothesis that Muscovites' subconscious attitudes to bribery are significantly less condemnatory than their public statements on the subject.[1] The methodology employed — that of the 'subjective semantic' — eschews direct questioning in favour of a more subtle and rewarding approach. The technique in question was pioneered by Charles Osgood, who in the 1950s began to search for 'evidence for a universal framework underlying certain affective or connotative aspects of language' (Osgood 1964: p. 171). Osgood drew up a list of substantives that were suitable for translation into numerous languages; his list was finally whittled down to a set of fifty bipolar pairs (good/bad, hard/soft, thin/thick and so on). The subjects of Osgood's experiments were asked to judge a set of concepts against this set of adjectival scales. When he began to process his results, Osgood found that there were many different ways of slicing up the semantic space generated by his subjects' responses, but that three dominant and independent factors kept reappearing: the Evaluative Factor, the Potency Factor and the Activity Factor. Osgood found that, 'contrary to [his] early expectations, these factors are more reactive in nature than sensory, more broadly affective than discriminatingly cognitive, and thus closer to connotative than to denotative aspects of meaning' (Osgood 1964: p. 173). The name for this method of measuring the subject's unconscious understanding of concepts is the 'semantic differential' (henceforth SD). It has by now been used to research many different aspects of society and culture: attitudes to birds and animals, the structure of meaning in different languages, the reception of works of art and evaluations of various political phenomena (the United Nations, the President of the United States of America, the US Congress and so on).

In our research we used a sixteen-scale SD (that is, an SD which consisted of sixteen pairs of adjectives: see Appendix for a list of the adjectives used). The experiment was conducted by anonymous written questionnaire which took from ten to fifteen minutes to complete. Three groups of subjects, all resident in Moscow, took part in the experiment:

1. Students at Moscow universities (sixteen people aged from seventeen to twenty-three).
2. Medium-level clerks at the Savings Bank of Russia (twenty-one people aged from thirty-four to forty-nine).
3. State officials of different levels and areas of work, all forming part of the Russian Academy of State Service attached to the President of Russia (eleven people aged from thirty-five to fifty-four).

The forty-eight people in the sample evaluated six concepts:

1. '*blat*'
2. 'the bribe' (*vziatka*)
3. 'the bribe-taker' (*vziatochnik*)
4. 'myself', or 'self-image' (*ia sam*)
5. 'the official' (*chinovnik*)
6. 'the person who knows how to live' (*chelovek, kotoryi umeet zhit'*)

The data were subjected to factor analysis with a view to identifying the predominant attitudes to the six concepts listed above.[2] I present here our preliminary results.

Results and Analysis

Our results indicate that, although bribery aroused strong emotions in the subjects, it is by no means regarded straightforwardly as a social evil. The attitudes of the three social groups are similar to one another in many respects, and they differ substantially from those that are usually expressed in public.

Close examination of the results suggested that the concepts were evaluated according to a particular 'system of coordinates'. Let us consider the main factors I indentified in my interpretation as underpinning attitudes to the six concepts — the factors which formed the two axes defining the coordinates. The first factor I call 'evaluation' (*otsenka*). The positive pole of this factor was represented by adjectives such as 'pleasant', 'good', 'young', 'clever', 'clean'; the negative pole by the adjectives 'evil', 'dirty', 'nasty', 'loud'. The second factor can be interpreted as 'successful but slightly dubious activity' (*uspeshnaia no otchasti somnitel'naia deiatel'nost'*). Here the positive pole was linked with adjectives like 'active', 'clever', 'replete', 'dirty', 'powerful'; the negative pole with 'unhappy', 'stupid', 'loud'. Our experimental results suggested, in other words, that the structure of meaning of the six concepts in question may profitably be analysed by considering the relationship between their location on two scales of assessment: the first scale is, roughly speaking, that of moral/emotional judgement, while the second mainly assesses the effectiveness of various social actors and actions.[3] Let us take a closer look at how the concepts fared on this system of coordinates.

The concepts 'bribe' and '*blat*' proved to be linked very closely, and were evaluated by all three groups as almost neutral. Extreme positive and negative evaluations are largely absent in both cases. Bribery and *blat* are regarded as the result of a successful but slightly dubious activity: they are both strongly associated with the adjectives 'active', 'clever', 'replete', 'dirty' and 'powerful'. The strong association between bribery and effective action is very striking. From the point of view of our subjects, 'bribe' and '*blat*' are the results of substantial and dedicated efforts.

The concept 'bribe-taker' is linked with those of 'bribe' and '*blat*', although it does receive a slightly more negative evaluation. A man who fills his pockets with bribes is not, however, a social bugbear. He is a somewhat negative figure, but none the less an absolutely normal element of real life. Here we find significant variation between the social groups that make up the sample: students provide the lowest evaluation of 'the bribe-taker', and officials, as might be expected, the highest.

'The bribe-taker' is clearly the most active and effective figure: he far outstrips 'myself', 'the official' and 'the person who knows how to live'. He is the only truly active person on the contemporary social scene. To take bribes is to demonstrate a certain degree of social status and influence.

In the mass media, bribery is usually associated with representatives of the state machinery — the state official, in other words. The *chinovnik* is accordingly the most negative figure in the estimation of the students and the bank clerks. 'The official' is psychologically the person most remote from them. According to the factor of 'evaluation', 'the official' and 'myself' are clearly opposed.

It is significant that students and bank clerks evaluate 'the bribe-taker' higher than 'the official'. They evidently find the behaviour of the bribe-taker easier to understand. He is more active and the action he takes is effective. The bribe-taker is located closer to 'myself' than to 'the official', so we can say that the motives underlying his activities are more attractive to our subjects. The bribe-taker, according to our results, is a surprisingly sympathetic figure.

'The official', by contrast, receives an extremely negative evaluation. He is a shady and enigmatic figure. The motives for his actions are much less clear than those of the bribe-taker. Our results also suggest, most unexpectedly, that to change people's opinion of him the official has to take bribes — to enter the world of give-and-take instead of standing aloof from it. The exception to these conclusions is the evaluation of 'the official' by the state officials. For this group 'the official' is an attractive figure who is located close to 'myself'. This can be explained straightforwardly by the tendency to give a positive evaluation to one's own profession and to manifest a certain 'corporate spirit'.

The evaluation of 'the person who knows how to live' stands out because it has clearly undergone a transformation over the last few years. In Soviet times this expression described a person who had adapted well to the shortage economy and could get hold of everything. This was generally an active and streetwise person. Now, however, the meaning of this phrase has changed radically. All three groups evaluated 'the person who knows how to live' positively. But for both the students and the state officials 'the person who knows how to live' is passive and not effective. He is not at all linked to 'the bribe' and '*blat*'. He is rather a contemplative type who is concerned with his soul and not his stomach. This conclusion is confirmed by the strong opposition between 'the person who knows how to live' and 'the official'. We find traces of Soviet attitudes only in the results obtained from the bank clerks. For this group, 'the person who knows how to live' is clearly regarded as active and is much closer to 'the bribe-taker', but to a marked degree is seen as better than he is.

The analysis of our results is completed by the concept 'myself'. All three groups evaluated this concept very positively. The subjects bring together 'myself' and 'the person who knows how to live', and oppose these two to 'the bribe', '*blat*' and 'the bribe-taker' according to the factor of 'successful activity'. In addition, the students and the bank clerks oppose themselves to 'the official' according to the factor of 'evaluation'.

'Myself' is thus a good but very passive person. In all three groups it is considered to be a more passive and less successful concept than 'the bribe-taker', 'the official' and 'the person who knows how to live'. It has the lowest evaluation according to the factor of 'successful but slightly dubious activity'. All the subjects feel distanced from bribery and all related activities, but only because of their own passivity.

The above results amply demonstrate the deeply ambivalent attitude of contemporary Russians to this area of their life. On the one hand, 'the bribe' and '*blat*' are psychologically desired things. The absence of negative evaluations clearly indicates this fact. The position of the concept 'myself' betrays obvious envy of the bribe-taker, who is more effective in life and better provided for. No group showed evidence of visible resistance to bribery and *blat*. On the other hand, they are closely linked in the subjects' consciousness with the notion of a dubious and dirty business. Here the public condemnation of bribery clearly plays its part. So the attitude of the subjects to bribery can be summed up by the saying 'forbidden fruit is sweet' (*i khochetsia, i koletsia, i mama ne velit*).

In conclusion, we can say that the negative evaluation of bribery and *blat* by the man in the street does not tell the full story. The associations that bribery and *blat* have for people are characterized by emotional ambivalence. Our subjects see no need to denounce these activities. They certainly do not regard them as morally repugnant. Bribery and *blat*, they perceive, can add to the social influence and material well-being of contemporary Russians, but these unofficial transactions require hard work if they are to operate successfully and they are certainly not available to everyone. For precisely these reasons, it seems certain that bribery, *blat* and the bribe-taker will retain a prominent position in the contemporary Russian consciousness — and subconscious.

Notes

1 I am extremely grateful to G. Marasanov for his help in organizing this experimental research.
2 Factor analysis is a statistical method of data processing which allows us to find out the structure of data and to discover the hidden links between complex data.
3 It should be noted, however, that the distinction between these two factors does not correspond precisely to that between moral evaluation and assessment of effectiveness. The factor 'successful but slightly dubious activity' clearly has moral/emotional colouring. But, although the two factors are not entirely distinct concepts, this does not disqualify their use: the aim of our research is to identify factors that might help us to model the structure of the human consciousness — and such factors will often not be as 'clean' as those employed in the social sciences.

Bibliography

Babichenko, D. (1997a), 'Brat′ nado po chinu', *Segodnia*, 21 October.
Babichenko, D. (1997b), 'Bor′ba s korruptsiei otkladyvaetsia?', *Segodnia*, 17 December.
Osgood, C. (1964), 'Semantic Differential Technique in the Comparative Study of Cultures', *American Anthropologist*, 66, 3, part 2.
Petrovskaia, I. (1996), 'Troe v odnom sude, ne schitaia Bryntsalova', *Izvestiia*, 25 May.
Zhdakaev, S. (1997), 'Sevriugin postradal iz-za poriadochnosti vziatkodatelei', *Izvestiia*, 14 June.

Appendix: List of semantic scales used in the experiment

(Note: the subjects were asked to evaluate the six main concepts according to the following sixteen pairs using a seven-point scale from –3 to +3.)
1. *Legkii — tiazhelyi* (light — heavy)
2. *Dobryi — zloi* (good — evil)
3. *Chistyi — griaznyi* (clean — dirty)
4. *Goriachii — kholodnyi* (hot — cold)

5. *Tverdyi — miagkii* (hard — soft)
6. *Staryi — molodoi* (old — young)
7. *Glupyi — umnyi* (stupid — clever)
8. *Gromkii — tikhii* (loud — soft)
9. *Medlennyi — bystryi* (slow — fast)
10. *Sytyi — golodnyi* (replete — hungry)
11. *Protivnyi — priiatnyi* (nasty — pleasant)
12. *Aktivnyi — passivnyi* (active — passive)
13. *Gor'kii — sladkii* (sour — sweet)
14. *Smelyi — truslivyi* (brave — cowardly)
15. *Neschastnyi — schastlivyi* (unhappy — happy)
16. *Sil'nyi — slabyi* (strong — weak)

14 Bureaucratic Encounters in Post-Communist Regimes: Evidence from 26 Focus Groups in the Former Soviet Union and East-Central Europe

William L. Miller, Tatyana Koshechkina and Åse Grødeland

Notoriously, under Communism, citizens could expect neither serious consideration nor fair treatment without some means of 'interesting' the official in their case (DiFranceisco and Gitelman 1984). Unfortunately, it is not obvious whether the fall of Communism should have improved the behaviour of officials or made it worse. The uneven mix of reform and chaos since 1989 has had both positive and negative consequences (Verheijen and Dimitrova 1996) and a 1993–94 survey showed that while 61 per cent of citizens and 79 per cent of MPs in the Czech Republic would personally expect fair treatment from officials without recourse to contacts or bribery, only 12 per cent of citizens and 21 per cent of MPs in Ukraine had that expectation (Miller, White and Heywood 1998: pp. 105 and 185).

This research was funded by the Overseas Development Administration under award number R6445, and the Economic and Social Research Council under award R222474.

In this new study we set out to investigate, in more depth, the nature of citizens' encounters with officials in the former Soviet Union and post-Communist East-Central Europe. Our analysis is based upon twenty-six focus-group discussions held towards the end of 1996 in the capital cities, towns and villages of the Czech Republic, Slovakia, Bulgaria and Ukraine. (Exact locations and other details are given in the Appendix.) The discussions were video-recorded and computer-readable transcripts allowed a degree of systematic analysis, using QSR:NUD•IST. (For a recent review of this methodology, see Weitzman 1995.)

We have chosen the 'text-unit' in these discussions as our unit of analysis, defined as the contribution made by one person at one point in the discussion, beginning when that person starts speaking and ending when the next person intervenes. By indexing each text-unit according to various classification schemes reflecting, for example, whether it mentioned arguing with an official or bribing them, we can calculate what percentage of the discussion fell into various categories.

It is important to note at the start that all our percentages are percentages of *text-units*, not of participants. So they tell us more about the discussions than about the speakers. And it is also important to note that, since a single text-unit can include several ideas, the percentages of text-units in different categories of a classification usually sum to a little over 100 per cent. This was especially the case in Bulgaria, where text-units were longer and more wide-ranging than elsewhere.

The Impact of the Transition

Wide support for the transition from Communism was combined with wide criticism of the way it had been handled: 'it is a good thing but I think it should not be the way it has started in this country' (Ky-B 1 — that is, a quotation from respondent number one in focus group B in Kyiv; the short names for the focus groups are given in the Appendix below). 'Democracy is something very nice, but we misinterpreted it. [...] instead of achieving [...] we kept destroying' (Te 4); '[it was] better under Todor Zhivkov' (So-A 6). There was also a perception, especially in Ukraine, that the transition was itself the final criminal act of the Communist regime and its officials. 'It's clear that [the transition] is being effected with the old Soviet methods — the same special shares, special distributions and special privileges everywhere' (Se 4). Elected deputies were accused of being in politics for their own personal advantage: 'power is necessary for money' (Ky-B 6); 'shielding yourself with the help of deputies' immunity is necessary when your pocket is full' (Vo 1); 'here politicians strive to get into the cabinet in order to gain financially' (Zv 7).

People were highly critical of the impact of the transition on the behaviour of low-level officials as well. Indexing text-units by whether they suggested the behaviour of low-level officials towards ordinary citizens was now better or worse than under Communism indicated some improvement in the Czech Republic, if only by the narrow margin of 8 per cent, but a turn for the worse elsewhere — by a margin of 20 per cent in Slovakia, 32 per cent in Bulgaria and 37 per cent in Ukraine (see Table 1).

Table 1: The impact of the transition on the behaviour of low-level officials

	Czech Rep %	Slovakia %	Bulgaria %	Ukraine %
Better now	31	10	15	8
Neutral	46	60	38	48
Worse now	23	30	47	45
Difference between better/worse	+8	-20	-32	-37
(Total no.)	(64)	(30)	(34)	(183)

Note: Percentages are percentages of relevant 'text-units' in the focus-group discussions, not of participants. The total number of relevant text-units on which percentages are based is shown in brackets at the foot of each column.

Citizens' Strategies for Dealing with Officials

How could citizens respond to officials? What coping strategies could they use when faced with unfair, or simply unacceptable, treatment? Participants in our focus-group discussions mentioned a range of possibilities, often drawn from personal experience.

Acceptance: 'I clearly understood from the very beginning that it would not do any good [...]. I came there, turned round, and went home' (Striy 4); 'Circumstances made me give up' (Ya 4).

Persistence: 'I drop in there every week and when they see me at the door they say to themselves "Oh God, she's here again, let's give it to her and get rid of her"' (Pra-B 6).

Argue/threaten: 'I succeeded in persuading them — maybe they were in a good mood, it was just after lunch' (Do 5); 'I had to throw a hysterical fit — then they gave it to me' (Kh 2); 'I phoned the KGB and asked "Who are you trying to catch? [...] we're not in Moscow, we're in Ukraine, on our own land!"' (Se 6).

Appeal: 'Go higher' (Hr 6); 'up the ladder' (Ho 2); to '[the official's] superior' (Br-B 7); 'the MP Boncho Rashkov' (Te 1); 'the village soviet' (Ni 1); 'the region executive office' (Vo 1); 'the mayor' (Pra-A 7); 'the minister' (Ol 3); or even 'the Supreme Council' (Ky-A 6). But appeals were 'easier when there was the first secretary of the party city committee [...] now there's no power like that' (Kh 3).

Bribery: Bribery could vary from a 'token present' of chocolates or coffee to money — and 'money as a rule is not "coupons" [Ukrainian temporary currency]' (Ky-B 4); 'people give dollars' (Sh 4). 'Now, anywhere you go, they can even tell you how much, whom to give to, and for what sort of matters' (Ho 1); 'they tell you a specific sum' (Kh 6); 'if a bureaucrat has even a slight chance to make something on you, he will do everything in order to get it from you' (Ky-A 4).

Contacts: Although contacts could be useful on their own, they were often a necessary precondition for successful bribery: 'I know roughly the price, plus the friend in the appropriate position' (So-B 2); 'I had the best entrance exam results, but they only admitted people according to their contacts. [...] my mum [...] knew someone there who knew the Dean. Money was even involved' (NZ 8). And even contacts might require payment in the new market economy: 'of course, acquaintances wouldn't do anything for you without money either' (Se 6).

Other strategies: Finally, there was a miscellany of other strategies: checking up on the law, 'knowing the ropes', politeness, a pleasant smile: 'It depends on sex-appeal or on psychology, yes, just that, how to talk the policeman round' (KH 7).

Bribery, however, was the most frequently mentioned strategy in all countries — in 26 per cent of relevant text-units in the Czech Republic, 36 per cent in Slovakia, 35 per cent in Bulgaria and 42 per cent in Ukraine, though it was also the most frequently denied. But other strategies were also mentioned frequently — including active strategies such as the use of contacts, argument, or appeals to higher authority, as well as the passive reaction of frustrated acceptance.

Strategies for Objectives

Indexing text-units on dealing with officials according to whether the citizen appeared to be seeking an entitlement or a favour showed that the Czech discussions focused more on seeking favours than fair treatment — by a margin of 10 per cent. But everywhere else discussions focused more on the minimum objective of obtaining fair rather than favourable treatment — and by even larger margins, of between 25 and 31 per cent.

Strategies were clearly related to objectives. In all countries, acceptance, persistence, argument and appeal were mentioned much more frequently in connection with attempts to get fair treatment than favours. Conversely, bribes and contacts were mentioned much more frequently in connection with attempts to get favourable treatment. 'Do you mean you need to pay only when you are doing something "illegal"?' asked the moderator in the Sholomia discussion; 'I think when everything is legal people pay less', came the response (Sh 2). But even in Ukraine, where bribes were mentioned in 28 per cent of text-units concerned with obtaining rights, they were mentioned in far more, 73 per cent, of text-units concerned with obtaining favours (see Table 2).

General Gossip versus Specific Personal Experience

We indexed all text-units according to whether they were about: (i) general hearsay and gossip about how people typically behaved; (ii) what people might do in various hypothetical scenarios that we put to them; (iii) the reported experience of friends and acquaintances; and (iv) personal statements.

Table 2: Strategies by objectives: 'fair' treatment (i.e. rights: Rts) or favours (Favs)

	Czech Rep		Slovakia		Bulgaria		Ukraine	
	Rts %	Favs %	Rts %	Favs %	Rts %	Favs %	Rts %	Favs %
USE:								
Accept	25	12	26	7	28	12	25	3
Persist	13	2	9	3	8	2	7	2
Argue	20	11	16	8	7	8	6	1
Appeal	7	4	10	3	12	1	17	2
Bribe	18	42	22	55	30	60	28	73
Contact	11	15	5	25	15	37	8	21
Knowledge	3	3	11	0	12	2	4	0
'Psychology' etc.	5	8	6	4	4	6	2	1
Court	0	1	1	1	2	0	4	0
DENY:								
Bribe	4	10	8	7	7	3	3	5
(Total no.)	(151)	(196)	(205)	(100)	(252)	(125)	(512)	(195)
Net assertion of bribery (% use minus % deny)	14	32	14	48	23	57	25	68

Note: Percentages are percentages of relevant 'text-units' in the focus-group discussions, not of participants. The total number of relevant text-units on which percentages are based is shown in brackets at the foot of each column. Shading highlights the greater frequency of 'bribes' and 'contacts' when seeking 'favours', in contrast to other strategies used when seeking 'rights'. See also Figure 1 (p. 268)

As the discussion moved from general gossip through hypothetical scenarios to personal statements, the nature of the discussion changed sharply. The emphasis on rights increased, and references to different coping strategies changed. References to passive acceptance increased, as did references to persistence, argument and appeals, while references to the use of contacts and bribes declined. Overall, therefore, there is a striking contrast between the repertoire of coping strategies mentioned in general gossip and that reported in more personal statements.

Table 3: Strategies by talk style: General gossip (GG) and specific personal experience (SPE)

	Czech Rep		Slovakia		Bulgaria		Ukraine	
	GG	SPE	GG	SPE	GG	SPE	GG	SPE
	%	%	%	%	%	%	%	%
USE:								
Accept	10	18	14	19	21	31	16	18
Persist	3	7	6	7	4	9	4	8
Argue	5	17	8	16	7	9	4	7
Appeal	3	4	4	6	4	9	8	17
Bribe	36	16	47	29	42	27	46	33
Contact	20	16	10	10	23	17	12	10
Knowledge	7	7	6	7	9	9	4	5
'Psychology' etc.	11	8	4	7	6	5	2	4
DENY:								
Bribe	7	13	9	15	3	9	5	4
(Total no.)	(277)	(275)	(192)	(215)	(235)	(236)	(612)	(314)
Net assertion of bribery (% use minus % deny)	29	3	38	14	39	18	41	29

Note: Percentages are percentages of relevant 'text-units' in the focus-group discussions, not of participants. The total number of relevant text-units on which percentages are based is shown in brackets at the foot of each column. Shading highlights greater frequency of 'bribes' and 'contacts' in the context of general gossip, in contrast with other strategies mentioned in the context of specific personal experience. See also Figure 2 (p. 269).

Personal Experience of Bribery

Since assertions of bribery always declined, and denials usually increased, as the conversation moved from gossip to personal statements, the *net difference* between assertions and denials of bribery fell sharply. The fall was particularly sharp in the Czech Republic. When people were gossiping in general terms, net assertions of bribery were about as frequent in Slovakia and Bulgaria as in Ukraine — and only around 10 per cent less in the Czech Republic. But when people began to talk more personally, net assertions of bribery occurred only half as often in Slovakia and Bulgaria as in Ukraine, and sank almost to zero in the Czech Republic.

Particularly in the Czech Republic, but also in Slovakia, a number of text-units actually combined a general assertion that bribery existed with a specific personal denial: 'not from our own experience, rather from what I hear' (Ol 4); 'everybody waits for something to be slipped into his or her pocket, a bribe, [but] I would never bribe anybody, I would not know how' (Prv 6).

In Slovakia, references to bribery were more frequent than in the Czech Republic. Some were, in the donor's eyes at least, not a bribe but 'just a little token' (Prv 2), though 'tokens' could add up significantly: 'My cousin [...], a customs officer [...] says: "I get so many chickens that I don't know where to put them — I need a second fridge." These are tokens for customs clearance' (Zv 5). Slovaks also listed monetary bribes quite explicitly: 'Sometimes [the police] give you a penalty without a receipt — sometimes this satisfies both parties — this has already happened to me' (Br-B 9). Bribery to get medical attention was mentioned particularly frequently: 'special deliveries, paid-for, fast, painless, and naturally the attitude of nurses to those patients was different' (Zv 1); 'When my wife went to the maternity ward, the obstetrician said 3,000 crowns for treatment and 1,000 for the delivery. I felt it would be better, that he would take care of her [...] I felt life was at stake' (Br-B 4); 'An acquaintance of mine came to me crying; she said she was afraid of an operation and did not know how much she should give them; so we went to those who had already been operated on to tell us — she wanted to give 5,000 crowns, I cut it to 3,000, and when we asked those people they said 1,000 was enough' (NZ 4). But other Slovak officials were also mentioned: 'The housing office — we could have had a flat but only if we had given 30,000 crowns — that is, 30,000 crowns to the officials there' (Zv 1). Sometimes what began as a denial ended as an admission: 'I didn't give [the dentist] anything [...] actually I must admit I did give her something [...] 500 crowns — otherwise she would not treat [my daughter] [...] 500 crowns beforehand and later [...] another 500 crowns' (Br-B 7).

Most references to the Bulgarian police involved real or imaginary traffic offences: 'I had enclosed in my passport 1,000 levs [...]. He took 200 levs [...] and recommended I take a brush-up course in driving' (So-A 5); 'The traffic police stopped the taxi. There was no reason to be stopped but [the taxi driver] explained to me that he should be ready on his way back to give the traffic policeman 500 levs [so that the policeman would return] his documents' (Ya 4). But there was one more serious allegation against the police. A gypsy woman reported: 'My daughter was raped a year ago, at the age of seventeen. Three months ago she was taken away [again]. [...] the bar girl told me "Your daughter cried her head off." [...] I went to the police department, beside myself, and they said "Maybe she wanted a man and that's why they took her." But if I provided 2,000 levs for petrol they would go looking for her [...]. I did not have the money so I went on my own' (Stral 5).

Health care was the other main focus of allegations about bribery in Bulgaria: 'Our health care has been getting corrupt for years, everybody knows that, it is a public secret' (So-A 2); 'I am a medical woman, I am friends with the dentist, the nurse — and yet I've got to invite them to a coffee shop and treat them. I wonder what people without connections can do?' (Ya 6). What they could do was pay large bribes, of course: 'The midwife's fee was 15,000 levs, whereas the doctor's fee was 30,000 levs' (Ya 6); 'I saw it in my room — doctors took money from those in the beds next to mine' (Ku 5); 'A doctor expects to be provided with the previously agreed amount of money to admit the patient [...]. They brought a child who had received many burns [...] and this kid was lying there for six hours [...] the doctor wouldn't even come out of his room' (Ku 1); 'Some time ago my father had to be placed in a hospital. We had to offer a bribe. [...] it was a question of 30,000 levs — a year and a half ago that was quite a sum [...]. I don't know where this sum of 30,000 levs sank, but two hours later a doctor came and my father was placed in the hospital' (So-B 8); 'A friend of mine is in [the surgery] and I can hear through the door how the doctor says "I don't have my set of instruments with me at the moment, why don't you come at such-and-such a time to my private surgery." Me, I go in after her, and I am told the same [...]. Out there [in the waiting room] we are gasping in amazement' (Stral 4).

But bribery was not restricted to police and health workers: 'I know the price is 300 dollars, but I've never given a mark without examining the student. So I've become the "black sheep" among my fellow lecturers and they've become nasty to me' (So-B 5). '[My friend's] son [...] is serving fifteen kilometres from Sofiya. [...] every two or three days he comes home — but that has its price, too' (So-B 3). Even MPs were involved: 'In accordance with the Law of Restitution, friends of mine [...] are entitled to the real estate [but the municipality would not hand it over] [...] so they decided to contact their MP. The MP found the guts and told them how much it would cost them for the favour [...] 10 per cent of the cost of the real estate' (Ya 4).

Sometimes, especially in small villages, Bulgarians reported that 'people know each other [and] bribes are not expected' (Te 1). Some could not afford to bribe: 'When I was in hospital, a guy whose father had to undergo an operation was told he had to give 20,000 levs. He said he could afford only 10,000 levs [...] and two days later his father died' (Te 5); 'I knew the price of my case in the hospital [...] plus the friend in the appropriate position [to pass on the bribe] [...] but I cannot afford it' (So-B 2).

More surprisingly, there were some tales of Bulgarian officials refusing to accept bribes. That even surprised and slightly disconcerted those who had offered them: 'I underwent two operations at the Medical Academy in Plovdiv. I was ready to pay, but the doctor I ran into turned down my offer of money [...]. Upon leaving I hinted about money, but he felt pained. Then he accepted, most unwillingly, a bottle of grape-brandy as a token of gratitude. [...] Now I am not sure what's going on there' (Ya 4).

Every group discussion in Ukraine, apart from that with the Crimean Tatars, produced specific personal statements about the use of bribery. Sometimes it was clearly for a favour: 'there was another instructor who had a tariff: a bottle of vodka for [an undeserved pass in] the mid-term test' (Kh 1). Sometimes it was at least partly out of gratitude and relief: 'I had an operation last year, a professor did it [...] we all knew, the patients talked about it, that he only took things after the operation' (Ky-A 1).

But on many occasions it was clearly a case of extortion by the official: 'they put you in a situation that you have to' (Ho 6); 'in the situation where you understand that you have to give' (Ho 2); 'the surgeon said that she was to give so much to the surgeon, so much to the neuropathologist, so much to the anaesthetist, and so much to the assistant. He directly said how much' (Ho 4); 'they told me straight out' (Kh 5); 'right away I told her, my wife, "give them something [for an operation in Donetsk] — it'll be solved right away". No, she stretched it out until the fourth time [...] and right away [when at last she did give something] everything was resolved' (Kh 1); 'they say loud and clear, how much for what' (Kh 3).

Sometimes the extortion came in stages. One unfortunate reported: 'I needed an operation [...] it [would, they said] cost fifty dollars. Okay [...] when I go in, she looked at me, all very pleasantly, then says "it'll cost a hundred dollars" [...] it's already gone up!' (Ky-A 2). Another reported: 'I sat in the chair and a doctor started to pull out my tooth [...] it was so painful [...] so I took out 100,000 karbovanets [...] the attitude changed immediately [...] but he caught me in a corridor [afterwards] and said "it is not being done for a thank-you, it has to cost two million" [...] he named the price openly' (Sh 5).

Extortion in Ukraine was not limited to health care: 'until I gave a bribe he did not receive me [...]. I gave him twenty dollars and he signed it' (Striy 2); 'yes, to have a position at school I have to give up my salary [...] for this whole year, if not longer, I will be earning money for them [those who had appointed her]' (Striy 5); 'my husband is in Belarus now and who's going to find him there? [...] I went to the People's Court [...] and they told me "let's start looking for him, but you have to pay for it"' (Vo 3); 'I faced it myself in the notary's office [...] if you haven't brought anything you will probably sit there for three days minimum if not three weeks [...]. I was there for five or six days. Until you buy something and bring it there, you are given no attention and no service' (Vo 5); 'she says "give me 500,000 to make a labour card for you" [...] and I never heard that you must pay for a labour card' (Vo 2).

And they paid frequently: 'twice in the last six months' (Ky-B 1); 'by my family, over the last six months, five times probably, not less' (Ky-B 3) 'I also had to do it frequently' (Ky-B 4).

Reform

Some of our findings might encourage complacency. Allegations about the need to use bribery or contacts in dealing with officials, though widespread, need to be treated with some scepticism. Allegations of bribery are at least twice as frequent in connection with attempts to win favours as to obtain fair treatment; and much more frequent in general gossip than in reports of specific personal experience.

But, rightly or wrongly, most people blame officials for extorting bribes; they interpret the present situation as a problem; and they propose solutions. Very few comments suggested that it was impossible to change the relationship between citizens and officials — the percentage ranged from zero in the Czech Republic to only 6 per cent in Ukraine.

A *better quality of official* was a popular suggestion: between 24 and 32 per cent of relevant text-units in each country mentioned it. Some comments about better officials were tautologous: in Ukraine especially there were calls for 'more responsible [officials]' (Ho 6); 'conscience' (Ho 3), 'competence' (Kh 6), 'understanding' (Vo 3), 'culture' (Ky-B 5) and — the ultimate in tautologies — 'honesty' (Striy 3 and 4). But other comments about better-quality officials suggested better systems of selection, better qualified entrants and more in-service training: 'state officials should [...] not pick their relatives' (Stral 6); 'where new [post-Communist] officials have taken over, they are often not experts' (KH 4); 'this has just happened to me — there's a beautiful computer there, worth say half a million crowns and [the official] finds it in the card index and writes the data by hand' (Do 2).

In the Czech Republic, 46 per cent of text-units — far more than anywhere else — mentioned a need to improve *administrative efficiency and organization* — which reflected the burden of the Czech participants' complaints: that they found the bureaucracy tedious and unhelpful rather than corrupt, forcing them to waste too much time on filling out forms, going to offices and standing in queues. So they proposed a better administrative structure, less bureaucracy ('fewer useless forms' [KH 5]; 'and above all fewer bureaucrats' [KH 4]), better located offices, or simply 'longer opening hours' (Pra-B 4). Slovaks made similar but less frequent suggestions for administrative reform; and there were also a few similar suggestions in Bulgaria and Ukraine: 'There should be computers everywhere' (Ya 5); 'they should tell you everything you need to bring the first time' (Ky-A 6).

Outside the Czech Republic discussion groups put more emphasis on other reforms, reflecting the different nature of their complaints which were more about extortion and rather less about mere time-wasting — *more pay for officials* to make extortion less necessary, stricter control to make extortion more dangerous, or some combination of the two. 'Insufficient salaries, that's the cause of all that bribing' (Br-B 8); 'if most of the officials are well paid, they might not be so easily tempted' (So-A 1); 'I think people should be paid according to their performance. [...] for doing an operation our doctors get small change, and when a plumber screws in a bolt in his house, he asks for money, worth ten operations' (So-B 4); 'if [officials] receive appropriate payment, they will work professionally in their positions and will not take bribes' (Sh 4).

Stricter control was seldom mentioned in the Czech Republic but quite frequently elsewhere: 'it's worse now than under the rule of Communism [...] you could lodge even an anonymous complaint and now there's no one to complain to. [...] now they are not afraid of anything' (Do 4); '[under Communism] they would be afraid of being sacked' (Prv 1). Ominously, one Slovak suggested: 'there should be, for example, a government service which would contact officials and hand out bribes. If the contacted official does not inform his or her superior of being bribed within five days, he or she will automatically be dismissed' (Zv 8). Another wanted: 'really harsh conditions, strict sanctions [...] we would have to start from the top and proceed downwards' (Prv 6). In Bulgaria participants complained: 'there used to be some order — people remember they could submit their complaints' (Ya 2); 'the control isn't there [...] there used to be isolated cases [of corruption] before as well, but most of them were promptly eradicated, especially when at lower levels [...] [though] at the top, you couldn't catch them. Now this order and discipline are ruined' (Ku 5); 'Now the situation is very bad — perhaps because we have no one to take our complaints of injustices to' (Ya 1); 'I do not approve of the former system [but] there existed some legal system, control. There was corruption but in other echelons, and people were not aware of it. In fact, I cannot say that the change we made is for the better: I think it was made for the worse' (So-A 6); 'I think control is the only thing that counts' (So-B 3); 'There should be control' (So-A 3); 'The stricter the control, the more offenders are caught' (So-B 2); 'Penalties should be severe [...] very severe' (So-B 1); though one participant insisted: 'by law only, otherwise no' (Ya 4). Ukrainians also emphasized the need for control, even fear: 'there was someone to complain to; there was power; now there's no power' (Kh 3); 'regulate more strictly' (Ky-B 1); 'we must do it rigidly' (Vo 3); 'a person has to be afraid' (Ky-A 6); 'there was discipline — everybody was afraid of the party' (Striy 3); 'not [by] the party [but] we need a control system' (Striy 4).

Sticks and carrots. Sympathetic attitudes towards officials' salaries were accompanied and often combined with less sympathetic suggestions. Pay rises could be combined with stricter control or a cut in the number of officials: 'raise their salaries but introduce strict punishments' (Zv 7); 'payment should correspond to adequate performance and qualifications' (So-B 4); 'If it were up to me, I would raise their wages; and if it were up to me they should be controlled' (Stral 2); 'if [...] he has a big, well-paid job, he'll be afraid for his position' (Kh 3); 'if the person received a normal salary they would be afraid to lose that position' (Ky-B 2); 'this position should be considered prestigious [...] they should be afraid to lose their positions' (Sh 6); 'Nothing terrible would happen if the official apparatus were cut back by two thirds' (Ky-A 4); 'And raise the salaries of the ones who are left' (Ky-A 5); 'Yes, and raise the salaries of the rest' (Ky-A 7).

Inevitably, the solutions proposed by ordinary citizens in our focus-group discussions are less complex and sophisticated than those prescribed by public administration specialists (Verheijen and Dimitrova 1997), and they differ considerably in the details, but both the academic specialists and the focus-group participants highlight the importance of a mix of encouragement, control and public information.

Conclusions

No doubt our focus-group participants held something back. We do not suppose that they revealed all. But it is remarkable how much they were willing to say in front of the video-cameras at our focus groups. Partly that reflected the expertise of our focus-group moderators, all of whom had extensive experience in leading group discussions. But it also reflected the openness of the participants themselves. Most did not seem over-inhibited by the long years of life under a Communist dictatorship. On the contrary, they seemed to revel in their new freedom to criticize the state — indeed, the participants in one focus group in western Ukraine could be overheard (on the audio-video link) before the moderator entered the room, happily remarking to each other than they would never have dared to participate in such a discussion ten years ago.

Of course, the opposite danger is that people might tell extravagant but untruthful stories to impress their fellow participants or to please the investigators. We did find a sharp difference between allegations made in general terms and those based on more personal experience. In the Czech Republic, general gossip about widespread corruption simply did not correspond to more personal accounts of experience and behaviour. But, by contrast, the discrepancy between general allegations and personal experience was less elsewhere, and very much less in Ukraine. We think it unlikely that this reflected greater reticence, more fear or less openness in the Czech Republic than elsewhere.

That has important implications: the difference between Czech and Ukrainian experience of interacting with officials was actually greater than was implied by more superficial questions about the general climate of corruption. A climate of exaggerated suspicion and criticism in the Czech Republic, influenced no doubt by press reports of high-level corruption, actually obscured the extent of the difference between Czech and Ukrainian citizens' own, immediate and directly personal, experience of dealing with officials.

We found evidence of a gradation in official corruption from the Czech Republic through Slovakia and Bulgaria to Ukraine. In terms of how citizens dealt with officials, there were clear differences between the Czech Republic and Slovakia — both, to varying degrees, 'Catholic' and both former Habsburg territories; and on our data 'Catholic' west Ukraine was actually more inclined to talk about bribing officials than 'Orthodox' east Ukraine. That contradicts any notion that we should simplistically divide the world into Catholic, Orthodox and Muslim cultures — or, more locally, into former Habsburg, Romanov and Ottoman cultures

(Huntington 1993; more crudely stated in Huntington 1996). While we do not suggest that long-established culture and history have no continuing impact, other factors may be still more important. Differences in the interactions between citizens and officials in the different post-Communist countries may reflect more recent differences in the way these states have actually treated their citizens — the half-century of direct experience of Soviet bureaucracy that applied equally to east and west Ukraine, for example. They may also reflect variations in contemporary post-Communist circumstances: economic collapse in Bulgaria and dislocation in Ukraine but better living standards and a smoother economic transition in the Czech Republic, and a greater discontinuity both of personnel and ethos in the administration of the Czech Republic, contrasting with more continuity elsewhere. Indeed, in so far as any one of our post-Communist countries stands out very much from the others in terms of the behaviour of its officials, it is the Czech Republic.

It is worth drawing attention, once again, to the infrequency of suggestions that it was impossible to improve the relationship between citizens and officials. And also worth recalling the widespread allegation that, except in the Czech Republic, the behaviour of officials had changed for the worse since the fall of the Communist system. Both those findings imply movement and change, whether for better or for worse; so both contradict the thesis that the relationship between citizens and officials is fixed and determined by an unchanging and unchangeable culture. Ironically, recent changes for the worse show that change is possible and therefore hold out the possibility of change, perhaps for the better, in the foreseeable future.

What is also clear from our focus-group discussions is that citizens in Bulgaria and Ukraine do not regard official corruption any more kindly than in the Czech Republic; they do *not*, for example, regard it as a curse in the Czech Republic but a blessing in Bulgaria or Ukraine. It may be a necessity for the individual citizen perhaps, but an unwelcome one: extortion by officials rather than a facility for citizens. And that also has implications for the possibility of reform. There is no dispute anywhere about the direction of 'improvement', no deep cultural attachment to corruption as a systemic virtue in post-Communist circumstances as it arguably may have been under Communism; and no shortage of suggestions for reform that take account of the specific circumstances and contemporary problems in each country. The concrete reality of variations in the behaviour of officials disguises more uniform aspirations on the part of citizens.

Bibliography

DiFranceisco, W. and Gitelman, Z. (1984), 'Soviet Political Culture and Covert Participation in Policy Implementation', *American Political Science Review*, 78.

Huntington, S.P. (1993), 'The Clash of Civilisations?', *Foreign Affairs*, 72.

Huntington, S.P. (1996), 'The West v the Rest', *Guardian* (London), 23 November.

Miller, W.L., White, S. and Heywood, P. (1998), *Values and Political Change in Post-Communist Europe*, London.

Verheijen, T. and Dimitrova, A. (1996), 'Private Interests and Public Administration: The Central and East European Experience', *International Review of Administrative Sciences*, 62.

Verheijen, T. and Dimitrova, A. (1997), 'Corruption and Unethical Behaviour of Civil and Public Servants: Causes and Possible Solutions', paper presented at the *NISPAee Annual Conference*, Tallinn, April.

Weitzman, E.A. (1995), *Computer Programs for Qualitative Data Analysis: A Software Sourcebook*, London.

Appendix: Design of the focus-group study

Ukraine (55 participants)

Capital city (higher education)	Kyiv-A
Capital city (lower education)	Kyiv-B
Medium town (east Ukraine)	*Khartsysk
Medium town (west Ukraine)	*Striy
Small town (east Ukraine)	Volnovakha
Small town (west Ukraine)	*Horodok
Village (east Ukraine)	Nikolayevka
Village (west Ukraine)	*Sholomia
Ethnic minority	Sevastopol (Tatars)

Bulgaria (45 participants)

Capital city (higher education)	*Sofiya-A
Capital city (lower education)	*Sofiya-B
Medium town	*Yambol
Small town	*Straldja
Village	*Tenevo
Ethnic minority	*Kurdjali (Turks)

Slovakia (49 participants)

Capital city (higher education)	*Bratislava-A
Capital city (lower education)	*Bratislava-B
Medium town	Zvolen
Small town	Presov
Village	Dolny Kubin
Ethnic minority	*Nove Zamky (Hungarians)

Czech Republic (38 participants)

Capital city (higher education)	Praha-A
Capital city (lower education)	Praha-B
Medium town	*Hradec Kralove
Small town	*Kutna Hora
Village	*Olesnice

Notes to Appendix

1 Focus groups were organized by Ukrainian Surveys and Market Research of Kyiv, Center for the Study of Democracy of Sofia and Opinion Window Market Research and Analysis of Prague (covering both the Czech and Slovak Republics).

2 All twenty-six focus-group discussions were video-taped. Computer-readable vernacular and English-language transcripts were made from these tapes. In addition, simultaneous translation was provided by Marichka Padalko in Ukraine, Mitra Myanova in Bulgaria, Zuzana Vrastiakova in Slovakia and Klara Flemrova in the Czech Republic during the sixteen focus groups marked with an asterisk, which were all attended by the authors.

3 Focus groups in east Ukraine were located in the Donetsk region, those in west Ukraine in the Lviv region, all chaired by Alexander Fedorishin, using the language chosen by the participants — Russian in Kyiv, Sevastopol and east Ukraine, Ukrainian in west Ukraine. Focus groups in Bulgaria were chaired by Andrej Nonchev (except for the one in Straldja, which was chaired by Elena Lazarova), all in Bulgarian. Focus groups in Slovakia were chaired by Patrik Minar in Slovak (except for the one in Nove Zamky, which was chaired by Ladislav Koppl speaking in Czech while participants responded in Slovak). Focus groups in the Czech Republic were chaired by Ladislav Koppl using Czech.

4 Underlining indicates the short form of town names used to identify respondents in the text. Thus, for example, a reference to (Ky-B 1) in the text indicates a quotation from the first participant in the focus group Kyiv-B.

Figure 1: Use of bribes by objective (% use minus % denial)

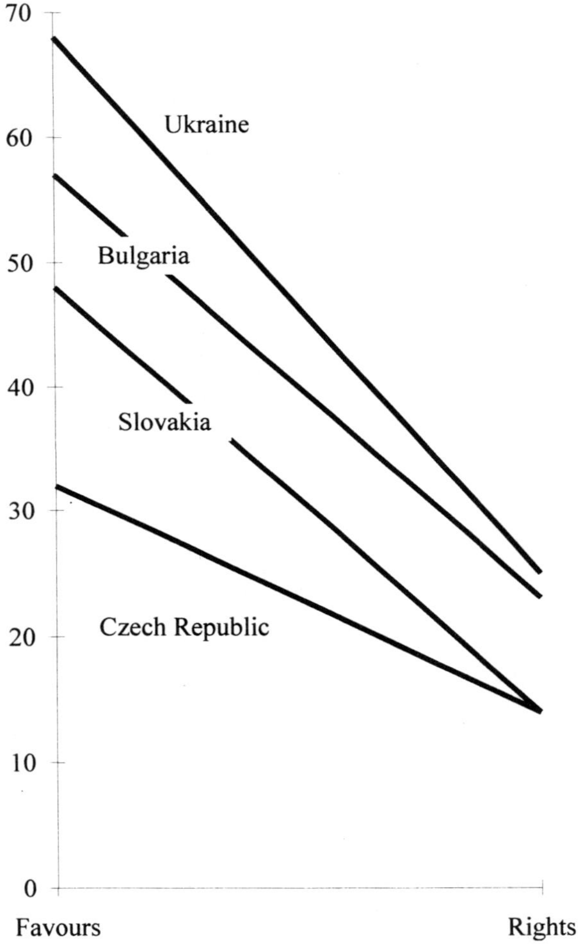

Figure 2: Use of bribes by style of talk (% use minus % denial)

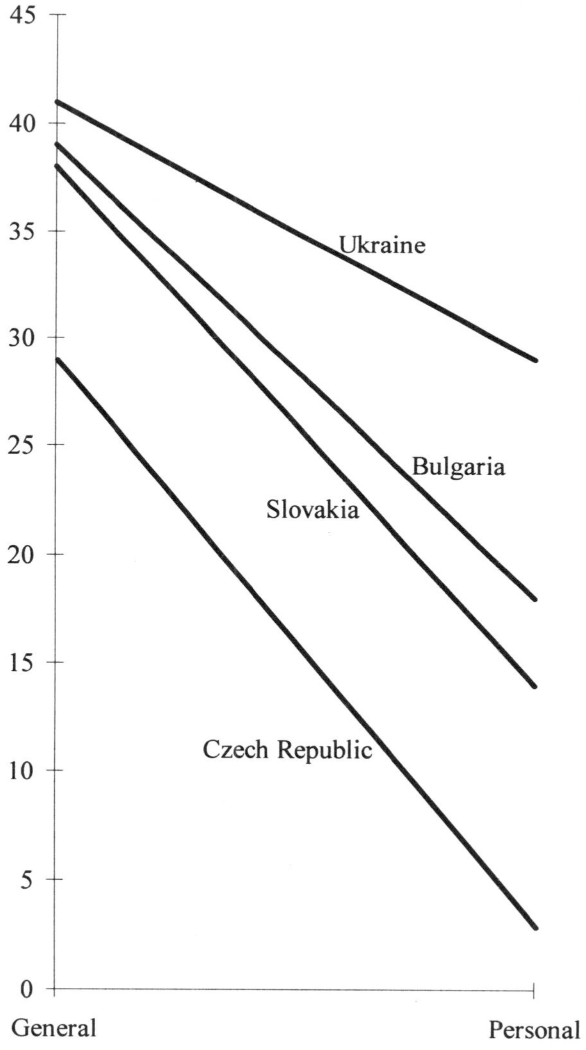

15 'Who's the Boss: Us or the Law?' The Corrupt Art of Governing Russia

Mark Galeotti

'Corruption', thunders Boris Yeltsin, is 'Russia's most serious problem' (*RFE/RL* 1997). He is hardly the first Russian leader to think so. In this context the surprise should be that corruption in Russia has survived — thrived — through the ages. Indeed, this tradition of corruption has shown itself to be deeply rooted and even entrepreneurial, adapting itself to new opportunities as and when they arise. The endemic but often rather insular bribe-taking of the tsarist élite became the institutionalized and rapacious embezzlement of the Soviet *apparatchiki*, thanks to the latter group's near-monopoly control of the economy. In the post-Soviet era, it has taken yet another form, as *apparatchiki* use their resources and connections to convert political clout into economic power.

So my main focus in what follows will be practices of 'give-and-take' (sometimes, it would seem, nothing but 'take') as they occur in the upper echelons of Russian politics — and in this respect the present chapter differs from many other contributions to this volume, which pay more attention to grass-roots reciprocity and non-official exchange of money and favours. But I make no apologies for the approach taken here: I will argue that the long Russian tradition of semi-legal or illegal exchange with office-holders has had far-reaching implications for the way Russia has been (and continues to be) governed. Any analysis of unofficial exchange in Russia would be incomplete if it failed to take into account this 'high political' aspect.

The classic definitions of corruption present it as the misuse of public office for private good. Samuel Huntingdon, for example, used the formula that 'Corruption is behaviour of public officials which deviates from accepted norms to serve private ends' (Huntingdon 1968: p. 59). Other approaches have sought to broaden out the concept to cover the wider transaction: after all, if a citizen bribes an official, then the citizen is as much party to the exchange and 'corrupt' (Clark 1993: pp. 3–10). Besides which, there is the whole question of the overlap with the black economy: how far is corruption more than simply another form of illegal exchange of service? Implicit, though, is that corruption — however widespread — is an aberration, a deviation from the official 'rules of the game'.

A more nuanced approach is to recognize that informal practices and formal bureaucratic structures coexist in any society, and to study their specific modes of interaction. Sampson (1985–86) distinguishes three such modes: 'benign', 'corrupting' and 'system-threatening'. Informal structures function as *benign aids* to the system when they help the bureaucracy to achieve its stated goals via unorthodox methods. In this sense, informal structures are just another means of achieving the desired result, or what Heidenheimer (1970) calls 'white corruption'. Informal structures may also lead to the achievement of goals quite contrary to those officially mandated by the organization or society. Here it operates *corruptively*, typical examples of such corruption being the petty bribe or more spectacular cases of nepotism or embezzlement. The corrupting aspects of the informal sector may also begin to generate their own alternative social hierarchies and value systems. That is, they may generate an 'unofficial ideology', a set of 'unwritten rules' and a 'dual consciousness'. In certain cases — particularly when political legitimacy declines and access to material resources becomes so inadequate that not even corruption will suffice — the informal structure takes on a *system-threatening* character.

In Russia, 'benign' and 'corruptive' modes have long interacted in interesting and distinctive ways (only occasionally veering towards the 'system-threatening'). Much of the literature has, rightly, concentrated on the degree to which the Soviet state's unholy combination of centralized economy and political monopoly provided fertile soil for corruption. While this study can do no more than set out a possible agenda for future research, it does appear important to take such accounts one step further and examine the *function* of corruption in modern Russian history. Viewed in this light, the active tolerance and use of illegal and extra-constitutional techniques of rule — including an acceptance, within certain limits, of bribery, patronage, embezzlement and the other manifestations of corruption — will often appear central to different regimes' approach to governing Russia.

After all, like organized crime, corruption is not always an entirely negative phenomenon. Instead, it can humanize an unresponsive political system, offer covert means to cater for and thus satisfy the wealthy (however this 'wealth' is defined — for most of the Soviet era, the real 'currency' was not the rouble but connections and infuence) and even cut through unnecessary red tape. It can also be seen as offering advantages to a regime or ruling élite. For a start, consider the unique challenges of governing a country such as Russia (Galeotti 1995a: pp. 3–21). The simple geography poses huge problems of management and, furthermore, this is a multi-ethnic land empire, even today a patchwork of municipalities, ethnic enclaves, densely populated regions and barren wilderness. Combine those challenges with the need to secure Russia's long, vulnerable borders and a relatively poor resource base, and it becomes hardly surprising that Russia's development of the machinery and culture of a modern state has been so sluggish.

Take a single but crucial example: revenue collection. It took tsarism a long time to outgrow tax farming, a system with huge indirect 'costs' (lack of central control, inefficiency, scope for local corruption), but with the key virtue of requiring no real up-front expenditure. Officials were granted areas of responsibility and revenue targets and cut loose to raise all they could without igniting rebellion. Even after the state had begun to acquire the resources and will to take direct control of the process, the all-important vodka taxes were still being 'farmed' until 1863 (Christian 1987). The post-Soviet state, facing a revenue crisis of its own, has established and unleashed the modern-day tax farmers of the Tax Police, a paramilitary organization deliberately under-funded and forced to rely on a share of the revenues it collects. In and of themselves neither is corrupt — but in practice both institutions lend themselves to the misuse of public office for private gain and, implicitly, rely upon it. Given the still confused and often contradictory nature of the Tax Code, the Tax Police know full well that any individual or business will have broken the rules it lays down in some way. It has thus become common practice for them to descend upon some firm, announce an audit, then make it known that if the firm suddenly 'realizes' that it has underpaid its taxes by a figure open to negotiation, then the audit will be closed. If not, the firm can expect an investigation which can range from the thorough to the downright intrusive. After all, not only must the Tax Police uncover some underpayment in order to balance their books, they wish to deter other businesses from refusing to reach a quick compromise. So most firms pay up, glad to see the Tax Police gone. On one level, this is a good result, as the ruinously under-revenued state acquires resources, but it has been achieved by using the methods of the criminal racketeer.

Corruption as a Tool of Governance

Who's the boss: us or the law? (Nikita Khrushchev)

The issue raised here by Khrushchev often creates a tension between short- and long-term expedients, or the micro- versus the macro-scale. Most Russian businesspeople, for example, would rather live and work in a stable, law-governed state. They will, however, generally not let this prevent them from giving bribes and paying for illegal protection, simply because it is necessary and because everyone else is doing it. Similar dilemmas have often faced Russia's rulers, and — to greater or lesser extents — they have chosen to adopt a corrupt style of governance either out of choice or because they felt it a necessary expedient. Corruption does, after all, offer certain advantages:

1. *Low start-up costs* As with the example of tax farming, a state which allows its élite to enrich themselves through their office can thus afford not to pay them much and unload much of the expense of government on them. Tsarist officials were historically underpaid, the presumption being that they would 'live off the land' (Pipes 1974: pp. 282–4; Clarke 1993: pp. 31–5). Even the two 'Greats', Peter and Catherine, while appreciating that this was a problem and seeking to do something about it, lacked the resources to undo centuries of tradition. Bribes were thus not only expected, they were an economic necessity for the officials, and eased pressure on the central treasury. David Christian (1987), for

example, estimates that a provincial governor probably received bribes from the local vodka-tax farmer alone approximately equal to his official salary and allowances.

2. *Insecurity and political control* The corrupt may become rich, but in a society marked by endemic corruption they must still stay on good terms with the regime, both to maintain access to corrupt benefits and also for their own protection. From the government's point of view, a corrupt élite is thus one both desperate to continue to serve and (because by definition it has broken laws) one whose members can be eliminated at any time simply by activating the machinery of law enforcement. This also helps explain the lack of support often given to honest officials: not only do they arouse the resentment of their peers, but they represent an implicit challenge to an ethos the state may wish to see preserved (Pipes 1974: p. 286).

3. *Getting the job done* Corruption may be sanctioned as a means both of getting round onerous legal requirements and of providing unofficial rewards for success. This was especially powerful during Stalin's times when, as one of his telling phrases put it, the 'victors of production are not judged'. There thus grew a whole network of *tolkachi* ('fixers'). Managers responded to the demand to meet (and exceed) Plan targets by sanctioning their fixers' use of techniques ranging from the covert exchange of services between enterprises to outright bribery in order to secure scarce materials (Berliner 1954). In many ways, this is a classic example of the sort of corrupt practices which it is possible (although ultimately incorrect) to describe as a public good, as it meant that Soviet managers and consumers were able to bypass some of the lunacies and distortions of the Plan. Today, corruption can be used to cut through the more tiresome swathes of red tape, such that some can share the view of Presidential aide Georgii Satarov that it is 'the grease making for speedier reforms' (*BBC* 1997).

4. *Reducing pressure for change* Ultimately, in O'Hearn's vivid image, the Soviet 'planned economy [was] held together by the baling wire and chewing gum of the parallel markets' (O'Hearn 1980: p. 223). A good thing for Ivan Ivanovich and his family, perhaps, as it meant that they could acquire commodities scarcely seen in the shop windows. But also a good thing for the pampered élite. After all, if ordinary Soviet citizens could gain access to the staples and luxuries they required (or even so long as they just

believed they could), then they had less reason to jeopardize their liberty to do so by challenging the status quo. Besides, the parallel market helped humanize the system; as Staats notes, people 'may have more faith in a system that they can influence to some degree, through personal action, than one they do not know how to manipulate or are unable to manipulate' (Staats 1972: p. 47). Or, in Colin Leys's words, 'the greater the corruption, the greater the harmony between corrupter and corruptee' (Leys 1965: p. 219).

5. *Co-optation* Corruption is a means by which the state can co-opt useful (or potentially dangerous) forces, by offering them hidden routes to influence or wealth. This is, really, a corollary of Huntingdon's thesis that corruption is often a by-product of modernization, as newly enriched groups and classes seek to buy themselves a commensurate say in a political machine which may not have evolved at the same rate (Huntingdon 1968). But it can also be a way to buy off new groups which might otherwise represent a force for political change. Thus, the tsarist state proved an assiduous co-opter of conquered local élites, from the Baltic to the city states of Central Asia. Similarly, Soviet practice soon came to extend the joys of *nomenklatura* privilege to powerful local clans and leaders.

So corruption does not simply happen, mysteriously and organically. There will also be instances in which regimes and élites actively foster corrupt practices as being in their interests or even in those of the state as a whole. This is, of course, hardly limited to Russia. The early-nineteenth-century British 'rotten borough' (a depopulated constituency retaining its right to elect a member of parliament) allowed the government or wealthy aristocrats to all but appoint their choice of representative, while the Habsburg Empire relied successfully on sinecures within its bureaucracy to co-opt potentially restive educated subject élites.

There are, however, some powerful counter-arguments. Corruption can actually be a distinct challenge to the state — as became visible in Soviet Uzbekistan (see below, p. 278), and may be becoming visible in today's Far East (Satter 1996). It is also, perhaps most importantly, macroeconomically debilitating. It encourages the formation of artificial monopolies, protected by political clout rather than economic advantage. But so long as the *perceived* or immediate interests of the élite or the leadership — rather than those of the abstract 'state' — appear to be served more by a judicious admixture of corruption, then this is a powerful temptation. Furthermore, once established, this is a difficult tradition to break, not least as those who benefit from it are by definition likely to be strongly placed to resist.

Corruption in Evolution

> 'I think,' says Ivan to Volodya, 'that we must have the richest country in the world.' — 'Why?' asks Ivan. — 'Because for nearly sixty years everyone has been stealing from the state and still there is something left to steal.' (Rosner 1986: p. 29)

This is, of course, not all that needs to be said about corruption in Russia: different élites have adopted different standards, and it is by no means entirely a 'top-down' phenomenon. Nevertheless, the incorporation of corrupt practices into a generic style, even tradition, of governance does help explain the phenomenon's longevity, despite the many campaigns waged against it. One problem facing the USSR, after all, was the extent to which the very organs of control were sucked into the *krugovaia poruka*, circles of mutual protection. Staats noted the irony that the close relationship between Party and state, designed to ensure compliance with central directives, actually worked to impede it by bonding the two rather than keeping them apart and watching each other (Staats 1972). Of course, this becomes a little less paradoxical once one accepts the notion of corruption being effectively encouraged as part of the style of governance.

The Bolshevik seizure of power in 1917, an operation more reminiscent of a coup than the later-mythologized 'popular revolution', saw a relative handful of revolutionaries capture the centres of Russia without either mass support or a clear blueprint for government. Once the Civil War exploded in 1918, the early idealism of 'commune democracy' was soon shouldered aside by a new creed of 'War Communism' and, indeed, a new generation of Bolsheviks. This was to prove the formative moment for the Bolsheviks, in which much of their internal democracy and Utopianism was to be sacrificed on the altar of victory. In their place came discipline, bureaucratism and a conviction that law must take second place to politics (Juviler 1976: pp. 15–25). This was a time of unparalleled possibilities for the so-called 'New Bolsheviks' who joined after the Revolution: not educated revolutionaries but to a large extent younger, poorly educated opportunists from the streets and the unions. They brought with them energy and ambition, but also a whole slew of traditional Russian values, from anti-Semitism (Jews were heavily represented amongst the 'Old Bolsheviks') to mysticism, from misanthropy to corruption (Fitzpatrick 1978).

The Bolsheviks passed their first decree against corruption in 1918, but by 1922 'Iron' Feliks Dzerzhinskii, Lenin's political police chief, was admitting that 'we are all well aware how prevalent bribery has become' (Chalidze 1977: p. 147). The New Economic Policy (1921–28), with its encouragement of small-scale capitalism, led to the rise of a new moneyed élite of NEPmen, traders and rich farmers. It was in part resentment within the Communist Party at the antics of these Soviet *nouveaux riches* that led to the end of the NEP and the rise of Stalin (1928–53), thus opening the next chapter of Russia's corrupt history.

If Stalinism was anything, it was not just the cult of state above society, but also that of pragmatism over ideals. Those in favour could do no wrong, but the corollary was that to fall out of favour was all but criminal of itself (Juviler 1976: pp. 43–6). As the USSR was thrown into the whirlwind of collectivization and modernization, the message that 'the victors of production are not judged' was put out in one form or another time and again. To meet their targets and simply to survive, managers turned to *tolkachi*, bureaucrats engaged in report-padding and mutual protection, which brought the recognition 'by political and legal agents that organizations must be given some leeway if they are to meet their targets or to create the appearance of success' (Lampert 1985: p. 177).

Indeed, under Stalin — who had robbed banks for the Bolsheviks before the Revolution and described gang leaders as 'the salt of the earth' (Glazov 1976: p. 142; Handelman 1994: p. 25) — the relationship between state and crime took on a whole new complexion. An increasingly obvious alliance was struck in the prison and labour camps whereby 'criminal' inmates were relied upon to police the influx of 'politicals'. In time this was to break down the traditional hostility shown towards the state by the criminal fraternity of the *vory v zakone* ('thieves within the law') (Glazov 1976; Serio and Razinkin 1995). The collaborators — *suki* ('bitches') — and the traditionalists finally turned on each other in an internal war which raged across the 'Gulag Archipelago'. What emerged after the victory of the 'bitches' was a new criminal tradition. It combined the discipline, dynamism and entrepreneurialism of the old ways with a new understanding of the opportunities to be found in co-operation with corrupt state authorities.

After Stalin's death, when the camp gates were opened, this tradition came to dominate the Soviet underworld. Already in the Khrushchev years, but most obviously under Leonid Brezhnev, an increasingly cynical and complacent élite encouraged a corrupt alliance with organized crime. But this was not just a case of a few rotten apples. First of all, this association with the criminal world had become so commonplace as to be almost the done thing (Vaksberg 1991; Simis 1982; Gurov 1995). The 'Uzbek Cotton Affair', for example, in which billions were embezzled from Moscow to pay for non-existent cotton production, involved not only almost the entire senior leadership of the Uzbek Communist Party but also highly placed protectors in the capital, including Brezhnev's son-in-law, Iurii Churbanov (Churbanov 1992; Clark 1993: pp. 185–91).

Secondly, there are considerable grounds for suspecting that the state itself was deliberately cultivating criminal connections as well as incorporating corruption into its style of governance. The Soviet public was wooed by the so-called 'Little Deal', a social contract which promised steadily improving quality of life in return for political quiescence (Millar 1985). Part of this was greater tolerance for the black market and a range of other illegal but common activities, from pilfering from the workplace to absenteeism (Whitmore 1998: p. 39). In effect, the state 'bribed' the population through an illegal transfer of resources. At the same time, the *nomenklatura* — especially the collaborator élites of potentially disruptive ethnic minorities — was promised an era of 'trust in the cadres', of increased freedom of manoeuvre and scope for enrichment so long as minimal targets were met and, importantly, discretion was maintained (Lampert 1985). Party shops were well stocked with subsidized imported goods, but kept hidden from view; leaders' luxurious dachas were built in restricted areas away from prying mushroom-pickers, and stately black Volga and Zil limousines, rather than imported cars, were still *de rigueur*. Corruption driven by the pressures and demands of the state became instead geared towards the direct interests of the élite itself.

During his brief time as General Secretary, Iurii Andropov showed some appreciation of the dangers, but even his anti-corruption campaigns were as much about the selective removal of political rivals as the imposition of legality (Clark 1993: pp. 145–97). The reforms of Mikhail Gorbachev, though, provided the next real test of the tradition and its ability to evolve. Even though he began with a wholehearted commitment to modernizing the Soviet system, the logic of his *perestroika* (restructuring) was to undermine the unity, political and economic monopoly and unaccountability of the Soviet élite.

This is the time when organized crime entered Russian life visibly. It is true that some of the reforms did encourage the spread of this home-grown *mafiia*. Gorbachev's anti-alcohol campaign, for example, did what Prohibition had done in the USA: give organized crime at one swipe of the pen a lucrative trade and a huge and eager market (White 1996). But the real reason why the 'mafia' became increasingly visible is precisely that, having worked within and behind the Party through the 1970s and early 1980s, it was losing this cover as the Party itself fragmented; not only that, it was increasingly free to develop and seize the new opportunities provided by reform (Galeotti 1998). Even to the very end, though, it was not just individuals and cliques within the élite who were resorting to corrupt practices. Gorbachev himself sanctioned an ill-omened secret programme to hide Party funds abroad or behind suitable 'front companies' for future use. In practice most ended up in private hands, with the only man who knew all the details, Party treasurer Nikolai Kruchina, conveniently and still controversially committing suicide right after the 1991 August Coup.

Contemporary Russia

> Judging officials on the basis of corruption [...] would result in the dismissal of all government officials, from the very bottom to the very top. Instead the existing regime has replaced this with assessing effectiveness and efficiency in achieving targets and implementing orders. (*Segodnia*, 5 February 1997)

Corruption obviously thrives in the presence of a state-controlled economy and massive and intrusive bureaucracy, and in the absence of democratic accountability. Nevertheless, the partial and distorted nature of post-Soviet Russia's 'democratization' and 'marketization' has left ample scope for the re-invention of the tradition of corrupt governance. The old *nomenklatura* has comfortably moved into a new role as a business and political élite, drawing on Party funds, connections and control over the privatization process to enrich and re-establish itself (Pleines 1995: pp. 11–12; Handelman 1994). If the Communist Party was so prone to corruption because it combined both an economic and political monopoly within the country, it seems clear that, in a much more diffuse way, the same could be said of today's Russian élite. The boundaries between private business and public office are very blurred — indeed, many Russians would not see any distinction at all. All politicians, most senior civil servants and even a large number of senior soldiers and police officers juggle their political duties with thriving entrepreneurial portfolios. This cannot help but continue to be a conducive environment for corruption, as rival 'clans' uniting key political, economic and sometimes criminal interests compete for power and resources. Furthermore, the Russian market remains uncompetitive, not least as the government rarely enforces anti-trust regulations or encourages foreign competition within its borders. This is 'crony capitalism', which Peter Rutland describes as dominated by 'an interlocking clique of business élites who use their political connections to shield them from domestic and international competition' (Rutland 1996: p. 3). To these political and business clans must, of course, be added the *mafiia*, enormously enriched by its participation in the privatization process and secure in its ability to 'buy' protectors, from the local police all the way to central government (Galeotti 1998).

But what about the notion of a 'corrupt tradition of governance'? Are there any grounds for suggesting that it also infects the post-Soviet body politic? Some. Considering the five issues discussed earlier, the first, the low apparent costs to the state of encouraging functionaries to 'feed' off their jobs, does appear to have some bearing. Admittedly, Russia's ruinous financial state precludes massive pay awards, but the almost derisory levels of salaries offered to public servants, who may at the same time have considerable powers and discretion, is almost a formula for 'feeding' (Glinkina 1998: p. 23).

Similarly, Boris Yeltsin's ruthless, personalized and pragmatic style of rule has not only permitted corruption, it has certainly kept the élite off balance and vulnerable. Yeltsin shares the present Russian fad for accumulating *kompromat* (compromising evidence) on potential rivals (Whitmore 1998: p. 36). He has a formidable record of building up allies, closing a blind eye to evidence of their misdemeanours (typically embezzlement) — whether through misplaced loyalty or political cynicism — only to cast them down when they become a threat or inconvenience. His reign is littered with such former favourites, from erstwhile Defence Minister Grachev, nicknamed 'Pasha Mercedes' for his fondness for German cars bought with diverted army funds (Turbiville 1995), to Yeltsin's tennis coach — and Sports Minister — Shamil′ Tarpishchev, whose National Sports Fund became a vessel for tax evasion and money laundering (Mil′man 1996). Perhaps the best example is Yeltsin's bodyguard-turned-Praetorian Aleksandr Korzhakov. By the beginning of 1996, his Presidential Security Service (SBP) had become the kernel of a new KGB, he was involved in a wide array of shadowy deals, and was widely rated one of the most powerful men in the Kremlin (Galeotti 1995b: pp. 17–19, 120–1). When a message had to be sent to millionaire Vladimir Gusinskii in 1994, it was by sending SBP gunmen to hold up his motorcade, with neither warrant nor authority, then letting them fade back into anonymity. On behalf of Yeltsin, Korzhakov (illegally) bugged Kremlin offices and gathered *kompromat* on all and sundry. Yet when he became a liability, his illegal acts were suddenly 'noticed', his deals with Tarpishchev were paraded before the media, and Korzhakov joined the ranks of yesterday's men (Hockstader 1996).

Contrast is provided by another scandal which exploded in late 1997 and concerned suspiciously large 'advances', for a book never likely to appear, paid to seven officials who had been central to the campaign to privatize state assets and by a company which had done rather well out of the campaign. Most were sacked — but the most senior, First Deputy Prime Minister Anatolii Chubais, was simply deprived of his additional post (Finance Minister) and otherwise survived unscathed until being dismissed along with the rest of the government in March 1998 for unrelated reasons (Glinkina 1998). Waste no pity on him, though: he quickly moved on to be appointed head of the giant firm United Energy Systems. Such uneven treatment has, after all, marked the Yeltsin regime, as one anti-corruption campaign or initiative after another either fades into obscurity or becomes simply an excuse for a few expedient sackings (Bernstein 1997). Arguably, then, corruption is accepted both as a means of rewarding and controlling members of the élite. *Caveat lector*, though: this is obviously a tricky matter to assess on anything but a very subjective level.

Does corruption also help bleed off potentially dangerous pressures for change? Here, the opposite appears to be the case, not least given the — for Russia unprecedented — combination of a relatively free press and mass access to it. There appears to be no lessening of the tide of investigative journalism, nor cooling of the tempers raised. But corruption may prove instead to be smothering what optimism was raised by the collapse of the USSR and the introduction of democracy. Russians may believe that all their leaders and public 'servants' are corrupt, but if they ever lose their belief that it *could* be otherwise, that they deserve honest representatives, then the corrupt tradition will have won a quiet but momentous victory. Even by the conspiracy-theory-rich standards of today's Russian reportage, though, it would be difficult to suggest that this is a deliberate policy

Finally, turning to the use of corruption as a tool of co-optation, there appears little doubt that the centre has either allowed or even encouraged a wide range of dubious practices precisely to win over or neutralize important interest groups. This applies not only to the new class of '*nomenklatura* capitalists' and the powerful industrial, financial and media empires. There is powerful circumstantial evidence suggesting a form of *modus vivendi* between the government and the most powerful and stable *mafiia* groupings, precisely because they are powerful and stable (Galeotti 1998). Indeed, part of the successful settlement of the 1994–96 Chechen War appears to have been a masterful piece of co-optation, whereby the bandit-turned-rebel chieftains of the Chechen government in Groznyi have been cut into a 'piece of the action'. Their guarantee of a share of the reconstruction budget and the income from oil through-traffic is also Moscow's guarantee that they will have a direct personal interest in remaining part of the Russian Federation and avoiding future conflicts.

Eternal?

> Russia is gradually getting used to living in an atmosphere of virtually legalized embezzlement. (Voshchanov 1996)

If one valid question for debate has been whether Sicily represents the future of Russia (Varese 1994), then it should be made clear that Colombia emphatically does not. While there is every prospect of new 'narcocracies' emerging in post-Soviet Central Asia, this will not be the model for Russia. After all, the Colombian cartels' economic (and thus political) strength is based on an explicitly illegal commodity. Russian organized crime — like its Italian counterparts — is highly diversified. It is thus far more able to operate within an apparently legal environment, reviving Soviet-era traditions of keeping dirty deals out of sight, while building a composite criminal enterprise operating right across the economic spectrum, from black (entirely illegal) to grey (mixed) to white (licit). The underground economy, for example, has not disappeared with marketization. As much as 40 per cent of Russia's economy may be staying 'hidden' to avoid paying tax or having to comply with inconvenient regulations on everything from employment conditions to environmental standards (Suetin 1997).

This is one possible future, and one which most Russians appear to expect. Yet there is also a more positive corollary: such a '*mafiia* incorporated' is also more able to begin to ease itself into an entirely legal existence. After all, study of the tenacious tradition of corruption in Russia cannot be taken as simple proof that Russia never will be able to outgrow it in the future. In this respect, there are already some grounds for cautious optimism. A generation of *biznesmeny* who made their fortunes plundering the coffers of the collapsing Soviet state now want security and respect to match. Perhaps they hope to bequeath a more stable legacy to their children, or appreciate the limitations to economic development within a corrupt society (Mauro 1995; Willer 1996). After all, while corruption can have its uses in making a distinctly sub-optimal political system a little more effective, responsive and efficient, this is still very much second best. Corruption is also profoundly alienating to any peoples who have begun to acquire a taste for democracy and thus a belief in their right to good (or at least responsive) governance and equal treatment under the law. Furthermore, the opportunities offered by full engagement in the international economy require Russian businesses and businesspeople — no matter how shady their pasts — to meet global standards and (given the prevailing hysteria about the imminent onslaught of 'criminal Russia') prove themselves 'cleaner than clean'. Already in 1998, for example, a desire to create a progressive image to woo foreign investors caused Sidanco, an oil firm owned by the powerful Oneximbank group, to reverse an original decision to limit a new bond issue to company insiders (Freedland 1998).

But if in the past corruption has survived precisely because of its usefulness to successive regimes, then this is where there will have to be real change. In this context, pressure from the new business élite — who now have a power base independent of the government, a first for Russia — may prove important. The government may also have to reassess the dangers inherent in using and sanctioning corruption. After all, the balance between the power of corrupt bureaucrats and that of organized crime seems to be shifting. In the Soviet era, the Party chiefs were very much the dominant partners, but today it is instead the *mafiia* which increasingly calls the shots (Williams 1996: p. 5). Thus, returning to the five factors outlined earlier, it becomes evident that the low start-up costs are illusory, the political control questionable, the practical advantages negligible, the pressures for change undiminished and that those whose co-optation is necessary are already on board. Also new to Moscow is exposure to a global debate on the costs of corruption, as well as, for the first time, internally generated statistics on its actual cost to Russia, for everything from corrupt tax evasion through embezzlement to the environmental damage caused by firms bribing inspectors: $10–11 billion annually (unpublished MVD data, 1997).

It will take a long time for Russians to cast aside their long-established perception of the state as little more than the arena for personal and factional duels for influence and a structure for the satisfaction of the interests of the victorious. Nor is the present depressing mixture of economic free-for-all and *mafiia* and ex-*nomenklatura* authoritarianism necessarily the first step on the way to the construction of a balanced and well-regulated capitalist democracy. But it could be. When organized crime and endemic corruption has been tamed — as in the United States in the nineteenth century — it has been as a result of the combined efforts of an élite willing to outgrow its anarchic roots, a public prepared to fight for change and the legal and political structures and institutions necessary to mobilize and respond to these demands, from the press to the judiciary. Russia has the skeleton of such institutions, although to date a lack of political will and public support has prevented them from becoming credible weapons in a battle against corruption and the *mafiia*. The rest is up to the Russians.

Bibliography

BBC (1997), Interview on *Ekho Moskvy* radio, 15 March, in *BBC Summary of World Broadcasts*, 17 March.

Berliner, J. (1954), 'Blat Is Higher than Stalin', *Problems of Communism*, 3

Bernstein, J. (1997), 'Sweeping Graft under the Rug', *Moscow Times*, 30 May.

Chalidze, V. (1977), *Criminal Russia*, New York.

Christian, D. (1987), 'Vodka and Corruption in Russia on the Eve of Emancipation', *Slavic Review*, 46.

Churbanov, Iu. (1992), *Ia rasskazhu vse, kak bylo...*, Moscow.

Clark, W. (1993), *Crime and Punishment in Soviet Officialdom*, Armonk, NY and London.

Clarke, M. (1983), *Corruption: Causes, Consequences and Control*, London.

Fitzpatrick, S. (ed.) (1978), *Cultural Revolution in Russia, 1928–1931*, Bloomington, IN.

Freedland, C. (1998), 'Shareholders Win Russia Bond Fight', *Financial Times*, 26 February.

Galeotti, M. (1995a), *The Age of Anxiety: Security and Politics in Soviet and Post-Soviet Russia*, Harlow, Essex.

Galeotti, M. (1995b), *The Kremlin's Agenda*, Coulsdon.

Galeotti, M. (1998), 'The Mafiya and the New Russia', *Australian Journal of Political Science*, forthcoming.

Glazov, Y. (1976), '"Thieves" in the USSR — A Social Phenomenon', *Survey*, 22.

Glinkina, S. (1998), 'The Ominous Landscape of Russian Corruption', *Transitions*, 3

Gurov, A. (1995), *Krasnaia mafiia*, Moscow.

Handelman, S. (1994), *Comrade Criminal*, London.

Heidenheimer, A. (1970), *Political Corruption: Readings in Comparative Analysis*, New Brunswick, NJ.

Hockstader, L. (1996), 'Gangland Scandal Reaches into Yeltsin's Inner Circle', *International Herald Tribune*, 6 August.
Huntingdon, S. (1968), *Political Order in Changing Societies*, New Haven, CT.
Juviler, P. (1976), *Revolutionary Law and Order*, New York.
Lampert, N. (1985), *Whistleblowing in the Soviet Union*, Basingstoke.
Leys, C. (1965), 'What Is the Problem about Corruption?', *Journal of Modern African Studies*, 3.
Mauro, P. (1995), 'Corruption and Growth', *Quarterly Journal of Economics*, 111.
Millar, J. (1985), 'The "Little Deal": Brezhnev's Contribution to Acquisitive Socialism', *Slavic Review*, 44.
Mil′man, Z. (1996), '"Sprut"', *Ogonek*, 43
O'Hearn, D. (1980), 'The Consumer Second Economy', *Soviet Studies*, 32.
Pipes, R. (1974), *Russia Under the Old Régime*, Harmondsworth.
Pleines, H. (1995), 'Organized Crime and Corruption in Russia since 1987', *Russia and the Successor States Briefing Service*.
RFE/RL (1997), Yeltsin's weekly radio address on 26 September 1997, reported in *RFE/RL Newsline* (email bulletin), 26 September.
Rosner, L. (1986), *The Soviet Way of Crime*, Boston, MA.
Rutland, P. (1996), 'Crony Capitalism in Russia', *Kennan Institute Meeting Reports*, 13.
Sampson, S. (1985–86), 'The Informal Sector in Eastern Europe', *Telos*, 66.
Satter, D. (1996), 'The Darkness Spreads from Primoriye', *Jamestown Foundation Prism*, December 1996 (accessible on the internet at: www.jamestown.org/publications/archive/prism/1296/satter.htm).
Serio, J. and Razinkin, A. (1995), 'Thieves Professing the Code: The Traditional Role of *vory v zakone* in Russia's Criminal World', *Low Intensity Conflict and Law Enforcement*, 4.
Simis, K. (1982), *USSR: The Corrupt Society*, New York.
Staats, S. (1972), 'Corruption in the USSR', *Problems of Communism*, 21.
Suetin, D. (1997), 'Ekonomika Rossii: Iz sveta v ten′ pereletaia', *Ekonomika i zhizn′*, 13.
Turbiville, G. (1995), 'Mafia in Uniform: The Criminalization of the Russian Armed Forces', *Foreign Military Studies Office Paper* (accessible on the internet at the following address: www.call.army.mil/call/fmso/fmsopubs/issues/mafia.htm).
Vaksberg, A. (1991), *The Soviet Mafia*, New York.
Varese, F. (1994), 'Is Sicily the Future of Russia?', *Archives européennes de sociologie*, 35.
Voshchanov, P. (1996), 'Rynochnaia reforma…', *Komsomol′skaia pravda*, 18 December.
White, S. (1996), *Russia Goes Dry*, Cambridge.

Whitmore, B. (1998), 'Russia's Top Crime Fighter', *Transitions*, 3
Willer, D. (1996), ''96 corruption strangled the achievements of '95', *St Petersburg Times*, 6–12 January.
Williams, P. (1996), 'Hysteria, Complacency and Russian Organized Crime', *PSBF Briefing*, 8.

Index